TOMORRO\

The Story of the Kingston Woman's History Club,
1861–Tomorrow

Dana E. Davis

Hamilton Books
A member of
The Rowman & Littlefield Publishing Group
Lanham · Boulder · New York · Toronto · Plymouth, UK

♾™ The paper used in this publication meets the minimum
requirements of American National Standard for Information
Sciences—Permanence of Paper for Printed Library Materials,
ANSI Z39.48—1984

To all the ladies of the Kingston Woman's History Club, past, present, and future . . .

Table of Contents

Preface

"When the Southern woman loses her reverence for truth, and honor; when her deepest affections change with the shifting winds; when memories, sorrowful and bitter as the waters of death, are cast aside and forgotten, then, and not till then, can she tear from her heart's core the memory of our glorious past." – Frances Thomas Howard, *In and Out of the Lines, An Accurate Account of Incidents During the Occupation of Georgia by Federal Troops in 1864-1865.* (This is the last paragraph of Miss Howard's book.)

While attending a summer session of political journalism at Georgetown University my junior year of college, my eyes were awakened to how the rest of the world viewed me. First, I looked a little different from the other girls. I certainly sounded different, and I had very different ideas about how the world evolved around me.

Our first night there, several girls went to dinner together, a kind of "get to know each other." We were all from different parts of the country. And, guess who was the only one there from a state south of the Mason Dixon Line? You get three guesses and the first two don't count. The first thing they noticed about me was that my makeup was perfect, my clothes were expensive, and not one hair on my head was out of place.

We went around the table describing our rooms at home. We thought this would give a little personal insight into each girl by the description she gave. I described my room as having six doors, a double window, four-poster canopy bed with white, French furniture. They stared at me in silence for a moment. I continued to explain that there were only two real doors to my room, one from the hall and the other one led to the extra bonus area over the garage. The other four doors concealed two, double, walk-in closets. More silence hung in the air.

Finally, one girl, I can only describe as a true Yankee, spoke up.

"You don't by any chance live at Tara, do you?"

Laughter and mumbles echoed around the table. Jeers were aimed at me with girls mockingly calling me "Miss Scarlett."

Now, I am a fan of Margaret Mitchell's epic work, *Gone With The Wind*. I also admit to turning it on each time it appears on television. I have until yet to buy the DVD, but admittedly, I am a huge fan. Despite being a fan, I was highly offended. I didn't want to be labeled with this stigma. However, I never gave them any more good reasons to change their opinion. It was just a matter of differences in upbringing that built walls between us.

Scarlett finally faded after about a week and was replaced by Suzanne Sugarbaker, not much better to me. If you don't recall, she was the dingy, pageant beauty, debutante on *Designing Women*. But, I accepted the name and always answered to "Suzanne." I could have handled it better had they called me "Julia" or "Mary Jo" in reference to the two smart ones on the show. To this day, I'm not sure exactly how many people knew my real name was actually Dana.

During my stay, I learned a lot, and I endured a lot. Many of the girls in my class saw me as a little backward. For starters, my accent did nothing to further my case that I contained one ounce of intelligence. One hot afternoon, we got caught in a sudden thunderstorm in downtown Washington, D.C.

"We better take cover cause it's comin' up a cloud," I shouted while running past a few girls.

"What did she say?" One girl looked at the other puzzled while they both stopped in their tracks.

"I don't know. Was that English?"

"Hey ya'll, I'm serious," I shouted. "That cloud's really bad. It's lookin' black and dangerous. Ya'll better take cover."

Finally, one of them got frank with me. "What in the hell are you saying?"

Stepping out from my bus stop shelter, I carefully pronounced my words, "I said, you should get inside or under a shelter because it is going to rain very hard very soon."

They got the picture. I should have learned my lesson, but you just can't help who you are, and it's hard to hide a lot of things about yourself. We had enjoyed a night of gluttony, ending with huge ice cream sundaes. Arriving back in the dorm room, I fell across the bed, spread eagle and began to moan.

"Oh, my gosh, I'm foundered!"

"I'm sorry, I didn't catch that," one of the girls retorted. "Is she speaking in a foreign tongue again?"

Remembering the thunderstorm, I tried to make things easy on them.

"I said, I have foundered myself, and I feel that I might die at any moment."

"We still don't follow you," she continued. "Should we take you to the emergency clinic, call a doctor? Is this something you take meds for?"

I had to lift myself into a sitting position and begin to explain the meaning of the term "foundered." I calmly explained that livestock, especially horses, have a tendency to eat until you stop feeding them. They don't have the capacity to control their own appetites. If you keep feeding them, they eventually just get very sick, which could be very dangerous for them.

After another long pause, the light went on for one of them, "You ate too much, didn't you?"

I just fell back into my pillow hoping they would go away.

They also thought I was setting back the Women's Lib Movement. I just merely pointed out that Southern women know how to make it work to their advantage. They always have.

You see, I can open my own door, get my own drinks from a machine, pick up my own briefcase, and the list could go on. However, I would always tell them, "I'm smart enough to know I don't have to." They still didn't get it. It was hard to convince them that women have more power and control over the opposite sex with charm and a smile than a show of nasty attitude and intelligence. Trust me, it was rare I had to carry my own briefcase or even purchase my own drink. I never had to do anything unethical or sleazy, I was just my Southern self.

As the semester went on, they softened a little when they saw how far that Southern charm could take me. Plus, I hardened a little, losing some of my accent. I was amazed by the diversity in the girls I got to know. I had never had a Jewish friend. My crowd was made up of all Southern Baptists or Methodists named Smith, Jones, or had a name that was the same as a color. I had never seen lesbians. Like all teens, we speculated at who might be "light in the loafers" once in a while, but this was all new to me.

Yes, a lot of diversity drifted in and out of my life that summer. I saw how the rest of the country viewed our lifestyle in the South. Although we are one nation, it seems we remain divided for some reason. I guess the notion of a great, old South is romantic and fascinating. To think that some things haven't changed or aren't going to change is comforting, I imagine. Maybe I wasn't the best ambassador for the South with my thick Georgia accent, my naivety, and my spoiled rotten, get anything you want, only child attitude.

However, they learned that I wasn't as "dumb" as I sounded. My grades far surpassed some, and I proved I had a place in advanced economics. All those "smarties" could name were eleven of the twelve Federal Reserve Banks. The teacher commented on how he didn't have to turn around to give credit for the last one named as I proudly said, "Atlaaanna." Properly said in the South, it has no "t" and about three extra "a's" accented by two extra "n's."

If you are wondering what this has to do with giving you a reason for writing this book, I'll tell you it has everything in the world to do with it. Once I returned home, I finished my publication management degree at the University of Georgia. Of course, I couldn't get the degree until everyone was satisfied I could properly pronounce "dawg" once again. No one will ever take that out of me!

I came home with a different view of my home state. I appreciated it a little more. I went to work at a small daily newspaper in North Georgia named *The Daily Tribune News*, in Bartow County. As a "cub" reporter, I was assigned some of the small outlying towns, namely Kingston. Insulted at first that my superb journalism skills were to be wasted on this minuscule dot on a map, I slowly acclimated myself to their way of life. Of course, this was an insult. I had attended Georgetown University where members of the Kennedy family had been educated. How dare they send me to Kingston! Alas, it was here that I finally found myself at home.

The other reporters made fun of me when I started to hang out in Kingston because they couldn't figure out why? At the time, the entire downtown business district looked much like a ghost town. There was no place to eat, nowhere to shop, and there certainly wasn't anything to do except maybe sit in the park.

That's just what I did. I sat in the park at the small Kingston Woman's History Club Museum. I sat, and I listened. I would go inside and wander around the exhibits and flip through their scrapbooks. I took in every word said to me.

The history of this club dates to 1861 at the outbreak of the Civil War. A small group of women began as a sewing group. They came to the aid of the soldiers who needed clothing and supplies. But, history would have them transform into so much more.

They established the first Confederate hospital, answering the need of sick and wounded soldiers left on their town's depot. They took care of these men and buried those they lost. They survived Federal attacks and raids as General William T. Sherman made Kingston his headquarters. It was here he got his marching orders to rip Georgia in half from Atlanta to Savannah. He began his march by burning much of Kingston and then moving onto Atlanta.

During Federal occupation, these same ladies sought and received permission to honor the Confederate dead with a ceremony and flowers. The only stipulation placed on them was to honor the Union soldiers buried there also. Today, Confederate Memorial Day, sponsored by the Kingston Woman's History Club, continues this tradition. It is the longest running ceremony of its type in the nation. And, they continue the ceremony in its original intent, including honoring the two remaining Union soldiers buried there.

After the Civil War, these ladies transformed into a memorial committee to maintain the soldiers' cemetery, and eventually became charter members of the Kingston Woman's History Club. They have rendered aid in all wars since 1861. When the school needed teachers, supplies, furniture, and books, the ladies were there. When the community needed a park, the ladies were there.

These women have been planted firmly in this community for more than a century. At times, they have been the bricks and mortar that have held this town together. When the interstate bypassed them, the railroad faded as main transportation, and time marched around the community, the ladies never let their heritage die. They have carefully and meticulously guarded the town's historical records, opening the doors of their museum to visitors and everyone in their community. They continue to teach and pass on their knowledge.

I have been given a rare and beautiful opportunity. I have been tutored by the best as to what it means to be a true Southern woman. She is a hard worker. She is diligent and persistent. She never gives up, and she never forgets. I was blessed to become a member of the Kingston Woman's History Club and hear the stories of generations passed down from the Civil War.

This book takes real people, the heroes, and combines them with a few fictitious characters to tell these stories I have been privy to hear. These characters are composites of the women who inspired me to tell their story. This book is a tribute to the spirit and tenacity of these women who have preserved their community's history and heritage.

Women of the twenty-first century, stand by your reverence for the truth and do what is right for those around you. Do not let bitter tears sting and blind you to your past. Cushion your heart with tears of remembrance and joy. Move forward with confidence in your Lord and Savior. And, walk in the footsteps of your ancestral sisters, never forgetting their pioneering ways. Make longer their path with your paving steps for those to follow you in goodness, kindness, and mercy for all. – Dana Davis, *Tomorrow is Better, The Story of the Kingston Woman's History Club, 1861-Tomorrow*, circa 2005. This is for you Miss Howard. I'm honored to take it from here . . .

Acknowledgements

This book would not be possible without the ladies of the Kingston Woman's History Club and the more than one hundred years of historical documentation they have collected. I would like to thank them for opening their hearts to me by sharing their stories. Their generations of these stories passed down from one to the other and their collection of records are the foundation for this book. Special thank yous go to Mrs. Martha Mulinix, a one-woman inspiration and institution to all of Kingston. For all the tireless hours of reading, verifying research, and efforts in obtaining a grant for the publication of this book, I thank Mrs. Emma Williams, Miss Jill Williams, and Mrs. Marty Mulinix. Words are just not adequate to thank Emma for all she's done. Without lodging facilities from the "Davis Hotel" and the "Hayes Inn," the hours of museum research from a long-distance traveler would not have been possible. Thank you Mimi and Poppy and Aunt B.B. For the many hours of free childcare and moral support, I thank my parents, Mr. and Mrs. Bill White. And, not least in any way, my husband and partner for life, Lance Davis, contributed more to this book technically and logistically than anyone. After many ten or twelve-hour days of work, he gladly took on the role of cook, maid, homework tutor, chauffeur, Cub Master, Den Mother, football and wrestling coach, and best friend when the going got rough. His behind-the-scenes efforts and never-give-up attitude are responsible for my part in seeing this project through to the end. Thank you, all, so very much.

Ghosts at the depot . . .

The clock was striking midnight just seconds after the last passenger train whistle pierced the cold, rainy night. With the steady noise of the wet downpour outside, Martha realized she didn't have to wear her shoes into the parlor. Each night, she put them on mainly to hear her heels clicking as she walked back and forth across the shiny, Georgia pine floor.[1] Fifteen-year-old Martha Malone hadn't slept an entire night since May 1861 when her father had marched off to war. Just before the clock would strike midnight, Martha would slip into her shoes, tiptoe past her mother's room, sneak down the stairs, and walk across the parlor. Staring into the blackness of Kingston, she would wonder where her father was laying his head for the night. She wanted to know if he were warm or cold, hungry or fed, well or sick, cared for or neglected, and the list went on in her mind.

And, it wasn't just her father she worried about. She thought about James too. James Litton became Martha's beau when they both turned thirteen. Against the wishes of his father, James enlisted with Captain Joel Roper's Company F 18th Georgia Regiment at Kingston along with Martha's father, and desperate for able-bodied males, he was accepted. Captain Roper's company became the first Georgia troops to march onto Virginia soil.[2]

Each night as Martha paced, the clicking of her wooden heels against the pine floor gave her comfort. It was a noise she welcomed. Because without the two men she loved most in the world, she felt life was too quiet and lonely. Hearing the last train whistle and the striking of midnight were also solace to her.

Tonight was a bit different somehow. It wasn't the rain that made it so different, but it was what she saw through the pitch black Georgia night. During the day, Martha could see the entire village from her parents' parlor window. Only the Malone residence had a panoramic view of the village. That night, she knew where she was looking, the train depot. She saw a light moving on the depot's platform, shining brightly through the rain. When the lightening flashed, she caught a glimpse of what looked to be ghostly figures moving along in a single-file line.[3] It wasn't at all unusual to see a light in the village coming from one of the town's four hotels or the bright illumination of one of Kingston's doctors' homes. People did get off of the last midnight passenger train and check into a hotel. Of course, since the war started, this was now a rare occurrence. Before the war, it was common to see many new, visiting faces in each of the town's four churches on Sunday morning. And, if the lights were on in one of the doctors' homes, Kingston was welcoming a new resident, or losing a sick neighbor.

Tonight the light was different and foreboding. It was a small, single light that kept an eerie pace. During one of the deafening clashes of thunder and blinding lightening flashes, Martha caught sight of armed men following the ghostly beacon. The next bolt of lightening flashed, and she saw several of them fall. Through the curtain of rain and more of nature's flashing lights, she saw men reaching for those who had fallen on the platform.

"What are you doing?"

Martha screamed at the sound of her mother's voice and the touch of her hand on her back.

"Martha," Catherine Malone said, "What are you doing?"

Startled, Martha regained enough composure to answer. "I'm just looking out the window, Mother. What are you doing?"

"I heard your usual pacing across the floor as I was drifting back off to sleep when I heard you stop. I thought something was wrong. You usually keep walking for about an hour or more," Catherine said.

"I've kept you awake?"

"Sure you have. Did you think your father's absence only affected you, Dear?"

"I'm sorry, Mother," Martha said. "I can't really explain why I walk the floor every night, but it sometimes helps me. Maybe I'm just tiring myself out so that I can go back to sleep."

"Well, why did you stop walking tonight? What could you possibly be looking at in the dark?" Catherine inquired.

Talking very fast, almost hyperventilating, Martha began recounting her experience at the window that evening. "It's so strange, Mother! I stopped walking to look out the window because I saw a small, bright light moving at the depot. It wasn't a train or the lightening. I know because I could see the entire depot every time the lightening flashed."

By now, Martha was making exaggerated hand gestures mimicking the lightening. "The small light was moving, and people were leaving the platform. I couldn't tell exactly where they were going, but some were falling down, and it looked like others carried guns!"

"Oh, Honey, I think your imagination is working harder than ever," Catherine said in a half laugh, half scared tone. "Why don't you go on back to bed. First of all, there is no way you could have seen anything out there. The rain is too heavy. And, second, we have seen no troops this far South. Besides, even if the passenger train stopped for coal or water tonight, I'm sure no one got off. People just aren't traveling. You know that."

Perhaps her mother was right. The people, the light, the guns, they had to have been just figments of her overactive and lonely imagination.

Mrs. Malone leaned over and blew out the lamp beside her daughter, took her by the hand and they used the candle she had brought with her to make their way back up the stairs and to bed.

Tiny drops of water still fell from the rooftop of the Malone residence the next morning when Camille came to wake Martha. Camille was the only slave owned by the Malones. The Malones preferred to do things for themselves. Mr. Malone was an attorney by trade and had no need of farm hands or house servants. Camille was a gift to Mrs. Malone from her plantation-owning father twenty years earlier. She had been offered her freedom, and the paperwork was kept in Mr. Malone's desk. Camille, however, opted to stay with the Malones because she received an education, home, and was considered a member of the family. When both of the Malone children were very small, Catherine became ill and could not take care of them. Camille became their surrogate mother.

This morning, her maternal instincts took over as she stroked Martha's hair until she opened her eyes.

"I heard you had a restless night, Angel, so I didn't wake you."

"Where is my mother?"

"She's already gone to the Presbyterian Church to help the Soldiers' Aid Society. Mrs. Woolley came by earlier saying there is a great demand for uniforms and socks for other Georgia soldiers, not just our own."[4]

"I'm going to head right over there now to help," Martha cried as she jumped from the bed and tripped over her own robe.

"Slow down, slow down," Camille said with a chuckle. "From what I hear, there's going to be plenty of war and plenty of sewing left by this afternoon. First, let's get some food into your skinny body."

Obeying Camille, Martha dressed and went to the dining room, but she didn't eat much. She was still haunted by the spooky images she saw on the platform the night before.

Getting up from the table and walking to the parlor, she stood just where she had the night before. It was clearly the depot's platform she saw through last night's storm. Today, it was busy with people shipping supplies of anything they could spare, from spices for the cooks to bedspreads and sheets for field hospitals. All of the uniforms made last week were packaged and placed on the day freight train. As usual, the passenger lines were half empty. Some soldiers on leave were switching trains on their way home to Alabama.[5] They were wounded and sick, probably discharged. Nothing out of the ordinary was happening. If she wasn't hallucinating, where did all the people go last night, and when did they leave?

Just as Martha was preparing to join the other ladies of the town for the afternoon sewing group, her mother opened the door and rushed past her up the stairs with her face half hidden in her handkerchief.

"Mother," cried Martha.

But, Camille grabbed her arm and stopped her while nodding to William sprinting up the steps.

"Wait, he probably knows something," Camille said softly.

William was just eighteen months younger than Martha and itching to join Confederate forces. Following the orders of his father to remain home as the man of the house, William was growing up too fast for a boy of his age.

"William, is it father?" Martha spouted in a fit of panic.

"No," he said flatly. "There have been several battles in Virginia, and many are dead and wounded. No names. The Reverend Hackett just received a letter asking for more supplies for the wounded and sick; supplies we may not be able to send. We just don't have them."

"There's more," William said. "The Union Army is pushing farther into the South, forcing retreats. It won't be long before East Tennessee becomes a battleground. Plus, fall and winter are coming which means many of the men will be returning to their homes to recuperate. If we keep sending supplies northward, what will be left when they get here?"[6]

Martha knew why her mother was despondent. The threat of war was coming closer, and her father could be among the mortally wounded, dead, or captured. And, to make it worse, he could be neglected and without proper supplies. At this point, Martha lost interest in William's news as she sank onto a parlor sofa, her mind traveling to the same hellacious places as her mother's. The only difference was Martha had two loved ones to worry about now.

William kept talking, and Camille was taking in every word the young man said. Martha stood up and moved to a chair near the window. She probably wasn't imagining things the night before. Those really were sick and wounded soldiers, but who was leading them? They didn't stay at the depot because it was locked during the night, and they probably didn't have money for a hotel room. They must have left with the early train since no one seemed to see them. So, who really was helping them find shelter for the night, and who put them on the morning train? This was a humanitarian miracle from Heaven for Martha. Her hopes deep inside were that if this be true, someone was doing the same for her father and James.

Notes

1. The character of Martha is fictional. She takes her name from an honored, long-time Kingston Woman's History Club member, Mrs. Martha Mulinix. The newest annex to the club's museum is named in honor of Mrs. Mulinix. The surname "Malone" is taken in loving memory of the late Mrs. Mattie Malone, another long-time, Kingston Woman's History Club Member.

2. *Random Notations About Kingston's Part In The War Between The States 1861-1865* are typewritten notes archived in the Kingston Woman's History Club Museum files.

3. Martha is looking at Kingston's depot as William "Doc" Tippin, leads soldiers left on the depot to shelter. This story has been recounted by members of the Kingston Woman's History Club, and it was inspired by *History of the Town of Kingston, Vivid War-Time Picture By a Lady Who Witnessed and Participated in Trying Scenes, The Cartersville News*, October 17, 1907, archived in the museum scrapbooks.

4. The Soldiers' Aid Society was organized in response to physical needs of soldiers rapidly deployed without proper supplies. Mrs. Ann Woolley was named first president. The Soldiers' Aid Society was the forerunner and appears to be the first ladies' organization to precede the Kingston Woman's History Club. Information taken from *History of the Town of Kingston, Vivid War-Time Picture By a Lady Who Witnessed and Participated in Trying Scenes, The Cartersville News*, October 17, 1907, archived in the museum scrapbooks.

5. Information taken from a letter to newspaper, *The Manassas*, Cassville, Georgia, written by C.W. Howard, Spring Bank, Georgia, August 7, 1862; handwritten copy on file in Kingston Woman's History Club Museum entered by Mrs. Wesley W. Roberts, March 27, 1975.

6. Information taken from a letter to newspaper, *The Manassas*, Cassville, Georgia, written by C.W. Howard, Spring Bank, Georgia, August 7, 1862; handwritten copy on file in Kingston Woman's History Club Museum entered by Mrs. Wesley W. Roberts, March 27, 1975.

Marching orders . . .

"Martha. Martha. Hey, Martha, are you all right?"

William's voice was becoming more and more clear like a distant train blowing a whistle and then is upon you.

"What?"

Now Camille spoke, "Martha, are you with us?"

"Oh, yes," she replied. "I was just thinking."

"New experience, Sis?" William was ribbing her in relief that she had not gone catatonic or worse.

"Listen, Sweetie," Camille began. "This was just a letter asking for assistance. I realize this news is scary, and I know your mother is just a fragile lady. We have to stay strong and carry on with our jobs and lives. You know men like to think they are in charge, right? Well, learn this today, a man has to receive his marching orders somewhere, and where do you think that is?"

Was this a joke? Why was Camille smiling and playing games at a moment like this?

"What are you talking about, Camille?"

"I'm saying a man gets his strength, his determination, and his marching orders from home and the good, strong, unbendable women there," she said firmly. "Your father's strength is coming from us at all times, and he knows his orders are to come home safely."

Martha was beginning to catch on and knew that James could hear her marching orders for him too, somehow.

"Now," Camille exclaimed loudly. "Private William Malone, where are you supposed to be right now?"

A surprised William slyly grinned and answered with a salute, "Eating lunch."

A half-annoyed Camille said, "Don't get smart with me boy. Aren't you supposed to be at the depot working?"

"Well, yeah, uh sir, ma'am. But aren't you supposed to feed me first? Remember, my strength and determination come from you women here at home! And, I feel the need for strength now."

Grabbing William and pulling him toward herself and Martha, they fell into a playful hug on the sofa.

"Okay, Boy, let's eat!"

At the end of the day, both William and Martha were relieved and tired. Martha had felt well enough after an enjoyable lunch to head off to the Soldiers' Aid Society daily sewing. It was hard to fathom that she had been doing this for months now. It amazed her at how fast the time was passing, and yet how every minute seemed like a painful hour.

She was glad she had gone this afternoon because she had learned that the women of Virginia were asking for more help. Many of the Confederate troops had been wounded and were sick. This was the main reason for the letter to Kingston. The Presbyterian Church would serve as a drop-off point for any donations that could be spared. Martha felt good knowing the "women" could help. Camille's words had been spoken in both truth and jest.

However, midnight would soon be at hand and another opportunity to spy on the depot would be arriving. Just before midnight, she awoke to the distant sound of the last incoming passenger train arriving at Kingston.

Doing her best this time not to wake anyone, she took off down the stairs barefooted and headed for the parlor window. Tonight was much clearer. There were just a few scattered clouds and a light drizzle. The same eerie light was shining on the platform just after the train labored off down the track. Just like the night before, she saw a single-file line of men hobbling and walking away from the depot following the same bobbing light. Then, as suddenly as they all appeared, they were all gone. The clock struck midnight; Martha tiptoed her usual mile and headed back to bed.

The next day, just before heading off to the sewing circle, Martha took a small detour around the depot. Nothing was out of the ordinary. It was business as usual. Boys were filling the trains with water and coal. The local merchants were unloading scarce supplies for the townspeople, and many collections of much needed military resources were being loaded for the Confederacy's fighting force. As luck would have it, she arrived in time for the mail train. She was looking up and down the depot's platform for any evidence that Kingston's midnight visitors had been there when the postmaster began to call to her.

"Miss Malone, Miss Malone, you and your mother have letters! Miss Malone, did you hear me?"

William had hopped onto the platform and began to nudge Martha into action when it registered with her that the postmaster was talking to her. She ran across the platform and down to the side of the depot where the mail workers were busy sorting incoming and outgoing letters and packages.

"I just saw you standing outside and thought I'd give you these immediately," the postmaster said.

"Oh, thank you so much," her voice trailed as she grabbed two letters and ran for home, forgetting all about her original destination.

She ran all the way up the street, past three hotels, one doctor's office, and crossed the tracks just as the afternoon train was pulling out. She never slowed down as her heart began to thump in her throat while she ran up the hill to her house.

She threw open the front door crashing inside. A startled Camille greeted her with a stern look of displeasure.

"You are supposed to be at the church for the Soldiers' Aid Society work," she scolded. "Where have you been? You look like you are outrunning the Yankee Army? You better be the way you look . . ."

Camille kept on chastising as Martha flung the letter to her mother into her hands. Camille's voice changed as she whispered a "Praise the Lord."

Martha didn't care about anything else Camille was saying because she continued to run up the stairs and into her room, slamming the door and falling across her bed. She recognized James' handwriting. She tore into the letter and began to read. For the first time in months, a smile crossed her face. His words gave every indication that he was all right. Times were tough but he was tougher, and he was determined to come home and marry Martha.

Following the light . . .

With a few steady letters from her father and James, Martha's days became a little easier. She sewed until her fingers bled onto the gray cloth, but she didn't complain. And, neither did the other ladies, even the ones who had not received good news. They were perhaps the bravest of all the women in the society. They had lost husbands, sons, and brothers, but they kept on giving because they were part of a society of soldiers unique among themselves. This was their way of fighting and winning the war. They dug trenches lined with cloth and armed themselves with needles and thread and fought the war with all they had.

August 1862 brought with it late summer rains and floods of pleas for more supplies. Many had sent their last blanket, quilt, and bedspread. Kingston residents began to send rugs from their floors as they made great bedding for bleeding soldiers.[1]

Those who still had means by which to make and replace the goods were hard at work. No one was still, and that included whoever stood on the depot platform every night, greeting the midnight passenger train.

On her usual stroll through the parlor, curiosity finally got the best of Martha. She didn't care that it was raining. She threw her father's old cloak over her head, strapped on her shoes, and headed out into the rain at a fast pace through the trees and the town square. She reached the depot platform just after the train lumbered into the Kingston darkness.

Martha finally saw the light up close. It was a lantern that was guiding dozens of injured and sick soldiers gasping for breath. Despite the humid mist, they were shivering and holding onto each other. Martha was compelled to step up on the platform, and as she did, one of the men fell onto her shoulder and said, "God bless you, ma'am for your help."

Taken aback and scared, she had no choice but to support the smelly, bearded man as best she could. She fell in line behind the others following the soft glow at the head of the group. They hobbled along, down the platform and across the wagon yard into an abandoned storeroom.

The soldier Martha was supporting fell to the floor and cuddled under his own wet cloak, but not before she saw the military emblems on his shoulders representing the U.S. Calvary, not the Confederate States of America. Through the darkness of the room, she saw the lantern moving toward her. Her heart began to pound, and her knees grew weak. She stopped breathing. She wanted to run, but she was paralyzed with enormous fear. What had she done? Had she stepped into a trap? Had the Union Army invaded Kingston already, disguised in a Trojan Horse?

"Hello, Martha," a hoarse, friendly voice broke the silence. "I've been wondering for the past month and a half when you might venture over and join me."

The lantern lowered, and it was none other than William "Doc" Tippin.[2] She was face-to-face with a friendly neighbor. But, what was he doing?

"Oh, child, I knew you were watching me. I could see the candle in your window every night. Didn't you think that if you could see my lantern, I could see your candle? Come on now, breathe and don't be afraid."

It had never occurred to her that the "whoever" moving under the cover of darkness knew she was watching. She remained silent.

"I knew it had to be you or your brother," he continued. "I figured it wasn't William because he's just too curious to sit around and watch. He'd have been down here the first time he saw my lantern."

When she regained her voice, she timidly whispered, "What are you doing?"

"Glad you can talk now," he smiled. "I was coming home from the mill late one night when I passed the depot and noticed about thirty men sitting in the rain, huddled under the small overhang. This just wasn't right to me. I asked the station master if I could have a key to let these men inside the depot overnight because they were all sick and wounded, but he said regulations wouldn't allow it. So, I took it upon myself to provide them shelter inside this old storehouse. They'll get on the first passenger train at daybreak, although many aren't able."

"You've been doing this every night?"

"Yes, I have," he continued. "You see they come from all over. Many are headed home to Alabama, and some are trying to get connecting trains up North."

As he finished, he gestured to the now asleep Union soldier at Martha's feet.

Before Martha could ask any more questions, Doc continued to explain how the number of soldiers had increased and how he feared there would be more coming.

"Why don't you ask for help?"

"Well, I know we have a great town, but our supplies are so limited and these fellows are just passing through. They only need a little help for the night," he said.

Surveying the room full of bearded, sick, and dirty men, Martha saw her father and James in the eyes that were staring back at her. These eyes were pleading for medicine, food, and compassion.

"We have to tell someone what you are doing," she said emphatically.

"I know," he agreed. "It has gotten to be too much for me to handle alone."

Martha pulled her cloak up around her head and turned to leave, intending to get immediate assistance when Doc Tippin grabbed her arm.

"Not now, Honey," he said gently. "I'll talk to your ladies group tomorrow afternoon. That's a good place to start. I promise. These fellows will be on the train in the morning, and a new group will be passing through tomorrow night. You need to get home before you are missed and in deep trouble I might add. Hold on and I'll see that you get home, and I'll see you tomorrow, right?"

She smiled at Doc, took his arm and allowed him to escort her home.

Martha decided to use the back door this time pulling off her shoes, now red with fresh, wet Georgia clay. She left them behind the door. Martha would just have to get to them before her mother or Camille found them. She climbed the stairs, shed her wet clothes and fell into bed.

Her midnight walk had taken her farther than she ever intended.

Notes

1 References to items shipped from the homes of Kingston residents; *History of the Town of Kingston, Vivid War-Time Picture By a Lady Who Witnessed and Participated in Trying Scenes, The Cartersville News*, October 17, 1907, are from museum scrapbook.

2 William "Doc" Tippin was one of the founders of the Wayside Hospital during Civil War. His grave marker was dedicated at his grave in 1951. Information taken from the article *Georgia Farmers' Market Bulletin, Confederate Marker*, editorial by Tom Linder, October 24, 1951.

First official patients . . .

Fortunately for Martha, her mother and Camille were preoccupied with preparing refreshments for the Soldiers' Aid Society meeting that afternoon. She was able to slip out her shoes and clean them as best she could.

William helped them to the church with their baskets of goodies and stayed behind when he saw Doc Tippin coming up the hill.

"What do you imagine he wants?" William half laughed.

"Who knows?" Martha lied.

"Good afternoon, Doc," Catherine said. "How are you today, and what brings you to our sewing group? Don't tell me you've given up milling for sewing?"

"No, ma'am," he said. "But, I do have some business with you ladies if I could pardon myself for a moment of your time?"

"Of course you can, Doc," she said. "Everyone is always welcome in church, and we would be delighted for you to join us."

William tugged at Martha's sleeve and whispered, "Would the mud on your shoes have anything to do with why 'Old Man Tippin' is here?"

Wiggling free of William's clutch, Martha ignored her younger sibling and marched into church behind her mother.

Doc Tippin, who was not a real doctor, made his way to the front of the sewing group. Word had reached Reverend Hackett that a visitor had joined the ladies, and he emerged from his office.

"Good afternoon, Doc," he said offering his hand for a gentlemanly shake. "What can we do for you this afternoon?"

By this time, all the ladies were seated, and William was hovering around the back of the church, suddenly interested in the sewing crowd's business.

"I'm here today to ask for your help," he began. His gaze fell on Martha. "I've been caught by a member of your group and urged to plead for your help with something. For some time now, I've been taking soldiers from the depot platform and sheltering them in the abandoned storehouse behind the mercantile. Last night, one of you caught me in the act and helped me. I know these men passing through need our help."

Silence fell on the group. Doc Tippin continued.

"I think it is unacceptable that these men, both our own and Union troops, are forced to stop here at midnight with nowhere to go until the morning connecting train. Many are sick, and most are wounded or both. I came upon them by accident, and God laid it on my heart to help. I just haven't said anything because I've done all that I can, and I know that you ladies have your hands full with your sewing and supply gathering.

"Anyway, anything you could do to help these men would be greatly appreciated, not by me, but by them. And, please remember that at one time we were all one country, a United States, and we continue to be one under God regardless of what uniform we wear."

Silence still hung over the group. No one moved or spoke for more than a minute. Then, the group's president, Mrs. Ann Woolley, stood and walked toward Doc Tippin.[1]

"Doc, speaking on behalf of the group, we would be glad to see what we could do," she said. "We have sat here day after day sewing for these troops that we can't see. We only get word of what it's like, but we don't know. It's time that we move on and see what we are facing. If it be God's will that we come to the aid of these men, then who are we to defy our Maker?"

She reached out her hand to Doc who took it. Mrs. Woolley smiled with a beautiful, inner Southern grace, straightened herself and asked that the group pray.

"Lord, we beseech You this day to give us endurance for the cause of humankind and compassion for healing acts and words. Lead us to do Your will and guide us to serve others. Bless our men on the battlefield and provide them with an angel like Doc Tippin to shelter them from the cold, harsh weather as they travel homeward. In Your most precious Son's name we pray, Amen."

With Doc's simple plea for help, these ladies began a journey into a series of compassionate, historical deeds.

For the first time in a few weeks, the night sky had stars, and the moon was shining as if to light the path to the depot platform for the angels of mercy. Doc was already there at 11:50 p.m. when a small group of ladies arrived. Soon, the whistle pierced the silent night. Several of the ladies jumped, their hearts beating rapidly as they knew some of their worst fears were approaching with the night train. They knew they were going to be looking into the faces of their husbands and sons. The sound of metal friction coming down the tracks announced the train's arrival.

Doc Tippin held up his lantern as a beacon for the wayward soldiers. The ladies followed him down the platform to the passenger car and watched as dozens of sick and wounded men de-boarded the train.

"This way gentlemen; this way gentlemen." It was Doc's deep, hoarse voice shaking the darkness and leading the men to shelter.

Following Doc's lead, many of the women began to support soldiers as they struggled to walk. Everyone arrived at the abandoned storehouse and settled in for the night. Without words to each other, the women walked from soldier to soldier, touching foreheads and administering quiet prayers and water that was brought from the nearest hotel's well. They held their emotions until everyone had been attended, and they exited the building.

Mrs. Woolley was the first to speak through tears, "We can't call ourselves Christian wives and mothers if we send many of these men on their way in the morning. They need medicine, food, and care."

"I know, Ann," said Mrs. Evie White. "But, how can we handle this? What are we going to do? We have nothing to offer except . . ."

"Except what, Evie?" Mrs. Woolley asked. "The Lord brought us here tonight and gave us a mission. Doc, you will be in charge of continuing to bring them to us."

Doc gave an approving nod.

"Ladies, at daybreak, we will help Doc load those who are able to travel back onboard the connecting train. They will all have a breakfast, anything our kitchens can spare, and then I'll start looking for a more suitable facility. We need something close to here that we can rent as a sort of temporary home for these men who are unable to travel. We can help them recuperate until arrangements can be made for their transfer to a proper hospital or send them home. Are we in agreement?"

A wave of nods from the group echoed her sentiment as she continued, "Rebecca, ask your father and Dr. Word for help."

Rebecca Mayson smiled in complete agreement. Through the night, they navigated the dark streets they knew by heart to find themselves home.

The next morning, many returned with baskets of food they carried by horseback. Rebecca Mayson returned with her father, Dr. Charles N. Mayson, and Dr. Robert Word. Dr. Word was destined to become dean of the Atlanta Medical College. But, for now, he was just another carrier of mercy to those in need.

The women began serving meals as sleepy men began to wake to the first smell of food they'd seen in many days, some weeks. The doctors each started at a different end of the building checking men to see who could travel and who would have to stay. Mrs. Woolley and Mrs. White began knocking on shopkeepers' doors looking to secure a more permanent and stable facility.

What began under the cover of darkness in the early, chilly, spring rains was coming full circle with the waning summer heat that precedes crisp, Southern autumns. Doc Tippin's one-man mission of mercy now had an army of followers armed with the kind of love and compassion that only the worst of wars can garner.

The immediate need for a more permanent facility was met as the ladies secured a building across from the depot. At their own expense, the group furnished what was to become known as the Wayside Home. Efforts made time speed up for the women of Kingston, especially Martha and her mother. Time began to pass quickly as they cleaned and scrubbed their new facility preparing it for wayward men. They did not discriminate on the basis of blue or gray. All men in need were equal.[1]

Bedding was in place; a system for bringing at least two meals a day to the soldiers was scheduled, and each woman had a job. Each night, Doc Tippin would lead a new group to the facility. The doctors would come free of charge and offer their services.

Much of this Martha watched from her window starting around midnight. Her mother was part of the late shift, but Martha was allowed to help during the day. She would bring meals to the soldiers who were able to board the connecting trains, and sometimes she and the other ladies would hold their hands while they wept. She busied herself helping others because it kept her mind off of her own worry because letters from her father and James were scattered and unsteady.

Sad cries of mourning and pain could be heard throughout the day, and soldiers' voices carried through the still night air. Sadly, Kingston had been drawn into a war it had not really wanted, and this was just the beginning. It seemed like more and more men came to Kingston's Wayside Home.

Unknowingly, the little Soldiers' Aid Society had created the first Confederate Hospital. The women had armed themselves with faith and cloaked themselves in Godly giving. They were truly fighting the war on the home front, and by all accounts, they were winning.[2]

Notes

1. References to conditions at the depot; seasonal weather; the sick and wounded soldier's arrival; the first president of the Soldiers' Aid Society; location of the Wayside Home; and references to physicians, including Dr. Robert Word, are taken from an article in Scrapbook 1, page 5, *Georgia Women Organized Way Back In The Sixties*, by Bell Bayless.

2. A letter from Miss Leila Darden to Mr. R.F. Burch, of Atlanta, Georgia, dated March 20, 1939, addresses a plea for the erection of a marker at the site where the first Confederate Hospital in South had been established.

Battlefields and front lines . . .

The South's first Confederate Hospital was in full swing. Soon, the one store building it operated out of was not enough. The ladies secured more rooms adjacent to the present site where a cook was hired, and more furnishings were placed for the rapidly increasing sick and wounded. Even the men of the town, who could not serve in the military, came to the aid of the soldiers by sitting with them at night. By now, a third doctor had joined the efforts of the other two physicians, and each continued to see soldiers free of any remuneration.

Without formal nursing training, the women learned medical skills on the job, assisting the physicians. Because of the enormity of running the two-building hospital, Martha, who was going on sixteen, was allowed to give more of her time to assisting the older women. Her first duty was to man a wagon with one of the ladies from the Soldiers' Aid Society. Martha found her days driving a wagon through the untouched and serene Southern countryside to be some of the best and most exciting times of her rapidly fading youth. She enjoyed learning from these strong-spirited women who could have convinced President Lincoln to join the Confederacy given half a chance. Their job together consisted of taking the wagons and riding throughout the Seventeenth District collecting any supplies they could from neighboring farms and plantations.[1]

Without fail, their weekly journeys would yield two full wagons. If anyone tried to deny them anything they could spare, the ladies would begin to preach about sinful selfish ways and lay unbelievable guilt trips on the farm owners. After a few weeks of fire and brimstone, many were waiting with packaged goods for the women to ride by in their wagons.

Martha was out of the house, out of the sewing circle and moving. She was going places and seeing people, and above all, involved.

As the months passed, hell and damnation sermons couldn't squeeze supplies out of those who had none left, so Martha's services were no longer needed on the wagon route. Now that she was sixteen, she was allowed inside the hospital. Her extra hands were to be trained by the town's only formally trained nurse, Lizzy Litton, none other than James' sister-in-law.[2] Like all of Kingston's women, Lizzy had a very independent spirit. She had insisted on attending nursing school when her then fiancé, Bradley Litton, left for medical school. When her father had flatly refused to send her, she and Brad eloped forcing her to follow her husband. As smart as she was, she had secured her own scholar-ship to attend nursing school. And now, she was using her skills to train the oth-ers.

Martha loved and respected Lizzy. She prayed that James would come home and ask her to marry him so that she could have a "big sister." She looked forward to learning nursing skills under Lizzy's watchful eye. Dreams of a fu-ture with James kept Martha going, and those dreams included running a small hospital in Kingston after the war. Just as Martha looked up to Lizzy as an older sister, James looked up to his brother and made plans to follow in his footsteps by becoming a doctor.

Martha had not been inside the hospital since she helped set it up with its initial furnishings. She remembered the clean smell of freshly laundered linens and the polished furniture collected and donated by the ladies. This place was nothing like she remembered. There was the stench of death looming in the en-trance. The smell of the sick and dirty was overpowering. Upon entering the Wayside Home, Martha had donned a smile filled with the joy at the thought of helping others, but the smile was replaced by tightly drawn lips and her own hand slapping her nose as a barrier to the scents of war casualties.

"Welcome to the real front lines." It was Lizzy with her usual jovial man-ner.

"Come on, let go of your nose. It's a horrible smell, but you will adjust, and soon you won't even notice," she said, grabbing Martha's hand from her face.

"What is that smell?" Martha grimaced and visibly gagged.

"Listen to me carefully," Lizzy said in a tone never before heard by Martha. "You cannot be faint of heart or weak of spirit to enter this place. This is a cold, hard fact of war and your mother has protected you from it up until now. I know this is difficult and a lot to ask of someone your age, but think about it in terms of James. You can go home in eight or ten hours and escape this carnage, but he's out there night and day in the middle of these deplorable circumstances watching his friends die. The least you can do is give a little care to these men and pray that someone is doing the same for James, just like I do for Brad."

Lizzy was gripping Martha's hand so tightly that it hurt as she continued her speech.

"If you truly are not up to this, speak now and walk out the door. There're plenty of other things you could be doing to help. If you wish to remain, then follow me. Your fresh hands and youthful energy are needed now."

Martha felt like she had no choice but to stay with Lizzy since she never let go of her vice-like grip on Martha's delicate hand.

"Your silence is a yes?" Lizzy nodded in an inquisitive gesture.

Martha never spoke as she took a step closer to Lizzy and began her train-ing as a nurse. Lizzy was right about one thing, the smell. At the end of her first training shift under Lizzy, Martha had become immune to the odor around her. She had assisted Dr. Word with a bandage, watched as Dr. Mayson removed a bullet from a young man's leg, and helped Mrs. White change the bed linen of a mutilated, dying young man not much older than James. It wasn't until she was ready to go that she realized her shoes now sported dried blood crusted across the top, and her apron was a light pink down the right side.

She barely waved good-bye to the others as she exited the building and broke into a run for her house. She hadn't noticed that she was crying until she reached her home. She immediately ran for the washstand, her pitcher already filled with water, which she immediately poured into the basin. She scrubbed her hands harshly enough to make them raw. Martha almost couldn't tell the difference between the leftover bloodstains on her hands and her own fresh blood coming to the surface of her skin from the excessive scrubbing. Her crying drew the attention of her mother and Camille who assisted her in silence. They knew their little girl had grown up to the horrors of an adult world in one day. Without a word, they helped her out of her clothing that Camille immediately took away and guided her into a hot, waiting bath in the kitchen.

Once inside her favorite warm dressing gown, Martha felt more at home, but Lizzy's words kept ringing in her ears about no escape for James. Martha began to weep again, wondering if she would have the strength to return to the Wayside Home tomorrow. What if she couldn't? She would be letting down James, her father, mother, Lizzy, and most of all herself. She fell asleep without supper as these thoughts and the bloody visions of the day continued to haunt her dreams.

She felt as if she had just fallen asleep when her mother, bearing a fresh dress, apron, and clean shoes awakened her.

"Charge," Catherine Malone said with a motherly smile and the forced push of a clenched fist.

Her mother's smile, thoughts of her father and James, and a simple prayer for endurance helped Martha out of bed and into her clothes for another day.

Notes

1. Information in the article in Scrapbook 1, page 5, *Georgia Women Organized Way Back In The Sixties*, by Bell Bayless, gives details concerning physicians, supply gathering, expansion, and operation of the Wayside Home.

2. Lizzy Litton is a fictional person and a character composite of many club members. Her purpose is to demonstrate the spirit in which the women handled the wartime tragedies.

One lonely homecoming . . .

After spending day after day with many of the same, sick soldiers, it was hard not to get attached. Once they were cleaned up, shaven, and speaking clearly, they weren't so scary, despite whichever uniform they wore. Martha always knew Mrs. Woolley was a very formidable person within her own right, but it wasn't until one day while making her own daily rounds to the troops that Martha saw her strong personality shine. The soldiers always welcomed her colorful visits and fancied her cooking.

Missing her own son, she took to a young man whom even both Doctors Mayson and Word had given up on. She had a few words with the doctors that afternoon as Martha witnessed the whole scene. It took all she had not to laugh in the face of all the surrounding suffering. Mrs. Woolley could fully compete in a theatre of war with the best of the best, including General Robert E. Lee himself. He'd surrender to Mrs. Woolley long before any Union general!

"Why is this young man still in this bed?" she inquired of Dr. Word, lips pursed with displeasure and fists folded on hips.[1]

"Well, Mrs. Woolley, his fever isn't breaking, and above all, his spirit is weak. War is a breaker of the human spirit, Ann, and I think our young man here has given in to it."

"Nonsense!" She knelt at his bedside and took his hand into her own. "Young man, what is your name?"

"Benjamin," he said weakly.

"Benjamin, we need this bed for other soldiers coming our way, and you are getting too well to lie in it anymore. The doctors think you need to get up now so that your recovery can be complete," she said.

"But I'm too sick," he whispered. "I can't even eat."

"God will get you for lying, son," she said.

Mrs. Woolley called for her carriage and raised up the frail young man by herself. She made him lean on her as she walked out of the hospital with him.

Martha thought she heard the doctors make bets with each other as to when she would be sending for one of them to pronounce him dead and remove his body.

That was starting to be the disturbing reality for the ladies. Martha imagined their hopes had been to nurse all back to health, but that wasn't possible in some cases. Instead, it became their jobs to hold their hands and offer the touch of an angel as they drew their last breaths, sadly enough some anonymously.

If it weren't enough for Martha to feel as though she had gone from sixteen to sixty overnight, William had just as hard of a job. When a soldier died, he was one of several called in to remove the body for burial. Local preachers were kept busy with many makeshift funerals for men they had only met once on their deathbeds or never even had a chance to meet.

One such young man became Martha's cross to bear. No word had come from her father or James in weeks when Doc Tippin brought in a very young, handsome Union soldier. Dr. Mayson discovered that the young man was wounded, not mortally, but badly enough that extra care was needed.

Martha spotted him the next day, and it became her mission to help him. Something about his eyes reminded her of her James. She took a pitcher of cool water and a clean cup to his bedside and knelt down, offering the young man a drink. He wouldn't take it. Instead, he stared coldly into her eyes and turned to look out the window.[2]

"What is your name?" Martha asked sweetly.

The young man in blue would not reply.

"Well, my name is Martha, and I'm new at nursing, but I'm here to help you any way I can," she said. "I can bring you medicine, or I can bring you food if you will tell me what you like. I have water now, but if you want, I might could find some milk or tea."

Still there was no response. She was talking to the back of his head.

"Sir, I could read to you if you like. Do you like books? My father has a library full of them. If you could tell me what you like, I could see if we have it. I could also read scripture to you. I carry my Bible in my bag."

Martha stopped talking for a moment, not sure if the young man were even listening to her. Then, she meekly whispered and hung her head in defeat, "I can go get it."

Then, she reached out to touch the young man. He only rolled out of her reach and onto his side. Clearly, he did not want her help. Martha stood up and walked among the rows of moaning men with tears streaming down her face. Looking into their faces was like staring into a freshly dug graveyard filled with the bodies of men who had to die for no reason. These were men who were loved by their families, and those same men who longed to see and love their families one more time. It was too much for a young girl to witness.

She made it to the fresh air of the outside. The familiar smells of Georgia pine and coal from the depot side of town made her remember she was at home. Instead of returning that afternoon, she headed for church where she could talk to God and gain some peace.

About two hours later, Martha remained silent and still on the front pew. She heard footsteps approaching and assumed it was Lizzy coming to retrieve her or her mother or Camille coming to baby her and take her home where she really belonged. But, the steps were heavier than a woman's. They were slow and deliberate. The weight behind the movement sounded like boots, large boots like a soldier might wear. Martha was too scared to turn around. She was alone in the church save for the intruder. She began to shake as the steps grew louder and harder, and she closed her eyes tightly as if doing this could make him disappear. Martha dared not look up and behind her as the noise stopped.

There was silence and she felt movement of an arm toward her back, and then a distressed voice spoke, "Martha, it's me."

It was James. She knew it was James despite the fact that he was much skinnier than when he left last year. His boyish face had faded into early manhood, and a scraggly misshapen beard replaced the soft baby fat that had left with him on his cheeks. He looked like so many men she had seen over the past year. His hair was matted and his clothes dirty. She couldn't believe her eyes, and she couldn't help herself. She leapt to her feet and threw her arms around his neck. They embraced through tears of joy and relief. Neither of them knew how long they held each other when they let go. Many questions raced through Martha's mind, the first being how was it possible that James were here?

"I have a short furlough," he said before she had a chance to ask.

Instead of replying to his statement, she responded with a question, "Is my father home too?"

"No. He decided to stay with the company, but I have a letter for your mother with me," he said.

Martha knew her mother would be crushed that her father wasn't with James, but that her father's letter would probably explain everything. Despite her longing to see her father, Martha couldn't help but show her excitement that James was home.

"Are you all right?" James asked.

"I am now that you're here," she said. "How long do you have?"

"Just one week," he replied.

One week, one day, it didn't matter to Martha. He was here, and all the things she couldn't and wouldn't say in a letter, she now had the chance to say to his face. Martha wanted to start talking and holding James immediately. She wanted to express all the feelings she had pushed to the bottom of her heart. She had seen too many men die without ever hearing how their loves felt about them, and she didn't want that to happen to James.

When she opened her mouth to speak, James silenced her with a kiss and said, "Wait. We have one week. Now, I need to deliver two letters."

"Two? I thought you just had one for my mother," she said.

"Brad didn't come home either," he said. "As a doctor, he felt it was his duty to remain with the company. He said if anyone would understand, it would be Lizzy. I need to see her first, and then I'll go up to your place."

They left the church arm-in-arm in silence. Inside her head, Martha was saying a silent prayer of thanksgiving for James' brief return and her father's safety.

Notes

1. A reference to a young man nursed to health in the home of Mrs. Ann Woolley is given in this article; *History of the Town of Kingston, Vivid War-Time Picture By a Lady Who Witnessed and Participated in Trying Scenes, The Cartersville News*, October 17, 1907, from museum scrapbooks.

2. A reference to an anonymous soldier in blue, who died without speaking, is given in this article; *History of the Town of Kingston, Vivid War-Time Picture By a Lady Who Witnessed and Participated in Trying Scenes, The Cartersville News*, October 17, 1907, from museum scrapbooks.

No good-bye needed . . .

Martha and James headed for the hospital to find Lizzy. It seemed as though she never left the place. Being the town's only nurse, she spent many nights on a spare bed. As soon as Lizzy saw the pair, she froze. It was obvious she was terrified that James was bearing bad news. James felt the panic fly from her eyes across the room and subdued it with one smile and the wave of Brad's letter. Lizzy grabbed the nearest headboard for support, regrouped her thoughts and embraced him.

Martha gave them a moment of privacy and decided to check on her Union soldier. As she approached his bed, she noticed he had not moved since she left him earlier in the day. She feared he had died and no one noticed, but then she saw his shoulder rising and falling with his steady breath. He was asleep. Forcing back tears, she reached down and touched his forehead. She wanted to give compassion to this man in any form, and if it meant that she had to do it while he slept, then she was going to give him the attention she felt that he deserved. She stroked his hair and prayed while she waited on James. Soon, he joined her, and they set off for the Malone' residence on the hill overlooking Kingston.

The same look of fear and anxiety came across her mother's face as she saw the pair approach. Catherine clutched her chest and temporarily stopped breathing until she saw the smiles that were plastered on their faces. To stop the fear, James waved the letter in Mr. Malone's writing so that Catherine could see her husband was well.

Putting his arms around Mrs. Malone, James softly said, "He wanted to be here, but the letter will explain it all."

Tears falling on her lips curled in a brave smile, Mrs. Malone took the letter and clutched it over her heart, kissed James on the cheek and walked into the house and up the stairs alone. Camille tried to force food on the boney James, but he insisted on heading to his own home, vowing to return for several Camille-original meals before his furlough was to end.

Although their first moments had been brief, Martha willingly kissed him goodnight, knowing he would be with her tomorrow. All that she wanted to say would be said.

For the first time in more than a year, Martha overate at dinner and slept without a midnight stroll. Although the mysterious depot light had been solved long ago, she still continued to walk, but not tonight. Only sweet dreams walked through her head throughout her slumber.

The next morning, both Martha and William sat across from their mother who had not been seen since James delivered the letter from their father. She wore the same brave smile.

"I read your father's letter until I fell asleep late last night," she began. "He decided not to take the same furlough as James. He said the lines are getting thin and many aren't able to fight like they did in the beginning. Conditions are harsh, as we imagined, and many of the young are considering desertion. Furloughs are being granted just a few at a time. Your father decided that we have had many, happy years together. He feels that we have many more to come.

"He has given up his furlough now so that other, younger men could return to their families and girlfriends, like James. He says the sight of home and those they love can only boost their morale. Your father said that we are all older, and he knows we miss him just as much, but he hasn't lost sight of what he is doing and why. He also knows what we are doing here and wants us to not lose sight of our mission. He wants us to all write to him and give our letters to James so that he knows we understand."

"Mother, do you understand?" William sounded like a timid child.

"Actually, yes I do, Will. Yes, I do."

At this moment, Martha loved her father more than ever. He unselfishly gave up a furlough so that younger men like her love could come home for a brief respite. As soon as her shift at the Wayside Home was over, she would start her letter to him and seal it with love so that James could carry her words to her father.

Just as Martha was leaving for the Wayside Home, James was walking up the hill.

"Good morning, Beautiful," he called.

"Well, good morning to you too," she replied. And, then added, "Handsome."

James had obviously bathed, shaved, and had his mother cut his hair. He resembled the James that left last year. However, he was in dire need of nourishment.

"Where are you headed this morning?"

"I'm on duty today. Oh, I wish I weren't, but maybe I can get off a little early?"

"Don't worry about it," James said. "I'll go with you. I've spent a lot of time with Brad in the field hospital. Maybe, I can help?"

James was just about perfect in Martha's eyes. So, just as they had trod up the hill the night before, they descended arm-in-arm.

Now used to the smell, Martha no longer gasped for breath or covered her grimacing face as she entered the Wayside Home. The two of them ran into Doc Tippin as he sat solemnly at the side of a dying man. He was scribbling down last words to a family and double-checking the address.

Doc was truly amazing to the women. He took his job very seriously. He continued to meet the trains and moved into the position as official record keeper. Doc kept very accurate records of all the men who were served at the Wayside Home. He knew their names, addresses, families, companies, and most of all, their siding in the war which still made no difference inside the walls of hope and healing.[1]

As Doc finished transcribing the man's final words, the Reverend Hackett stepped into the picture with a final prayer for passage of the dying soldier. Mrs. Woolley and Mrs. White solemnly covered his body and wiped their own eyes. Martha left the scene and headed for her lonely Union patient. She could still hear the same weeping that all the ladies endured as each man died, as well as a quiet greeting exchanged between Doc and James, when she approached a terrible sight. Still lying in the same position as the night before was the Union soldier she tried so hard to reach. Only this time, he wasn't breathing, and he had been covered with the white death shroud that had become commonplace all too often at the Wayside Home.

She was too mortified to scream, too shocked and angered to cry for him, so all that was left to do was shake. Martha began shaking. She felt every emotion she had ever had while in the Wayside Home rush through her body like some uncontrolled demonic force. She was angry with him for dying. She was angry with him for fighting against her father and James. She was angry with him for never telling her his name. She was mad because he hadn't let her help him. And, she was grieving because someone that young had to die. Who was he? Now that he was gone, his mother would never know what happened to him. Did he have a fiancé like James had her? How would she handle not knowing what happened to him? Would she wait until her dying day to be reunited with him in Heaven? Was he saved? All of these burning questions would never be answered and for no reason.

"Honey, what's wrong?" Doc asked as he embraced her shoulders from behind. "Martha, talk to me."

But Martha still could not speak. Instead, she did something so out of character; it seemed to silence the room. The usual quiet, meek, and observant but speechless Martha shouted, "Tell me why, why, why did he have to die? I was here! The doctors were here. I prayed while he slept."

By this time, James and Lizzy had joined Doc at Martha's side and were taking her to the nearest seat. In silence, they stroked her hair and tried to calm her. Still, she could not shed a tear for the Union soldier.

"Martha, I tried myself," Doc began. "We're not sure exactly what happened to that young man. I stayed with him last night until he died. He wasn't alone. He never spoke. Dr. Mayson said he was probably in too much shock to talk. Since we don't know anything about him, there is also the possibility that he was mute and unable to write. Sweetheart, we just don't know. But, I can promise you one thing. He won't be forgotten here."

How could Doc say that? Martha was wondering just what Doc meant. They didn't know his name, his family, or where he was from. How could he be remembered?

"I have a feeling he'll always be in your heart. And, he'll have a final resting place right here in Kingston. I know you will be personally responsible for a few flowers every now and then, won't you?"[2]

Doc was unbelievable. He could always see something being done for someone else no matter what the circumstances. He opened his ledger and began writing on the next line. "Brave, Union, Young Man, Family Unknown, Friend Known, Miss Martha Malone." He continued to record a physical description of the young man just in case someone inquired about him after the war, as well as catalog all of his worldly possessions. Then, his body was hastily prepared for burial, and actually to Martha's delight, James assisted in removing the young man. He and Martha accompanied the wagon carrying his body and several others to the cemetery on the hill for burial.

It was a hard day for Martha despite James' presence. James busied himself carrying supplies and moving beds and bodies. He looked quite at home in this task, which made Martha wonder what he was enduring on the battlefield. They had both grown up entirely too fast.

Notes

1. Personal writings of Miss Leila Darden, Kingston Woman's History Club charter member, and local historian, reveal William "Doc" Tippin kept records of all the men who died in the Wayside Home. He recorded the number of their grave, their wartime affiliation, home address, and next of kin. After his death, and the war, the records were never located. They are believed to have perished in a fire; *History of Kingston Memorial Day*, personal writings by Miss Leila Darden, archives, Kingston Woman's History Club Museum.

2. The Kingston Cemetery, soldiers' section, contains two hundred forty-nine unknown Confederate soldiers, one known, and two unknown Union soldiers. Information taken from *The Daily Tribune News, Cartersville, Looking 'Em Over, 93rd Memorial Day at Kingston*, April 25, 1957, by Thomas Spencer, reprinted in the *Commemorative Program for the 125th Confederate Memorial Service*. One of the unknown Union graves could be linked to the eye-witness account of a silent Union soldier brought to the Wayside Home who died without giving his name. (*History of the Town of Kingston, Vivid War-Time Picture By a Lady Who Witnessed and Participated in Trying Scenes, The Cartersville News*, October 17, 1907, museum scrapbooks)

Too many farewells . . .

Having James home for an entire week was wonderful. However, for Martha, the wonderful was constantly overshadowed by a looming sense of departure. Lizzy stepped in and took one of Martha's shifts at the hospital giving her a full day with James. Martha felt blessed beyond the means of many women because of her opportunity to say all that was in her heart. She and James made a peace with each other and their situation. They knew this might be their last moments together on this earth. Nothing was left unsaid between the pair as James prepared to leave on the Saturday morning train.

As luck would have it, James wasn't the only man leaving Kingston that morning. Heading back into battle was Benjamin, Mrs. Woolley's "sick little Benjamin." Inside her head, Martha was thanking the Lord for the sight of Benjamin who joined James in a makeshift send off parade to the depot. The reason Martha thanked God at that moment was the sight of Benjamin made not only Martha laugh out loud but everyone who saw him including Doctors Mayson and Word. The two physicians who had given up hope probably laughed the loudest. Was he a sight! The frail, sick and skinny lad, who was swept away by Mrs. Woolley months ago, was now about twenty pounds heavier, and it appeared, a couple of inches taller. This in itself wouldn't have been funny except that his clothes were bulging at the seams, many of which had been expanded by Mrs. Woolley, and he was wearing the most ridiculous-looking hat. It was apparent that Mrs. Woolley had tried to modify it into a man's headpiece but failed. Through the joyful and playful jeers, Benjamin smiled and waved to the crowd as he marched to the depot side-by-side with James.

"At least his head will be warm, and I pray I won't see his return to our Wayside Home," Mrs. Woolley shouted above the laughter.

People weren't being mean, and she knew it. She was just a little annoyed that her handicraft hat was getting a little too much attention. In fact, someone stepped onto the platform to pay for Benjamin's ticket, none other than Evie White.

The memory of Benjamin's appearance and the fact that he survived gave Martha hope. The darkest days of the war were steaming down the track, undetected and deadly. Despite the promise of spring coming in 1863, everyone kept a cold shiver.

After James' brief visit, Martha's life went back into a routine of hospital duty. Small gunfire could be heard from time-to-time, but the only evidence of war was the casualties brought to the Wayside Home.

In fact, the most exciting event had taken place a year earlier on April 12, 1862, when Andrews' Raiders hijacked the General in Kennesaw. Their Yankee mission was to destroy the railroad lines in North Georgia. However well planned their strategy, they hadn't counted on getting side railed in Kingston where they lost a good bit of time. Thanks to this temporary derailment, the pursuing Confederates were able to recapture the General before any real harm could be done. It was in Kingston where the Confederates hopped aboard the Rome Railroad locomotive named the "William R. Smith" and continued their pursuit north.[1]

As usual, the Georgia spring weather was unpredictable. Comfortable days often led to cool or cold nights. Without the comfort of loved ones, they seemed even colder. Words on paper were poor substitutes for warm hugs from Martha's father or soft kisses from James.

Despite the droll times, business as usual continued for the Soldiers' Aid Society. Doc Tippin had only left his duties with the ladies once to serve as a private in Company K of the 41st Regiment of Volunteer Infantry, Georgia. He was transferred to Company "C" within that Regiment and later discharged from Confederate service in Lauderdale, Mississippi, in July 1862. Although he only saw about four months of active duty, he returned home a well-respected Confederate veteran.[2]

Doc hit the ground running when he returned to Kingston, and nothing could slow him down, not even the doctors. Martha had noticed Lizzy and Dr. Word giving Doc Tippin a serious talk about slowing down a little and allowing some of the younger men, like William, to help. Doc was adamant that he was fine and could do his job. About a week after this little talk, Martha saw Doc finish a letter for a dying soldier, fold it, and prepare it for the mail. Doc stood to walk to the makeshift office when he collapsed beside the man's bed. Martha and several others rushed to his side. Lizzy and Dr. Mayson assisted by three ladies carried Doc to the nearest bed. Martha began to put his papers back in order and secure the letter he had readied for the mail.

"He's burning up," Lizzy said.

"I knew this was going to happen eventually," Dr. Mayson said. "Bring some ice and rubbing alcohol now, Ann. We have to get his fever down."

As Doc woke, he began to cough uncontrollably. Doc had contracted pneumonia. The ladies kept a twenty-four hour bedside vigil with their dear friend, but to no avail. Doc died that terribly depressing May in 1863. As resources were limited for all, he was buried in an unmarked grave in his home soil. Sadly, this brave humanitarian and soldiers' friend would sleep unceremoniously in an unmarked grave for the next eighty-eight years.

However painful and devastating to the women, their mission had to continue.

"If we give in to grief and our own self pity over our loss, we will desecrate the memory of the real hero of our Wayside Home," Mrs. Woolley proclaimed the morning after Doc's funeral. "We cannot let him down. He gave his life for this place and his country. We should do well to follow his lead."

And, follow his lead they did. Young William Malone was proud to assume many of the beloved William "Doc" Tippin's duties. Times and supplies continued to get slimmer as the war pushed farther South. The rest of the spring and summer passed almost uneventful for Martha. Letters were fairly steady from James and her father as they were encamped now in Georgia.

Soldiers were recovering at the Wayside Home, and some could be seen walking the streets from time to time looking for food and milk. Because food was scarce, they would go door to door and beg. No one turned away a hungry man even if it meant doing without a meal themselves. As soon as they were well, they would graciously say thank you and hop aboard a train to fight another day.

Martha's heart broke every time she would see a grown man, looking like a hollow shell of his former self, wandering the streets of Kingston just to knock on a door to ask for food. It was painfully obvious that each man had been a strong and able-bodied provider for his family before the war. How much more was this war going to cost in human blood and dignity? All she could do was smile at the men and give them what they needed when they knocked on her family's door.

Time was limited for the Wayside Home's existence. After more than two years of service, the small, community-run "hospital" was commandeered by the Confederacy and an official military hospital was established. Kingston became a military medical site. All of the women, except for Lizzy who was drafted into nursing service, were excused from their nursing duties. Many of those who had been involved with the sewing group returned to being seamstresses.

For more than two years, the women had diligently served as nurses, mothers to dying men, cooks, maids, and general errand girls. Now, they were asked to return to sewing and waiting; a pattern to be repeated throughout the history of war in the United States. And, so they returned to their pre-Wayside Home days. However, they never abandoned their group as the Soldiers' Aid Society.

In the coming winter and spring months, many of them, including Martha and her mother, sewed as cloth became very limited. They waited for news and letters, many of which rarely came. The Yankees had pushed into Georgia and loud skirmishes could be heard all over the area.

By May 1864, real combat had moved to Kingston, and all of hell's fury was about to be unleashed.

Notes

1. Information taken from *Andrews Raiders at Kingston*, Georgia Historical Marker, Kingston, Georgia.

2. According to the *Georgia Farmers' Market Bulletin*, *Confederate Marker*, editorial by Tom Linder, October 24, 1951, "'Doc' Tippin served-without pay in this hospital-and was away from his duties there only once, and that was during his service in the Confederate Army."

Hell hath no fury . . .

It did seem that the floodgates of hell had opened and unleashed such a beast, as the women had never seen before. The battles around Resaca, Dalton, and Calhoun raged. Little did Martha know how near her father and James actually were, and that they were both involved in these bloody confrontations. Many of the women had the general idea from the last letters they received that their men might be fighting close to home. They would question Lizzy after all of her shifts to see if she recognized any of the Confederates who were brought in for treatment.[1]

The ladies thought they had seen the worst of the worst, but the moans and cries of anguish could be heard twenty-four hours a day coming from the Goulding House. In 1854, Dr. Francis R. Goulding, a Presbyterian minister, purchased land in Kingston and built his beautiful, gabled house. He was an author, teacher, and inventor who is said to have invented the very first sewing machine.

However, Dr. Goulding ran a boarding school for boys and authored several children's books including *The Young Marooners*.[2] Now, his beautiful, boarding school home had become the official hospital site for the worst of the worst, gangrene and amputees. The dining room table was transformed into an operating table. Those who didn't survive were buried in mass graves in his back yard, and his handsome floors were now stained with blood.[3] With the lack of morphine and other painkillers, the continual cries of agony were almost unbearable. Many began to leave Kingston and flee to the countryside, but Martha's family, many in the sewing circle, and several members of the Soldiers' Aid Society stayed firmly planted in Kingston.

Traditionally a month that culminates with the promise of spring, May was as unkind to Kingston in 1864 as she had been in 1863. With hell's gates now open, many believed Satan had come to town. Martha thought that a very unkind and unbending Union general pompously paraded the streets with a band of marauders never before set loose in Georgia. General William T. Sherman made

Kingston his headquarters, commandeering the home of Thomas V.B. Hargis from May 19-23, 1864.[4]

These three days were only the beginning of months of skirmishes between Confederate and Union troops. Although Sherman left Kingston in pursuit of Confederate forces, he decided to return after the fall of Atlanta to make Kingston his headquarters again.

During this time, several incidents became unbearable such as the treatment given to Kingston residents. Their places of worship were torn apart, their pews were thrown into the wagon yard where Union soldiers allowed their horses to feed from them. Martha thought this was a slap in the face to a people who had given so much to not only their own, but to their adversaries. Sherman and his officers would allow this type of behavior, and only stop it when it reached proportions of complaint that could later be used against them.[5]

Those who fled to the countryside during these months were in more danger than those who remained in and around the village. Plundering and pillaging took place every night. When the complaints would come, some of the residents' possessions would be returned however damaged and destroyed they were. Most all of the Malones' food had been confiscated and many of Mr. Malone's books and legal papers destroyed. A particularly nasty Union private grabbed Camille once he found her freedom papers. He drug her into the Malone's front yard where he ripped her dress for sport and kicked her on her backside leaving an enormous bruise.

"You dumb girl," he began to shout. "Why are you still here? What have I been fighting for all these years? It's your stupid kind."

Martha and her mother were held back as they raced for Camille. For safety, William was perched high above the property in a tree, as he was an excellent tree climber. The men were more likely to have killed William with any resistance from the young man. Little did Martha and her mother know, William was pointing a loaded rifle at the soldier's head. The boy had hidden the weapon inside a hollowed out branch in May when Sherman's men first arrived in the village. Now, shaking and raging with anger, William almost took his shot at his surrogate mother's captor. However, he maintained self-control as he was afraid of shooting Camille instead.

The private continued to terrorize Camille by knocking her around despite the cries and protests from the Malone women. Finally, in one terrifying moment, the private produced a single match, struck it on his belt buckle, and held it close to Camille's skirt. For a moment, they thought he was going to burn Camille, but instead he burned her freedom papers.

To Martha, the private performed an act of brutality and power over the women. The filthy and ill-groomed private shoved Camille to the ground one final time, spat in her face, and then drew her near by the collar and said in a sinister voice, "You are now free to go."

With a nod of his head, the others released Catherine and Martha and left with most of their food rations. All that remained was a malnourished cow, two skinny chickens, and a baby pig. William scurried down the tree red faced and hot tempered. They all clung to each other and thanked God for life.

As if this weren't bad enough, Sherman's occupation meant a near halt to all mail. If there were any letters from her father or James, Martha and Catherine rarely if ever saw them. The women were determined not to be defeated, no matter what the costs. In fact, their bravery became bolder in the face of adversity.

With Union occupation of Kingston and the surrounding areas, Martha and her comrades could feel the presence of these sinister minions draining little bits of joy each time one passed. It was obvious being in the village was easier than on the outskirts of Kingston. Tales continued to filter in about how bands of soldiers, without the accompaniment of officers, would sporadically enter homes, terrorizing and robbing its residents. Much of it was senseless now that they had robbed the villagers and farmers of their food. Many times they took nothing but destroyed everything they could lay their hands on.

Members of the Soldiers' Aid Society remained faithful to their sewing even though very little, if anything, could be shipped. It may have been lovingly packaged, but it would be savagely torn apart and taken by the Union troops before it could reach the hands of needy Southern men. In fact, the women had very little if no cloth left, so they just made socks and undergarments, as well as, wrapped bandages and bed clothes from whatever they could salvage. Later, cotton would be called "king" in the South, but for now, its abundance was wearing thin. Everything had been made of cotton right down to a soldier's shoes, and these supplies were now limited.

One particular afternoon, the group gathered at Evie's house. Lizzy and her mother brought the afternoon's refreshments from what rations they had left. The ladies also began to meet in private homes, as the church was too public for their mission. Plus they could not stomach what the ignorant heathens, the ladies concluded, were doing to their sacred place of worship. The Yankees thought they were dealing the group a blow that as frail women they wouldn't recover from. Little did they know how well equipped the female spirits were to handle anything they could dish out.

The ladies hadn't been one hour into their sewing on the last remaining piece of now grayish, brown cloth they could muster when there were loud, rough footsteps on the White's porch. With one token, rude knock, three Union privates entered. You could tell the privates from the officers by the way they conducted themselves, badly in the ladies' opinions.

Once they had busted in and grabbed what food was left on Lizzy's silver platter, one shoved the platter under his coat while looking around for anything else he could take. Martha was privately calling the man a "scoundrel" in her mind. Then, the lead private eyed the group's handiwork and snatched it from the circle, needles and all still attached. He took a knife from his boot and began to shred the last, precious piece of Confederacy gray they had. Tears of anger rolled down several of the women's faces. Then, the most amazing thing happened.

Softly, gently, and with more grace than Martha had ever seen, Lizzy stood up and seemed to glide toward the severely uneducated private.

"My dear sir," she began, "there is no need to be so rude. Obviously, you need to give great gratitude to whomever directed you to our little sewing soirée for much needed repairs to your most impressive uniform."

Three puzzled looks emitted from the faces of the intruders. By this time, Lizzy had walked up to the grizzly-looking man and was close enough to kiss him Martha thought. If the men had not been so caught by surprise by Lizzy's brazen actions, they might have dared look at every woman's chest to discover that hearts were collectively beating out of control with fear. No one moved or spoke, except Lizzy, who continued her little speech.

"I mean you have certainly come to the right place for uniform repair. I'm so pleased that you are here. Are all of you in need of tailor services? We are not professional tailors, but we do a fair job."

"Huh," was all that came out of the foul, toothless mouth of the lead invader.

Lizzy was now closer, and she began to touch the man's uniform pulling at every button and seam all over the nightmare in blue. He squirmed and wiggled as if he were a child being tickled for the first time.

"This is disgraceful," she said shaking her head. "These poor buttons are so loose and dirty. Why, this seam is ready to burst any moment. Look at these holes and tears."

Suddenly, her gentle tickling turned to buttons flying off the man's coat. They were landing with gentle pings on the floor.

"What in the..." was all he could say through his squirming.

"Oh my," she continued. "See what I'm talking about. This uniform is about to fall off of you. You got here just in time."

Then, the most unexpected event of the entire war for Martha took place. No one had noticed that Lizzy was holding a pair of shears in the folds of her skirt. And, until the day she died, Lizzy never disclosed exactly how she did it, but in one felt swoop, she used the sewing tool better than a master swordsman when she let out a squeal and somehow cut the waist of the man's pants making them fall to the floor exposing a very nasty and torn pair of long johns. There he stood, more vulnerable than the women he came to terrorize because his manly honor had been disgraced in front of his fellow soldiers and a bunch of Southern women.

If heartbeats could be heard aloud, the noise coming from the women would have been deafening. Everyone was frozen, including the three Union men.

"I told you that uniform was falling apart," Lizzy said calmly. "Why, I was just trying to trim a loose string for you. I sure hope you have a spare suit in your camp. You better get there now and change, and then head straight back here with this torn rag for repair. Of course, it may have to be stitched in gray thread. Will that be acceptable?"

There was no answer from the disgraced soldier who was now bending down grasping for his britches. Lizzy moved to the left of him and went toward one of the other men who quickly retreated for the door.

"Come back," she said. "I think I can fix you up too."

Many of the older women were beginning to fear repercussions, and Martha was just trying not to laugh too loudly as the men ran from the house. They heard the stolen silver tray hit the porch steps. It became obvious that the men feared Lizzy most. Still holding the sewing shears, she followed them to the door shouting.

"Wait, don't leave. I haven't finished the repairs."

The women heard laughter from some passersby, as the lead thug must have been a sight running while holding his pants.

The women let this "theft" incident slide and did not report it to the Union authorities. They feared what might become of poor Lizzy if all of this were to come to light.

Hearts began beating normally, and the group started to move once again when Lizzy walked into the room holding her silver platter in one hand and the now-famous sewing shears in the other.

Martha eyed the prized Union buttons still resting on the floor and knelt down to pick them up. Lizzy saw her putting them in the pocket on her sewing apron and gave her one final prize that was still in her hand with the scissors. All that ran through Martha's mind was how amazing and brave Lizzy was. She cut that man's pants loose while still holding one button.

Lizzy's mother gave her a token scolding, and Mrs. Woolley pretended to be annoyed with her, but couldn't help herself from fits of uncontrolled laughter. Although the enemy had shredded their last piece of cloth, the women considered this a small victory in the war. One of their own had forced a shameful retreat. They had proven themselves worthy adversaries for the Northern occupants of Kingston. Their men would have been proud.[6]

Notes

1. Information about locations of battles and experiences during the Civil War for the fictional character of James Litton are taken from stories retold to a local newspaper by Dr. John D. Goodwin, dated August 20, 1925, in an article titled, *Dr. John D. Goodwin Tells War-Time Stories of Past*. Article archived in Kingston Woman's History Club Museum, Scrapbook 1. No newspaper source was saved or cited in the scrapbook files.

2. *Homes on Tour*, Kingston, Georgia, April 24, 1976; program supplement was sponsored and printed by the Kingston Woman's History Club.

3. *Random Notations About Kingston's Part In The War Between The States 1861-1865* are typewritten notes archived in the Kingston Woman's History Club files.

4. Dates and information are taken from the house site of Thomas V.B. Hargis, Maj. Gen. W.T. Sherman's Headquarters, May 19-23, 1864, Georgia Historical Marker, Kingston, Georgia.

5. Incidents like the one described where soldiers were allowed to feed horses from church pews have been passed down as part of the town's history from club member to club member. This account taken from personal interaction and recollections of various club members.

6. Inspiration for all of the above fictional incidents revolving around the characters telling the story were inspired by the writings of Frances Thomas Howard, *In and Out of the Lines, An Accurate Account of Incidents During the Occupation of Georgia by Federal Troops in 1864-1865*; and a letter to the editor of the *Cartersville Tribune News*, March 9, 1922, from Joe T. Jolly. The letter describes his family's experiences with federal troops, as well as, one of his neighbor's. Typewritten copy of letter on file in Kingston Woman's History Club Museum archives. Please note, many club members also verbally repeat similar incidents that have been told to them via word of mouth, passed down through many generations. This chapter merely adds the book's characters to represent interaction with Union soldiers and the characters' feelings about them.

The end begins . . .

Lizzy found out what happened to the men with whom she had done battle. They met the same fate as the tyrant who had terrorized the Malones. These men were stripped of what little rank they had held and sent North where they were promptly put to work with other prisoners.

As for the women who were waiting, each day was longer than the one before it. News and letters had ceased to come. The summer was long, and the cooler weather of fall was a welcome change. Soon, Sherman's men became more restless than ever. There wasn't a whole lot more they could do to the people of Kingston, or so Martha thought, until November 7, 1864.[1]

On this fall day, Sherman received the official orders from General Ulysses S. Grant and President Abraham Lincoln to move forward with his plans. Grant gave Sherman permission to destroy the state. And, the way to do this was through a new warfare so horrible that Georgians found even the thought of it unimaginable, "total war." This meant nothing was sacred, and all was fair game. Cities, towns, farms, homesteads, and all civilians were now targets. This was the plan for dividing Georgia and ending the war.

Sherman's goal was to march to Savannah. In Martha's mind, Sherman was a dangerous man. Her heart was sick with fear for her home state when she learned of these orders. She had witnessed his cruelty first hand, and she knew that history's account of this war would not end well for the South.

History would record that Sherman's *March to the Sea* was from Atlanta to Savannah, but the first smoldering piles of rubble and desperate cries of pain originated in Kingston that November. With the news of the orders spreading like wildfire throughout the village, everyone headed for home. The Malones' plan was much the same as it was the day they had been terrorized. They would not resist, and William would hide in the tree above the house. Only this time, Martha, Camille, and Catherine felt a little better knowing the young man was brandishing a loaded gun. They just had to lead the soldiers with lanterns to a moonlit spot where William could get a clear shot.

Praying for the best with Sherman's departure and expecting the worst, the Malones waited as the sun drifted downward. The silence of night fell with a deafening crash, and the screams began. For Martha, the cover of darkness unleashed the cowardice of many of the Union soldiers. The Malone women and Camille watched from the front porch as lights scurried all over the village and into the outskirts. There was no reason to hide because the soldiers knew where everyone lived.

That night, a couple of residents suffered the most. Twelve-year-old Jimmy Norris' father met the troops at their front door when they demanded food, whiskey, and tobacco. His father insisted there was none in the home. Jimmy, his mother, and siblings watched in horror as Mr. Norris was dragged from the house and a rope tied around his neck. They found this rope under the side of the home. It had been used to drag off an old army horse turned out to die. Amidst the screams from his family, Mr. Norris was dragged off into the woods and the rope thrown around a branch of a tree where the soldiers tried to frighten him into giving up his goods. Convinced he had none, they let him go.

While in the woods with one group of Union soldiers, Mrs. Norris was being robbed of all her tableware, all clothing that was wearable by troops, and a small stash of sweet potatoes from their front porch.

A few hours later, the Malones could still hear the cries in the night as the rampage continued. Around ten o'clock, someone came up the hill masked by darkness. The Malones were prepared for anything. A nervous William slowly and deliberately cocked his gun and raised it with shaking hands. He was prepared to shoot until he heard a familiar Southern drawl. It was an unshaken Mr. Norris who was asking about their well-being. The nervous teenager in the tree almost dropped his gun as he un-cocked it, and then lowered it to his lap. They were glad to know that the town's men were braving the night's terror to check on the women.

Little did Mr. Norris know that his family was being terrorized once again. While at the Malone residence, a separate set of Union soldiers knocked at the door of his residence, insisting they were ordered to search the houses. Mrs. Norris and the children had gone to bed, so she asked if she could dress and dress her children. The two oldest boys, Ray and Jimmy, were dressing when Mrs. Norris opened the door and a large Union soldier entered with a pistol drawn. He demanded she show him the entire house. Once satisfied no one was there, he said he had information that gold was somewhere inside the house, and he came to confiscate it. If she didn't give it up, he would burn her house with the smaller children in it.

She confessed she had ten dollars in greenbacks and about two hundred dollars in Confederate money buried in the back yard. The soldier took the terrified mother and the two boys at gunpoint into the back yard where the boys dug up the currency. The foursome returned to the house where Mrs. Norris gave the man her last penny. Then, he demanded the gold. When she cried there was none, he said he would burn the house to the ground, and headed for the fireplace where he took a large glowing coal. He turned and headed for the bed of sleeping young children.

Mrs. Norris forced her way in front of him, begging him to allow her to get her children out of the bed, but he shoved her aside and into the wall with a hard lick to her shoulder. Jimmy later described his mother as having superhuman strength as she swept all of the children onto the floor. Finally, convinced the family was not hiding anything, he threw the coal into the fireplace and left.

A few days later, Mrs. Norris would recount her shocking story to Martha and Catherine. Catherine fully understood the woman's feelings and emotions as a mother when she said, "As a Christian, I do not believe in taking the life of another person. However, if that man had harmed one hair on any of my children's heads, I would have killed him with my bare hands. God help me, but I would have taken his life any way I could have."

The Norris family had narrowly escaped death and disaster that night, however, one of their neighbors didn't fare as well. After this band of soldiers left their house they headed for Phillip Greene's. Some of the very screams heard on the hill by the Malones were coming from his place as Phillip's daughter watched the near death of her father in horror while being held down by the Union soldiers. She was forced to look as they placed a rope around her father's neck and tied it to the horn of a saddle.

They continued to run the horse back and forth in front of their house until Mr. Greene could barely breathe. They weren't finished with the Greenes until they committed an unthinkable crime against the beautiful, young woman they were restraining.

No one ever knew for sure, but Martha could only imagine what the mongrels did to the poor girl. However, they topped off their terrorism by burning her severely. In the days and years that followed, she was never seen in town again because she was severely disfigured. Her aging and sickly father, whose neck bore the scars of near death, stayed with her until she died. Lizzy visited regularly as did Mrs. Malone. Lizzy and Dr. Mayson provided the necessary medical treatments to make her as comfortable as possible.

Martha never saw Miss Greene again, but some of the screams she heard that night, she knew for sure came from her. When the war began, Martha had seen a single light of hope drifting through Kingston. It was the light of love and compassion coming from the late Doc Tippin's lantern, lighting the way for help. That night, she saw many scattered lights piercing her beloved Kingston. They were like fiery arrows of death and destruction puncturing the very spirit and soul of those who had unselfishly given to others. Martha kept going with the attitude that Sherman only thought he was bringing Georgia to her knees with his devastating and dastardly campaign. Little did he know, the only knee bending done by the women of Kingston was in reverent prayer, and no matter how much he destroyed, he could never break them. Martha had seen all the goodness and kindness the war extracted from her friends and neighbors in this small town. She was thinking that none of them were perfect, but still, she wondered what had they done to deserve this? [2]

Notes

1. Sign erected in the front of Kingston Woman's History Club Museum gives directions and dates as to where and when General William T, Sherman received his orders to begin his campaign, and it describes his new "type of warfare."

2. Inspiration and information provided in a letter to the editor of the *Cartersville Tribune News*, March 9, 1922, from Joe T. Jolly. Letter describes his family's experiences with federal troops, as well as, one of his neighbor's. Typewritten copy of letter on file in Kingston Woman's History Club Museum archives.

So begins remembrance . . .

Dawn gave birth to a harsher reality than fear conceived the night before. Lives were shattered for miles around Kingston. It appeared that Sherman had temporarily won. As Thanksgiving and Christmas approached, there wasn't much to celebrate. People were trying to put their lives back together as best they could. Hunger and desolation set in throughout North Georgia. All communications were cut off with the outside world, or so it felt. The Malones spent Christmas alone with barely enough food for the four inhabitants of the house. Like all of Kingston's remaining citizens, they sang Christmas carols and prayed for the safe and rapid return of their loved ones. Despite the limited communications, word reached Kingston about Sherman's success and his capture of Savannah. This news left the people of Kingston feeling like the torn and discarded fragments of once celebrated wrapping paper left on the floor.

The New Year came and passed into winter without any celebration or news. The winter months were harsh, and still no word from anyone made life very difficult. Once in a while, a drifter would pass through with snippets of disjointed information. The Battle of Peachtree Creek, which had been fought last summer, had been bloody, and it appeared that with James and Mr. Malone entrenched in Georgia, they quite possibly could have perished there, but when would Martha and her mother know?[1]

Spring 1865 began to bring forth a new hope for Kingston. The weather seemed to fare better than the previous two years, budding hope among the women. Easter bloomed with renewed life and the promise that the war was ending.

On April 9, 1865, General Robert E. Lee surrendered the Confederate Army of Northern Virginia to Lieutenant General Ulysses S. Grant at Appomattox Court House. Coupled with this news was word that many troops had been ordered to Kingston for surrender under Brigadier General William T. Wofford, of Cassville. Cheers of elation that the ordeal was finally done overshadowed the fact that the Confederacy had been crushed. Confederate and Union troops alike began to drift into Kingston. With each new straggling company marching into town, Martha and Catherine eyeballed every passing soldier for a spark of recognition of James Litton and Robert Malone.[2]

During this time of hope in early April, the women met as the Soldiers' Aid Society once again. Mrs. Woolley and the others were hatching a new idea. The women decided it was time to honor their fallen, brave soldiers. The only question was how to do that while under Federal occupation.

Fate and destiny were on their side. Brigadier General Henry Moses Judah was the commanding officer of the Federal brigade sent to Kingston for Wofford's surrender. Judah and Wofford had met in Resaca where their terms had been negotiated. A native of Cass County, later named Bartow, Wofford made arrangements with Judah for relief efforts of Kingston and the surrounding areas. The ladies finally felt like they had a humanitarian Union officer in the area.[3]

In mid-April, the ladies asked to see Judah, and they were granted a visit. Accompanied by other citizens, they were on a mission to ask permission to decorate the graves of all the soldiers buried in Kingston.

"General, the Union is once again one, and our cause has been defeated," Mrs. Woolley began with the grandeur of a politician. "May we honor our fallen men with hand picked flowers this Sunday, and hold a brief service in memory of their bravery?"

For a tense moment, General Judah was silent. However frightening he may have appeared in his blue uniform, the ladies got the impression that he wasn't a man to be feared. Instead, he looked like one who commanded respect with dignity.

"Ladies," he began by taking off his hat and giving a gentlemanly bow. "This has been a long and bloody confrontation among brothers. This is a war that should have never been fought. Too many of our countrymen have died and forever been scarred. You are correct; we are once again a Union. Therefore, I would be very pleased if you ladies would take it upon yourselves to decorate the graves of the men, that I understand many of whom you cared for in your hospital.

"However, I will make one request and requirement of you. Please do not overlook the graves of the Union soldiers who are buried in your Southern soil. Remember, they too fought and died for what they felt was right."

Mrs. Woolley took one step forward with an outstretched hand in General Judah's direction. Taking her hand like a gentleman, she gave him a small curtsey.

"General, while they were patients in our care, we gave them the same kindness and treatment as if they were our own Confederate troops. Their memories are now our responsibility as some are unknown. From this day forth, they will not go unremembered."

Satisfied with her answer, General Judah bowed to Mrs. Woolley and all the citizens who had come to see him.

The women and other residents busied themselves with gathering flowers all day on Saturday, April 22, 1865. Word spread throughout the village that there would be a memorial service, and that flowers were to be placed on all the graves in the military portion of Kingston's cemetery on Sunday.

Sunday morning, April 23, 1865, everyone attended church and had a meager lunch together. At two o'clock that afternoon, they gathered on the hill where a brief eulogy to all the brave men buried there was given. Generals Judah and Wofford stood side-by-side and placed flowers on their respective men's graves. The ladies and children followed suit until all graves were overflowing with beautiful spring colors.

Martha stopped to take a little more time at one particular grave. It was the grave of her unknown Union patient; the one James had helped bring to his final resting spot. Martha made sure that his grave had more than a dozen different colors of flowers scattered over its head. She said a prayer for him, and just called him "friend" as she talked to him about the war's end, telling him that his side had won. Doc Tippin was right. Martha smiled through tears because she knew he had been telling the truth when he said the young man would never be forgotten.

It was a day of peace and brotherhood in the village. No one talked much of the upcoming surrender, and no one was angry. To the delight of the ladies, the Union soldiers were respectful and kind, unlike those who had marched through with Sherman. It would come to be retold that every soldier both North and South who was able to walk, sit on his horse, or be carriage driven to the service attended, and Martha heard rumors that even some of General Lee's men who had been temporarily stranded in Kingston were said to have attended.

Little did the ladies know what a historic day they had planned and executed. Once again, they unknowingly made history as they held the first Confederate Memorial Day. They weren't the only ones with the idea; they were just the first to spring into action. Many others throughout the South followed suit. They began a tradition that would be carried on for many generations to come, and they would be given credit, a century later, for starting and perpetuating the longest continual service of its kind in the nation. But for them in 1865, it was just one more thing they could do for the men they had buried.[4]

Notes

1. Stories retold to a local newspaper by Dr. John D. Goodwin, dated August 20, 1925, in an article titled, *Dr. John D. Goodwin Tells War-Time Stories of Past*. Article archived in Kingston Woman's History Club Museum, Scrapbook 1. No newspaper source was saved or cited in the scrapbook files.

2. Information obtained from *Looking 'Em Over, Surrender In North Georgia*, by Thomas Spencer. The clipping is archived in the Kingston Woman's History Club Museum. No newspaper source or date attached. Information found at *Appomattox Court House, Virginia, The Surrender, April 9, 1865,* nps.gov/archive/apco/surrend.htm. (June 4, 2007)

3. Information obtained from *Looking 'Em Over, Surrender In North Georgia*, by Thomas Spencer. The clipping is archived in the Kingston Woman's History Club Museum. No newspaper source or date attached.

4. The Kingston Cemetery, soldiers' section, contains two hundred forty-nine unknown Confederate soldiers, one known, and two unknown Union soldiers. Information taken from *The Daily Tribune News, Cartersville, Looking 'Em Over, 93rd Memorial Day at Kingston*, April 25, 1957, by Thomas Spencer, reprinted in the *Commemorative Program for the 125th Confederate Memorial Service*.

Finally home . . .

Three days after the memorial service in the cemetery, General Joseph Johnston surrendered to Sherman near Durham, North Carolina.[1] This would make the flock of men crowding into Kingston for their final surrender, the last contingent of Confederate troops to surrender east of the Mississippi River.[2]

By the first day of May, more and more soldiers were arriving via wagon, foot, horseback, and train. Still, no James or Mr. Malone. On May 3, 1865, Martha, her mother, and Camille were sitting on the front porch enjoying a cool breeze and reading just to pass the anxious time of day, when they spotted someone coming up the hill. At first, his form resembled that of William, but Will was inside the house at the time. Mrs. Malone did a double take on the figure walking up the hill. As he approached, she took note that it was a soldier. He was dirty, ragged, and tired. It was Mr. Malone.

"Greetings, family," he shouted while waving his hat in the air. "I surrender, Daddy's home!"

"Robert!" Catherine shouted back, and did something that left Martha and William, who had now joined the group on the porch, just plain speechless.

Very un-lady-like, Catherine grabbed the tidy netted hair from the back of her head and set it free, lifted her layers of skirting and jumped the rail of the porch and began to run down the hill to greet her long-lost husband.

First of all, William and Martha had no idea exactly how much hair their mother had or how much she looked like a teenager at age thirty-seven with it bouncing around her shoulders. Second, at what point in her life had she learned to run? The very proper, polite, and serene Catherine never raised her voice let alone her skirt. They were shocked to see their mother had legs! But, that wasn't all. Catherine knocked the poor unsuspecting Robert to the ground when she leapt into his arms and began to hug and kiss him uncontrollably.

"Gee, ladies," William began, "I'm not sure Father saw that much combat and danger during the whole war. What a shame to be killed in front of your own home, by your own wife."

"Oh hush, William," chuckled Camille as she may a playful slap with the back of her hand at the young man's chest.

Martha remained still, silent, shocked, and speechless. There were her parents rolling around in the front yard in plain site.

When Mr. Malone regained the use of his legs, he stood up and gave a hearty wave to the threesome on the porch who, impatiently, was waiting their turns to welcome him home. Once a little closer to his family, everyone remaining, including Camille, ran to him and nearly knocked him down with just as much force as Catherine had shown, alone.

After hugs and greetings were exchanged, Martha tearfully asked about James.

"Honey, we were separated more than a year ago at the Battle of Peachtree Creek," he said. "I know Bradley didn't make it. The Littons are being told now, but as for James, I know he didn't die there. But afterwards, I just don't know."

Martha didn't know what to say. All joyous laughter ceased for a moment.

"Sweetie, why don't you let William take you to the Litton house. Camille should go too. I think your presence would be very helpful and wanted now," Robert said.

"I was cooling some sweet cakes," Camille said. "I'll leave one and take the rest to the Littons. Will, give me a hand please?"

William and Camille headed inside to gather the meager refreshments while Martha waited silently with her parents not wanting to let go of her father.

When William and Camille returned to the front yard, all three left the Malone residence and somberly trod toward the Litton home, which was now in a state of grief. They could see a gathered crowd and hear the weeping emitting from the open windows of the house. The trio wasn't sure how they would get close enough to pay their respects and possibly learn more of James' fate when they saw a figure dash from a side door. Martha knew at once that it was Lizzy.

Camille motioned her on while she and William kept forging their way toward the Littons' front door.

"Lizzy," Martha called, but the figure kept running. She was headed for the cemetery. Lizzy was a faster sprinter than Catherine Malone. Martha could barely keep up. Finally, out of breath and about to collapse, Martha slowed down as she approached the now slumping figure at the cemetery's entrance.

"Lizzy," she said softly while reaching for her shoulder. "I'm so sorry."

An already red-eyed, teary-faced Lizzy looked squarely into Martha's face and said, "James is probably dead too, you know?"

Martha's heart sank faster than her knees as she slumped to the ground beside Lizzy. There was now a painful silence between them, they just held each other and wept in privacy for more than an hour.

"Why did you come to the cemetery?" Martha finally asked.

The pair had begun their descent back into the village and toward the Litton residence.

"I came here to mourn because there is no grave for me to visit for Brad," she replied.

A shocked Martha listened intently as Lizzy continued. "He was buried near the battlefield at Peachtree Creek where he and James were wounded. The officers who came to the house said James made arrangements to have Brad buried with a marked grave, but when one of James' friends returned to find the grave for him, the marker was gone. He is now in an unmarked grave."[3]

The tears between them began flowing again. Martha didn't want to ask the next question, but she had to know.

"Lizzy, you said that James made the arrangements for Brad just now, but when I first found you, you said he was probably dead too. Did the officers mention where he might be buried?"

"No one knows," Lizzy began. "James was badly injured and taken off the field to a hospital, then transferred, then released. He vanished."

"What!" Martha exclaimed and stopped in her tracks. "Vanished? How can an injured man vanish?"

"Martha, it is mass chaos in most of the hospitals, and when someone is able to be released, sometimes, they just go. Now that the war is over, they might not return to their company, or they may be so badly hurt, they choose to go elsewhere and die. We may or may not ever know where James is, or if he's even alive," Lizzy said.

Just the thought of an injured or badly deformed James roaming the country alone was enough to make Martha sick at her stomach. Why didn't he just come home so that she could take care of him? Say good-bye and I love you? Where was he? Through her despair, Martha was glad in her heart that she and James had their final week together. She knew there was nothing left unsaid that she would regret if she never saw him again.

She and Lizzy wandered back into town where Lizzy began her mourning period for Brad.

May 4, 1865, saw many more Confederate troops straggling into poor little Kingston. She was busting at the seams with people. Union and Confederate officers alike were on every corner and in the middle of the street shouting orders and trying to round up men into their perspective companies for the official surrender and pardon. To keep her mind off of her own situation, Lizzy walked the streets with Martha and checked each train that came into town for any sight of James. By mid-afternoon, the pair began questioning Confederates as to his whereabouts.

Martha stayed at the Litton house that night with Lizzy. They were good company for each other. Early on May 5, before anyone was up, they saw a lone wagon coming into town. The Litton home sat just on the outskirts, which gave it a prime location for watching the troops pile in from Atlanta. A shiver ran down Martha's spine, and she began to shake Lizzy to wake up. The two women watched as the mule-drawn wagon approached and slowed down when it came up to the Litton property.

Once it stopped, two men helped another off. He walked very slowly, with a cane. He was slightly bent over as if holding his stomach. It was undoubtedly James.

Martha clamored for her robe and shoes, but ended up wearing Lizzy's unnaturally small ones out into the yard. Lizzy followed Martha barefooted and hobbling on some of the stones from the walk. Despite the excitement and anticipation, when everyone came face-to-face they all froze, and for a moment, no one could move. They were all paralyzed where they stood.

Notes

1. Information found at *Appomattox Court House, Virginia, The Surrender, April 9, 1865*, nps.gov/archive/apco/surrend.htm. (June 4, 2007)

2. Website information about the city of Kingston, Georgia, found at notatlanta.org/Kingston.html. (June 4, 2007)

3. Stories retold to a local newspaper by Dr. John D. Goodwin, dated August 20, 1925, in an article titled, *Dr. John D. Goodwin Tells War-Time Stories of Past.* Article archived in Kingston Woman's History Club Museum, Scrapbook 1. No newspaper source was saved or cited in the scrapbook files.

A terrible journey...

Martha didn't know what to do. By now, Mr. and Mrs. Litton joined the group in the front yard. Martha wanted to run to him, but knew his mother would want to hold her son first, so she hung back.

"James, oh, my baby," Mrs. Litton cried, as she was the first to embrace her wounded son. "I have no tears of joy to shed for you. They all left me yesterday when I found out about your brother."

James interrupted his mother and said, "Before you all speak, I have the answers to your questions, but right now, I'm starved."

A few faint smiles crossed their faces when it dawned on all of them how he liked Camille's cakes, still lingering in the Litton kitchen.

Finally realizing that Martha was standing behind her, Mrs. Litton released James into Martha's quivering arms. He was back. He wasn't the same young man who left her. Instead, he seemed much older than his age and much more subdued. Youth had faded, only to be replaced by an adult demeanor unfamiliar to Martha.

Inside the kitchen, some of Camille's leftover cakes were promptly served with hot tea. James began to smile as he recognized the unforgettable taste of her cooking.

He began to speak, and no one dared interrupt, "Brad was doing what he always did, helping and administering to others. We were at Peachtree Creek; you probably know that by now. Anyway, I took a bayonet to the leg, and I was on the ground. I saw Brad helping the other wounded men, and I called to him. He headed my way when there was a blast, and several men went down; Brad was one of them. I saw him bleeding, and I knew I had to get to him."

Lizzy began to cry and moved a step closer to Mrs. Litton. They held hands.

James continued, "I couldn't stand completely straight, so I thought that it would be okay to kinda hunker and walk to him that way, but they got me again. This time, it was bad. I took a bullet to my middle just inches away from being able to reach out to Brad. We fell on the battlefield just as the Confederates fell back. We were left there for what seemed like hours.

"I was taken to the field hospital, from there to a division hospital, and then on to Atlanta." James paused to sip some tea and take another bite of food. Still, everyone was silent.

"I remember getting hungry, and not having anything to eat until I was on the depot platform in Atlanta. A lady was checking on soldiers, and when she came to me, she gave me a cucumber pickle from one of the jars she had in her bag. She also gave me a hat."

He paused again to touch the crumpled and dirty headpiece on the seat beside him.

"Brad died on the field before they got him to the division hospital. I made arrangements to have him buried and his graved marked, but when I was well enough to look for it, I couldn't find it. I'm sorry, Mama, Lizzy."

Both women reached to hug James. To Martha's surprise, all three cried together. She had never seen James cry. She didn't know how to handle it. She had seen men cry in the Wayside Home but never James. Later, he would confess to Martha in private that in his mother's and Lizzy's arms, he finally felt safe enough to mourn for his brother.

Mr. Litton interrupted, "Son, where have you been since last year?"

"I was sent to the hospital at Barnesville, stayed there until I was sent to Macon where I stayed for about three months. A local judge who offered aid to any soldier cut off from home took me in. I was sent to his house where I stayed for a few more weeks.

"While I was there, my crutches slipped, and I fell and hurt my knee. There was no doctor, so they called in an old farmer. He put a clay poultice on my knee, and the next day the pain was about gone. The people were very kind to me while I was there."

James had to take another break while he assessed the level of stress on his family's face. A few moments later, he picked up where he left off.

"The judge told me I could stay longer, and he would make arrangements for my expired furlough to be extended. I told him, thank you, but that I just wanted to go home. He gave me some money, and I left. He offered more, but I didn't feel right in taking it," he said.

James continued his treacherous adventure story through Jonesboro and back to Atlanta, and finally his encounter with a couple of local Kingston men who gave him a final buggy ride home.

"Why didn't you just come home from the beginning?" Mrs. Litton was in a serious mode now.

"I wanted to," he started. "But, you have to understand the confusion, the suffering, all of it. I was in so much pain most of the time that I just blacked out. They would move me, and I would wake up in a different place each time. One time, I woke up in a dirty, smelly room where gangrene patients had been left to die. They thought I was dying and hopeless. I found enough strength to get up and walk to the door to ask for help.

"After that, I must have started to recover. I don't even remember when I was taken for surgery or where exactly that was."

No one knew what to say. There wasn't a lot of rebuttal to any of his story. Their collective, deep breaths spoke a thousand silent, joyful words of thanksgiving for his return.

Finally, Lizzy spoke. "It's all over now. You're home. Just move on, James."

She left the room without another word.

After James was fed and tucked safely into bed, Martha left too. James needed lots of rest now. She could rest too, knowing he was safe, and that their future together finally had a fighting chance.[1]

Notes

1. Stories retold to a local newspaper by Dr. John D. Goodwin, dated August 20, 1925, in an article titled, *Dr. John D. Goodwin Tells War-Time Stories of Past.* Article archived in Kingston Woman's History Club Museum, Scrapbook 1. No newspaper source was saved or cited in the scrapbook files. The information about Dr. Goodwin's journeys and his experiences in battle were used as the basis for this chapter about James' return and his injuries during Civil War service.

Choices . . .

"It is over!" Martha's mind repeated these three words as she made her way home, knowing that James was tucked safely into his own bed. Everyone could return to his or her pre-war lives. Little did she know nothing would go back to normal. Everything and everyone was going to change, especially the women of Kingston. They were just getting started.

Sleep came easier that night and all the nights to follow for the rest of Martha's life. No problems of life ever compared to those endured during the War Between the States. Everything was to be considered a "minor" issue to Martha and James. Even the May 5, 1865 surrender of James and her father, along with thousands of other Confederate troops, at Kingston was a joyful event to both the Littons and Malones. It was bittersweet, tears of joy mixed with tears of relief. Of course, it was hard to see their men led away by Federal troops, forced to take an oath to the U.S., and admit defeat. Through this humiliation, both families mourned because Brad wasn't there.

Lizzy whispered to Martha, "I'd rather see him in shackles now than to never be able to visit his grave."

Lizzy disappeared into the crowd and wasn't seen for several days.

Martha didn't see James or her father again until the paroles began on April 11. The official surrender was May 12, but the Federal authorities began the process a day earlier. By mid-May, it was estimated more than six thousand men had been paroled. Although stripped of most everything, the men were allowed to keep their horses, if they owned them.[1]

James and Robert were among the first to be pardoned, and Martha noted a Union band's mocking music could be heard as the hoards of Confederate soldiers were marched through the village. They were playing and singing, "We'll all drink stone blind *When Johnny Comes Marching Home.*"[2]

The people of Kingston had choices to make. It seemed during the war that circumstances had dictated their lives and made choices on their behalf. Now, the townspeople could see there was hope that tomorrow would be better, and a small group of women now had the opportunity to make a choice. And, so did Martha.

She spent the next few days in a mode of closure in her mind. Everyone was going about the task of rebuilding and readapting to their pre-war lives as best they could. However, many changes made this difficult.

A few days after the final surrender, Martha found herself at the depressing, burned out shell of her church. She knew in her heart this beautiful house of worship had fallen victim to Sherman's cruel beginnings of his *March to the Sea*. To Martha, this was proof he began his terrible campaign to destroy Georgia right here in her village. His new "total warfare" left its scars not only on the landscape but also on the hearts of those who endured it both physically and mentally.[3]

Choices for the future and putting the past in perspective were all that mattered now. Many names had forever entwined themselves with Kingston. William T. Sherman rang spine-tingling fear among those who had witnessed his first-hand destruction and cruelty. It occurred to Martha that all people were put on earth by God and given roads of choice in life. To her, some made bad choices by brutally destroying lives in the name of righteousness, while others used righteousness like a beacon of light to heal, restore, and remember.

Walking away in tears, Martha headed to the grave of Kingston's "beacon of light," Doc Tippin. Her thoughts drifted back to a time when his lantern would light the way at the depot. He chose to bring light into others' lives, not snuff it out with the flames of hatred. His name rang chords of joy in her heart.

Yes, choices, life was all about choices now.

Some of those came a little easier thanks in part to the Federal Government, and another name to be remembered with gratitude in Kingston. Like everyone else who endured the War Between the States, Brigadier General Henry Moses Judah battled his own demons of alcoholism and unsuccessful battlefield commands. However, unlike Sherman, Judah was able to see beyond the battlefield and into the homes and lives of those whom the war destroyed. Not only did he give the permission for the remembrance of Confederate soldiers that eventually led to Confederate Memorial Day in Kingston, he sought permission to distribute corn and bacon to needy Georgians. He saw the destruction of cornfields where no crops had grown because of bloody battles. With this humanitarian act, Judah aided in getting Georgia's economy back on its feet. Sadly, the ladies would learn that General Judah would pass away just a little more than a year after helping them start Confederate Memorial Day. He was never able to return to see what he helped form.[4]

Yes, choices came easier in the months and years to come. James left Martha again. Only this time, it was not a sad good-bye. Instead, he left for medical school. Martha was never totally sure about his decision. She knew he wanted to be a doctor just like his brother, but somehow she thought this might have changed after the war. Later, as husband and wife, James never discussed his decision with Martha; just like he never spoke about the war in as much detail as the day he came home. Instead, he focused on the future and encouraged Martha in her endeavors, and together they worked to make tomorrow brighter for all they met.

Martha had seen enough bloodshed in her days at the Wayside Home. She abandoned thoughts of becoming a nurse to become a teacher. She didn't want to remember the bad parts of Kingston's past, but she felt it was important to teach the children about their history so that it might never be repeated. Yet, there were other lessons she wanted to come out of her experiences. She wanted to teach them about the goodness and human endurance of their hometown. Martha didn't want those who had given character to Kingston to be forgotten. Once again, choices were made, and time began marching again.

Home from school, both Martha and James attended the very next Confederate Memorial Day ceremony in April 1866. By now, the ladies were transforming themselves into the Ladies' Memorial Association. There was much work to be done, and once again, Martha was drafted into service.

Notes

1. Information obtained from *Looking 'Em Over, Surrender In North Georgia*, by Thomas Spencer. The clipping is archived in the Kingston Woman's History Club Museum. No newspaper source or date attached.

2. Stories retold to a local newspaper by Dr. John D. Goodwin, dated August 20, 1925, in an article titled, *Dr. John D. Goodwin Tells War-Time Stories of Past*. Article archived in Kingston Woman's History Club Museum, Scrapbook 1. No newspaper source was saved or cited in the scrapbook files.

3. "Notes On School," *We Remember Kingston . . . Woman's History Club & Others*, Third Printing Courtesy of The Etowah Valley Historical Society, Cartersville, Georgia, May 1998; page 2 states, "After Sherman's troops left Kingston, only one church building remained standing – the Methodist Church . . ."

4. Information obtained on Henry Moses Judah (June 12, 1821-February 14, 1866), in his biography found at en.wikipedia.org/wiki/Heny_M._Judah. (June 4, 2007)

Moving on . . .

The years began to pass quickly, and James' absence was only slightly difficult this time. Martha was busying herself with her education to become a teacher, and she was helping the newly formed Ladies' Memorial Association with plans for the continuation of Confederate Memorial Day. She always kept in mind that James was just a letter away. Besides, he always managed to make it home for major holidays like Thanksgiving, Christmas, and in Kingston, Confederate Memorial Day.

For some in town, this day was almost as big as Christmas. The spring flowers and words of remembrance were refreshing and renewing. They were cleansing and healing to those who had suffered. This ceremony gave the people of Kingston a chance to remember the loss and suffering with thankfulness at the chance to move onward with their lives.

Each ceremony became more and more colorful as the years progressed. Martha and James were among the fortunate to hear one of General Wofford's addresses and socialize with his daughter known as the "Sweetheart of the Confederacy."

Another tradition during the early years of the ceremony would be for Captain A.F. Woolley, clad in full uniform, to ride into town on his horse, followed by more than one hundred Confederate veterans. Also joining the march were members of the famous Company F 18, Georgia Regiment, formed in Kingston. These men would keep perfect step with a band playing *Dixie*. Captain J.C. Roper's Company F 18, Georgia Regiment earned its fame as the first Georgia Company to land on Virginia soil during the war.[1]

Although James patriotically attended, and seemed to enjoy, each Confederate Memorial Day service until his death, he never participated in uniform or with speech. He was always somber and reverent. Martha would hold his hand and just assume that he was honoring his brother and the others in his own way.

As the years went zooming by, both Martha and James fell into a routine of hard work, letters to each other, and recapturing what was left of youth before their final step into adulthood. The Malones moved to Rome, Georgia, where Robert worked as an attorney in the downtown district until his retirement. Camille didn't want to leave the only "family" she knew, so Catherine and Robert bought a home with a private guesthouse residence just for Camille. She went on to teach black children to read and write. She did this from the Malones' home where Catherine would cook and assist Camille in taking care of the children. When she wasn't teaching, Robert would trust no one other than Camille or Catherine to assume the role as his legal secretary, filing, and corresponding.[2]

Later in life, after their deaths, Martha would laugh to herself thinking of her parents and Camille, especially in their later elderly lives, as they would snap and gripe at each other due to senility. She always saw Camille as the one in charge since she was instrumental in taking care of both Robert and Catherine through elderly illnesses. She would be the last to pass away. James and Martha would be her caretakers in her last years when she moved into their home where she was loved as the surrogate mother she had been to them both for many years. Watching these three, Martha decided she would never get old and "crotchety" like her parents and Camille.

Just before the Malones moved in 1867, William decided not to follow in his father's footsteps by becoming a lawyer. Instead, the young man went to work for the railroad. He had developed a love of the rail as a young boy during the war while filling trains with coal and water. Eventually, he became an engineer who would pass through Kingston. Martha would make sure that she was standing by the tracks to catch a wave and a blown kiss from her brother from time to time. He would enjoy a long career with the railroad.

But for now, Martha was on the move just as she was during wartime with many of the same ladies from the Soldiers' Aid Society. They were on a different mission these days as they were planning a concert and tableaux to raise funds for better grave markers and a Confederate monument near the cemetery. Just as it had been during the days of the Wayside Home, no one could say no to the ladies' tenacity and spirit. Besides, the whole town participated in the Confederate Memorial Day services and had lost close relatives or friends to the war.

On September 4, 1867, the concert and tableaux drew crowds and raised the funds needed for the cemetery improvements. The bright colors of the costumes and music brought life back to Kingston. Joyful noises were broadcast throughout the village. Sounds of jubilation that had not been heard since before Sherman introduced himself to Kingston were resounded through the hills. Spirits were lifted and laughter pierced the evening, even drowning out the usual lonely cry of the night train's whistle. Good times were being reborn in Kingston.

After the concert and tableaux, the work continued to appropriately mark the graves in the cemetery and care for their perpetuation. Many of the soldiers were being moved to their home states while a few remained interred in Kingston at families' requests, including Martha's unforgotten friend whose grave she frequented.

And, once again, in 1874, it is believed that the women of Kingston made another first when they were able to erect the first monument in Georgia in memory of the Confederate dead.[3]

The perpetual care of the cemetery continued, traditions took form, and life was improving in Kingston. As for Martha and James, after a decade of living with the people who "should be" Martha's in-laws, the pair was ready to marry.

Martha had moved into Lizzy's room at the Littons' house years earlier when her parents left their home on the hill. She started out living there to train as a teacher. Living with the Littons allowed her to remain in Kingston, and it made it easier to be near James when he came home from Atlanta. Ironically, she had remained with the Littons while James had to find another place to live and work after his graduation.

Both of them had agreed James would set up his doctor's office and secure a proper residence for the two of them, but there were times Martha got a little annoyed with this arrangement when she saw all of her friends marrying and having children. She was beginning to feel like the old-maid schoolteacher of Kingston. So, finally, just shy of their thirtieth birthdays, Martha and James set a date for what residents joked about being the "long-awaited wedding of the century."

Notes

1. *Random Notations About Kingston's Part In The War Between The States 1861-1865* are typewritten notes archived in the Kingston Woman's History Club files, and *History of Kingston Memorial Day,* the personal writings of Miss Leila Darden, Kingston Woman's History Club charter member and local historian, reveal information about the early days of Confederate Memorial Day celebrations.

2. The characters of Camille, Catherine, and Robert Malone are fictional, and their exit from Kingston to Rome, Georgia, is just that, a fictional end to their impact on the view of the Kingston Woman's History Club story. No such characters and residents of Rome are known to have existed to the knowledge of the author.

3. *Kingston Women Erect Memorial To Confederate Dead*, published article by Bell Bayless, Kingston Woman's History Club scrapbooks, no date or newspaper source preserved cites information about the declaration attributed to Mrs. J. A. Rounsaville, of Rome, Georgia. She was the former regent for the Daughters of the Revolution, and was considered an authority on this subject.

Life moves forward . . .

Martha missed her mother and wanted her closer when it came time to plan for the wedding. However, she was just a train ride away to the next town. And, she had Mrs. Litton who by now considered Martha more of a daughter ready to be pushed from the nest. Mrs. Litton helped with wedding plans, as well as Lizzy. Lizzy had married a veteran from Captain Roper's company and they were happily living just north of Kingston on Hall Station Road with their two children. A couple of months before the wedding, Mrs. Litton, Lizzy, and Martha boarded a passenger train to Rome where Mrs. Malone met them.[1]

The foursome enjoyed a day of shopping for the wedding. New fashions were trickling into Georgia via riverboats, and Rome was a center for steamboat travel in those days.[2] In addition to a gorgeous wedding dress that required few alterations, each lady acquired a new fashion. Catherine even purchased a surprise dress for Camille and just hoped she would sport it for the wedding. Camille pretty much refused new clothes as she considered them frivolous for some reason. She chose to make her own and never changed her style. Camille had stayed at the Malones' residence preparing one of her famous meals. Eating a Camille-prepared meal was much more satisfying than going to a restaurant. Even Mr. Malone joined the "cackling hens," as he called them, for a fabulous meal. After lunch, Mrs. Malone and Camille set about measuring and pinning the dress for alterations. In a couple of months they would bring it to Kingston for the big day.

A few days before the wedding, Camille arrived via wagon with a very annoyed William and his wife, who had taken a vacation for the big event. Camille insisted on holding on to the dress the entire ride. She spent the next few days with Mrs. Litton cooking and preparing for the reception. Mrs. Litton was a gracious and patient host and partner to Camille who overtook her kitchen.

James and Martha had wanted to have a fancier, catered affair at one of the local hotels, but Camille made such an argument, they decided it was best not to upset her. They felt like they would be insulting a parent not to allow her to furnish the reception food.

The spring day was beautiful. Camille and Mrs. Litton had gone above and beyond on decorating the Littons' home and yard. Everything was like a dream to Martha from the time her father walked her down the staircase at the Littons' to the time she and James boarded an afternoon train for a brief honeymoon in Chattanooga. Even after an argument, and leaving the dress at the Malones' home in Rome, Catherine brought it with her and Camille looked beautiful, strained and uncomfortable. Camille's appearance was the only one Martha could clearly remember from her wedding day because she stood out the most.

Back home, life became busy for the newlywed Littons. Martha spent her days homemaking and teaching. She only helped with office paperwork for James. After her years at the Wayside Home, she could only assist James in desperate emergencies. Lizzy worked for James on occasion. As a formally trained nurse, she was very helpful. Finally, Martha and James were expecting the birth of their first child. James intended to deliver the child himself, but when Martha's time came, she was thankful Lizzy arrived because James became so nervous and excited, he fainted! The tough Confederate veteran and educated physician who had already delivered about one-fourth of Kingston's young population, fainted. Lizzy delivered their first child, Bradley William. Bill was a joy and a gift for both families. Martha took a brief break from teaching to raise Bill and his two siblings that followed, Benjamin James, or Ben, and Martha Elizabeth, or Martie.

Martha just couldn't help herself with the name Benjamin. She and James had often wondered what became of the boy Mrs. Woolley had literally willed to live, and then overfed. The next years passed happily and fruitfully for the Littons. Unless he had an emergency, James would take all three of his children on walks, horse rides, or he would just stay home and play games with them while Martha would attend Ladies' Memorial Association meetings. He would help out when it came time to working in the cemetery and preparing for Confederate Memorial Day.

When little Martie was old enough to begin school, Martha went back to work. James teased her that she was only going back to teaching so she could continue to dote on her baby girl. This annoyed Martha.

However annoyed she would become when James would tease her, she forged ahead as always and resumed what would be a long and fruitful career as a well-respected educator.

In March 1887, Martha saw the destruction of her childhood home to fire. No one knows exactly how it started as the house had been empty and abandoned for more than a decade. Mr. Malone had plans to use it as a type of summer home getaway for the family. However, work had kept him from following through with those plans. So, he had the debris cleared and put the property up for sale. In September 1887, the Samuel Lewis Bayless family purchased the property and established a fine residence. Mr. Bayless was a civil engineer who relocated to the Kingston area. The family had come south seeking a warmer climate for health reasons.[3] Martha was both delighted and sad to see another family on her old home site. The Bayless family were welcomed and remained for many years.

The Litton children were growing and learning more each day. Both boys were showing interest in medicine and spent a lot of time with James and their Aunt Lizzy in James' office. Martha and Martie remained in a world of their own. When they weren't at school, Martie would spend hours listening to Martha tell about the Ladies' Aid Society days and the years of the war. She would memorize and write down her mother's memories in a diary each night.

She was fascinated learning about her hometown and recognizing many of the names of the people who had shown such patriotism during the war. By the time she was sixteen in 1898, Martie felt as though she had lived her mother's life through all the vivid stories she would recall. Since birth, Martie had not missed a Confederate Memorial Day at the cemetery, nor had she been absent from one Ladies' Memorial Association meeting since age fourteen. She was just as saddened by the more frequent deaths of some of the original Ladies' Aid Society members as her mother. She felt as though she had known them personally too.

During her years growing up, Martie was known as a little tomboy who loved to get into trouble. Having no older sisters, she made one, Miss Bell Bayless. Martha had gotten to know the Bayless family since they moved onto the site of her childhood home, and they became friends. Bell would take the rambunctious Martie off Martha's hands from time to time and let her help out at the post office where Bell served as postmaster. Nearly eighteen years Martie's senior, Bell would spend hours sorting mail and talking with the younger lady about town history. Sitting and talking to Bell about everything her mother had recounted to her kept the young lady out of trouble. Martha, James, and the entire town breathed a collective sigh of relief when Bell would take her away for the afternoon.

Together, Bell and Martie discovered a friendship that would endure decades. Their common love of history and Bell's affections for her adopted hometown brought them together. As Martie grew and matured under the watchful eye of her mother, and adopted sister, Bell, people soon forgot the age difference of the women. Bell certainly never acted her age when it came to fun and good-natured humor.[4]

Notes

1. A marriage of the fictional character, Lizzy, is not based on any documentation of a Confederate veteran of Captain Joel Roper's company.

2. "Rome becomes a hub for railroads and steamboats serving much of the southeastern interior," is an excerpt from the Website, roadsidegeorgia.com/city/rome.html. (June 4, 2007)

3. A letter from Mrs. C.L. Bradley to Mrs. Louise Hood, Dalton, Georgia, January 24, 1963, entered into club records by Emma Williams, October 30, 2006, includes notations from Mrs. Virginia Bayless Irby that indicate the family relocated to Kingston in September 1887 seeking a warmer climate for health reasons.

4. A letter from Mrs. C.L. Bradley to Mrs. Louise Hood, Dalton, Georgia, January 24, 1963 entered into club records by Emma Williams, October 30, 2006 includes notations from Mrs. Virginia Bayless Irby that indicate Bell was postmaster as of June 4, 1900. The information into Bell's personality is drawn from the author's conclusions when reading her writings and the manner in which she began the Kingston Woman's History Club. A relationship with fictional character Martie Litton is merely a way to tell the women's story through another composite of the women's personalities in the club.

Hatching an idea . . .

By the turn of the twentieth century, life for Kingston residents had returned to a comfortable pace. Business was booming once again, and the railroad was in full swing. Commerce was good for the little town. Storefronts were stocked, and merchants had most anything townspeople could want. The ladies had restored their afternoons to pleasant conversation and their community service working hours to the memorial association.

One January afternoon in 1900 while at the post office, several ladies were having a discussion about afternoon entertainment and how they could achieve this. During this conversation, Miss Bell Bayless and Miss Martie Malone stopped sorting mail long enough to listen in on the ladies' conversation.

Out of the corner of her eye, Martie carefully scanned Bell's face. She began to see the wheels turning inside Bell's head through the bright, glassy look that came over her.

"What are you thinking?"

"Shh, I'm trying to eavesdrop," Bell replied. "And, I'm getting an idea."

Known for a little spirit and spunk, Martie began to worry about where this conversation and idea might be going with Bell. She promptly scolded Bell in an audible whisper about the evils of eavesdropping.

"What are you planning?" Martie asked a little annoyed as the ladies left the building. "Is this going to get us in trouble?"

"Heavens no!" Bell exclaimed. "But, I have to run. The evening mail train won't run for a few hours, so just finish getting that batch in the corner box ready to go, and then lock up for me. I have a spare key at the house."

And, with that, Bell tossed a key at Martie, and she made a dash for the door forgetting the Bayless' mail.

Being a kind friend, and out of curiosity as to what Bell might be plotting, Martie quickly finished Bell's afternoon sorting job, grabbed the Littons' mail as well as the Bayless family's, and made a dash for the Bayless home on the hill.

She wrapped her coat and scarf tighter around her to block the cold January wind as she proceeded up the path to their home. Bell must have wings like Pegasus was all that Martie could think as she trudged forward.

Finally, she arrived at the home and knocked on the door. Mrs. Bayless opened the door, and she was surprised to see Martie shivering on the front stoop.

"Get in here before you catch something other than a spanking for being out in this cold," Mrs. Bayless laughed. "What on earth brings you up here on this windy day?"

"Bell forgot your mail," Martie exploded through gasping, frosty-burned breaths.

"Well, thank you, but this could have waited I'm sure," Mrs. Bayless replied. "Bell, get down here. Martie obviously finished your chores for you today. I think you owe her a big thank you and a cup of hot tea!"

Mrs. Bayless took Martie's coat and scarf and herded her toward the sitting room fire. She heard Bell racing across the floor upstairs and then loudly pounding on the steps as she entered the lower level of the home.

A very cheery, pink-faced Bell entered the room, her eyes still sparkling brighter than the fire. By now, Mrs. Bayless had left the room with the mail. Bell looked through each entrance into the room, closing the two of them off before she began to speak.

"What?" Martie half yelled at Bell. "I'm about to burst out of curiosity. You know I didn't really care about the mail. I just have to know what you are up to!"

"Well," she began with a giggle. "I'm not going to tell you my entire idea. It's a surprise, but I do need your help, just a little. By the way, did you lock up the office?"

"I'm not going to help you because you are probably going to get me into trouble. Again!" Martie fished the key out of her pocket and threw it at Bell, just short of her head. It hit the floor with a clinking sound. "Yes, I locked up!"

"No, no. This is nothing like last time." Bell paused to laugh a little louder as she thought about the two of them trying to hop a train to Rome. What were they thinking? Why were they even going?

"You know, it was kind of funny when you bounced off that boxcar, Martie."

Martie had no fond memories of that fateful afternoon when her dress nearly ripped clean off as she tried to hop aboard the moving train from the depot. She ripped the entire bottom off her skirt as she hit the boxcar and not the entrance. She must have fallen backward about twenty feet. As luck would have it, her Uncle William had been inside the depot and witnessed the entire thing. Bell was of no help as she stood on the platform laughing, not even seeming to care if her friend had been injured.

Uncle William had been kind enough not to tell the Littons what Martie had attempted. He had wrapped his overcoat around Martie and rushed her home where his wife, now most assuredly Martie's only and favorite aunt, Louise, had made hasty and necessary alterations to reattach the skirt. Of course, Martie, William, and Bell had to ride on William's horse about a quarter of a mile down the track to find it first. Luckily, it had snagged in a small tree as the train thundered out of town.

Okay, thought Martie, the site of her entire skirt detached at the waist lumbering down the train tracks, flapping in the wind was funny, but also horrifying. What a caretaker Bell turned out to be!

Aunt Louise had done such a fine job of alterations that her mother never knew. Her limp and the bump on her head were a little harder to explain. The other bruises and bumps were easier to cover. She explained them away by telling her parents she and Bell had been "horsing" around on the hill when Bell pushed her and playfully swung a big stick at her and actually knocked her down.

"Yeah, that was it," she had thought. "I'd love to get Bell in trouble for a change."

But, as usual, the Littons just chalked this one up to nonsense and went on about their business without another thought into the matter.

Recalling the memory, Bell was wiping a few laughing tears from her cheeks when she noticed the not-so-friendly scowl coming from Martie's face.

"Okay, this is not going to get us in trouble, and I will take full responsibility for the entire thing," she said. "I'm actually serious about what I'm going to do. And, it's a good thing. Just do me a couple of favors, please."

At this point, Martie could not turn down her friend. The innocent look and sweet pleading convinced her that Bell was serious, and she was not into any type of mischief this time.

"What do you want me to do?"

"Great. Don't say anything about this to anyone until around January 20. You and some other ladies of this town will receive a surprise invitation," she said. "On January 24, bake a very large batch of teacakes using Camille's recipe. I know you have it even if you and your mother won't share it."

Martie was becoming very puzzled. Surprise invitation and bake teacakes.

"So, that's all I have to do?"

"Yes, just don't tell anyone that I'm up to something is all I'm asking this time," she pleaded.

"I can do that," Martie gladly agreed. No knowledge was good knowledge this time she thought.

Bell had gotten Martie off the chair and was guiding her toward the door. She was rewrapping her in her coat when Martie said like an offended guest, "Where's my hot tea?"

Bell stopped in her tracks and shot Martie a semi-nasty and playful look.

"You didn't want any tea. You came here just to find out what I was doing."

"You're right, but your mother told you to make me some tea," Martie demanded. "So, where's my tea?"

"Oh, you'll get your tea soon," Bell said and shoved Martie out the door and slammed it behind her.

"Well," was about all that Martie could think about as she stepped off the Bayless porch and back onto the trail down the hill home. At least this time, she hadn't been shoved into a moving train. However, the feeling in the pit of her stomach was very similar to the one she had as she bounced off a slow moving train to Rome.[1]

Notes

1. Dialogue and "Rome train incident" are fictitious. The spirit of the conversation and incidents are based on Bell's personality depicted in writings about her, and by her, including *God's Acre Reclaimed*, torn newspaper clipping about the Kingston Woman's History Club beginnings and civic works, Kingston Woman's History Club Museum scrapbook, no newspaper recorded, only handwritten date, 1909.

Goober hulls . . .

Martie couldn't say that she wasn't just a little relieved that she did not know what Bell was up to. However, over the course of the next week, she saw Bell at different merchants around town, not buying peanuts, but picking up empty goober hulls and carefully placing them in a small purse as if they were made of pure gold.

Perhaps it was because Martie was constantly watching Bell for any signs of "trouble," that she noticed this behavior. No one else seemed to notice. Soon, things began to make sense. Just as Bell had promised, there was a very unusual delivery to the Litton home. It was a goober hull. A small invitation, handwritten on tissue paper was enclosed in the gilded peanut shell for both Mrs. and Miss Litton to an afternoon tea to be held from two until four o'clock in the afternoon on January 25, 1900.[1] This would be very out of the ordinary Martie thought, except she knew the name of the hostess before she read it, Miss Bell Bayless.

Martie got a good laugh out of Bell's creativity and follow through with an idea that appeared on the outside to be another good joke. Just as she had been instructed, and now that she got the hint of why, Martie made two batches of teacakes on January 24.

Martie and Martha set out together to attend this afternoon tea. When they arrived, Martie couldn't help but feel a little bad about her suspicions of Bell as she handed her the teacakes. Bell wasn't at all the mischievous friend who had talked Martie into jumping a train a few years back. Instead, she had evolved into a true lady who made a gracious and kind hostess. Her manners were impeccable and her demeanor was unobtainable to many. Martie was proud of her friend.

The parlor at the Bayless home was full of women in their finest attire; all curious about the mysterious goober hull invitations they had received. Martie recognized everyone and was most impressed by some of the ladies from her mother's wartime stories like the unstoppable wagon driver who collected supplies for the Wayside Home. Once the high-pitched buzz of the room settled to silence, Bell and her sister, Virginia, welcomed everyone and began explaining the purpose of their meeting.

"I recently overheard a few of you talking about afternoon entertainment," she began as Martie recalled their afternoon at the post office a few weeks earlier.

"I thought it would be very appropriate for us to meet and discuss our own heritage and history," she continued. "We all share an interest as some of you were original members of the Soldiers' Aid Society during the war, and others of you have helped form the Ladies' Memorial Association."

Bell paused to look around the room and find the older faces such as the devoted wagon driver and Mrs. Martha Litton. Then she eyed her friend, Martie.

"We all share a common interest in community service, preservation, and history," she said. "So, this afternoon, we will begin our tea with a history of Georgia as a colony."

The ladies were surprised and delighted as Bell began to conduct a lesson and discussion on Georgia history, literally from the beginning. The young and energetic Miss Bayless perpetuated her discussion by carrying her "goober hull" party theme through the afternoon when she passed out Georgia history questions enclosed in more goober hulls. The ladies laughed and were delighted to open them and take part in the lively historical discussions.

A squeal of delight and surprise came from one of the guests when she grabbed for one goober hull and broke it open to find the prize for the tea, a beautiful enameled brooch.

Bell had at least entrusted her secret to one other lady who read a paper she had composed on John and Charles Wesley. Virginia, also known as Mrs. Claude Irby, delighted the ladies with a few musical selections.

As the discussion, history lesson, and entertainment wound down, Martie stood up to assist Bell in distributing the refreshments. Martie told her friend how proud she was and apologized for her suspicions.

The afternoon was such a raging success that the next meeting was set for February 22, 1900. These ladies organized themselves as the Woman's History Club with the intent to meet monthly. A home was selected, and the topic, "Georgia as a Colony" was decided.

For the next two years, the women enjoyed fabulous teas and lively discussions at each other's homes. Many of them continued to serve double-duty with the Ladies' Memorial Association. The Woman's History Club began assisting with the Confederate Memorial Day as they discussed more of their history forever entwined with the war and Wayside Home. Some of them didn't have to learn about the war, they had lived it.

As the next two years progressed, Martie found herself in the company of two other prominent sisters from Kingston at these club meetings, the Misses Bell and Leila Darden, both of who were always present at Confederate Memorial Day with their father, a celebrated Confederate veteran.[2]

Also during these first two years, Bell was informally recognized as "chairman" of the Kingston Woman's History Club. The ladies spent their time studying historical figures important to Georgia such as the Reverend Sam P. Jones, Dr. W.H. Felton, Charles W. Smith, the Reverend Charles Wallace Howard, Dr. Francis R. Goulding, and Mrs. W.H. Felton. They also studied Irving's *Sketch Book* and other notable men and women of the state.

In 1902, the ladies entered the next era of the club when they held an election for president. Bell's sister, Mrs. Claude Irby, became the club's first president. Under her leadership, the women joined the Georgia Federation of Women's Clubs in 1903.

After joining the state federation, the women were instrumental in forming the Bartow County Federation. Members of the Kingston Woman's History Club had the honor of being the first elected district officers in the state. Their district, the Seventh District, was the first to be organized in Georgia.

Martie and Bell were both carried away with how organized and energetic the ladies had become. Instead of just an afternoon social club, the women ran full-steam ahead in a very business-like direction.

By this time, the club needed to adopt a formal constitution. Very simple and straightforward rules were outlined concerning the club's name, its goals and objectives, its meeting dates, and dues not to exceed $1.20 per year.

Life was bustling and the town was growing and prospering. Business was good, and life was becoming easy compared to the days of the past. Despite the prosperity of the town, the members of the Kingston Woman's History Club did not sit back and let the afternoon breeze blow by them. Instead, they stirred up their own whirlwind of work keeping their hands, their minds, and their hearts always flowing into the next day and the next project at hand.[3]

Notes

1. Information obtained from *God's Acre Reclaimed*, torn newspaper clipping about the Kingston Woman's History Club beginnings and civic works, Kingston Woman's History Club Museum scrapbook, no newspaper recorded, only hand-written date, 1909; and *History Of The Woman's History Club*, written by Mrs. Louise Pratt Hood, *Commemorative Program for 125th Confederate Memorial Service, April 23, 1989.*

2. Information about the early days of Confederate Memorial day taken from the personal writings of Miss Leila Darden, Kingston Woman's History Club charter member, and local historian, *History of Kingston Memorial Day.*

3. Information obtained from *History Of The Woman's History Club*, written by Mrs. Louise Pratt Hood, *Commemorative Program for 125th Confederate Memorial Service, April 23, 1989.*

Plowing the way in red clay . . .

By 1901, Martie was more active with both the Ladies' Memorial Association and the Kingston Woman's History Club than Martha. Martha had been busy the last years with ailing parents as they passed away and now an ailing Camille. Martha spent much of her time enjoying Martie's news of the latest ideas emerging from the club. She was also enjoying her grandchildren. Martha and James did what they could when they could, and they always contributed financially to the good deeds of the club.

Of course, Martha was always encouraging Martie to settle down just a little and find the right man. But, Martie rarely had time for such social functions as she and Bell were always on the move, working and actually staying out of trouble.

Martie had taken the time to follow in her mother's footsteps in becoming an educator. She was working in the large wooden school in 1902 when the Woman's Club took on the project of starting a free library for the students. Club meetings were buzzing with ideas and means by which to raise funds for the library. In May 1902, the ladies gave a book tea. This one tea started the library's collection. Enough funds were given to the ladies to purchase a twenty-five-volume set of *Encyclopedia Brittanicas*. As a teacher, Martie was very proud to have been a part of such a worthy community cause.

At the start of the May fund-raising tea, Bell pulled Martie aside and whispered in her ear, "Feel like you've hit a train lately? Or, have you been hit by a train?"

She giggled and sauntered off to socialize.

Martie could only hang head while smiling and laughing to herself. She read between the lines of Bell's comment. Age had started healing those pride-crippling wounds of silly youth, and the whole thing was quite funny now.

The ladies took no time to read the books they furnished for the library, so to speak, they had another task. The plight of a young orphan girl was brought to their attention. Just as many of them had opened their doors and hearts to soldiers many years before, they opened their hearts and purses to this young girl. Since Georgia only had five months of free school in those days, the ladies picked up the slack and purchased books and paid her tuition during the pay school term.

As if this weren't enough, the school trustees took note of the Woman's Club and entrusted them with the duty of selecting teachers. The club even contributed toward teachers' salaries.

County fair time rolled around in Bartow. The club entered exhibits and won several prizes. The ladies also entered the Southeastern Fair in Atlanta with their exhibits. They walked away with eight prizes.[1] The ladies were beginning to make a difference and bring notoriety to their town. And, they were gearing up for another run on history. Some days, Martie felt like she barely had time to catch her breath, let alone socialize. Besides, she would think after another droll conversation with Martha about "finding the right man," I socialize with the club all the time.

Once again, Bell and Martie found themselves in another perfect position to overhear a now famous Kingston conversation. The pair had just finished lunch at the hotel with Martie's Uncle Will on one of his Kingston stops when they returned to the depot to find the depot agent and his wife in a deep discussion.

Bell's sister, Virginia, was the newly elected president of the Kingston Woman's History Club, and she had an idea to run by her husband, Mr. Claude Irby.

A few days earlier, she had been looking over the muddy, barren, red clay patch that appeared to have been plopped in the middle of town from a gigantic spoon. After hard Georgia rains, it always looked like a morning portion of red-eye gravy gone very wrong. It was a very unappetizing site for the eyes. Truly, instead of rich, red-eye gravy, it appeared more like eyesore muck.

Virginia was just starting in on her spill to her husband when the lunchtime crowd appeared.

"Poor little Kingston! It will never amount to anything with that old clay patch in the middle of the town," she said. "Some clubs build a club room, some plant flower beds in conspicuous places, but some turn an eyesore into a park!"

A silence filled the small depot office until her husband began a boisterous laugh that rattled the timbers. Virginia's face fell hard as if his laugh had literally shaken a rafter from the ceiling and smacked her in the head with it.

"Where'll you get the money for such a job?" Bell didn't appreciate the leering look on her brother-in-law's face by now. "It takes cash and hard work to bring up land."

"I thought the town might contribute. It would be worth something to the whole community to have a pretty, green park around the depot; show what could be done with the poorest kind of land," she said fighting back tears, not of hurt, but anger.

"A half-carload of green paint is the only thing that would make an impression," he continued to laugh and speak. "The town has nothing to do with it. The land belongs to the state of Georgia for railroad use."

He paused, now realizing they had company. The group could tell he felt bad that he had unintentionally hurt his wife's feelings, and that he was just caught off-guard by her idea. His tone softened a little.

"The Western & Atlantic Railroad has just leased it to the N.C. & St. Louis for fifty years. You'd have to get permission from that company before you could stick a toothpick into that red clay."

For now, the conversation was over. Virginia left the depot silently, deep in her thoughts. Bell and Martie just looked at each other. This was one argument to hide and watch just to see how it would turn out.

Later, Martie and Bell would discover that Mr. Irby only thought the conversation had ended that afternoon at the depot. Virginia made a polite written request to President Thomas of the railroad company, and in return, a courteous note of permission to proceed with a park was granted.

It wasn't long before a strange site appeared in Kingston. Mr. Irby was astonished as he saw his wife standing on the depot in her "gardening" clothes overseeing track hands working the land. Huge gangplows chewed through the red Georgia clay and the scrapes leveled off clods. Gullies deep enough to hold teams of mules were filled, and a fence was built around the entire plot of land.[2]

Martie and Martha would watch these activities while Martha recalled with a defiant smile the use of the land during Sherman's occupation.

"You know, girl, that's the old car yard where Sherman would let his men throw our church pews out," Martha said bitterly. "Those jackasses would throw good grain in them that we could have used and let their filthy horses feed on it. They didn't even eat all of it; they were too well fed."

Silence.

Martie had never heard her mother utter any sound of vulgarity. And now, calling Union troops "jackasses?"

Martha looked Martie in the eyes and said, "I've held that in a long time. I've also held in something else, a thank you to General Sherman. Despite my feelings, I can say that he did his job well. He ended that war and sent my family back to me. I don't like how he did it, but he did it."

More silence. Martie began to see her mother's point. Then, she began to speak and giggle again.

"Yeah, that felt good," Martha laughed. "Horses asses, all of them."

"Mother," Martie began, but it was too late. Martha had endured all of the afternoon sun she could bear. She headed back home slowly, laughing. Martie could hear a little something different in Martha's laugh. It was a solid sound, robust with healing tones.

Martie then knew that for years, her quiet, strong, well-versed mother had harbored some deep resentment in her heart for the cruel injustices brought on Kingston by outsiders who didn't understand their peaceful, kind-hearted way of life. Watching the land torn to bits, tilled up, buried, pierced, and filled was like a final farewell for Martha.

The ghosts that had haunted the land for so long were going to be buried beneath the middle of the very ground they had desecrated. Forever, in Martha's mind, the ugliness they wrought would be entombed so deservingly beneath what promised to bring beauty and joy to the people they set out to destroy.

That land would eternally spring forth color and life for all to enjoy. How appropriate and timely for Martha. Now, Martie smiled and understood.[3]

Notes

1. Information is referenced in *History Of The Woman's History Club*, written by Mrs. Louise Pratt Hood, *Commemorative Program for 125th Confederate Memorial Service, April 23, 1989.*

2. The story with detailed, direct quotations from Mr. & Mrs. Claude Irby and in-depth details about the beginnings of the town's park is detailed in the article, *Lady Was Laughed At When She Mentioned Park For Kingston, Weekly Tribune News,* Bell Bayless, July 29, 1954.

3. Story of Sherman allowing horses to feed from church pews is one that stems from word of mouth with ladies who have heard the stories passed down from generation to generation.

Pea pickin' park . . .

Curious onlookers would gather at the edge of the muddy pit to watch the work. Virginia finally quelled some of the curiosity by starting her own survey. She seriously needed to know how to make the grass grow once the land was prepared. She started with several successful local farmers. The general consensus and conclusion was to plant field peas and plow them under green for several seasons. Next, a winter crop of rye should ready the soil for planting grass.

She had her plan. However, the club didn't have the manpower or the seed in which to execute the next phase of the park. When the land was ready, she approached a local farmer, who like her husband, laughed at her. However, he gladly took her money for the job and began plowing up the lower part of the park opposite the depot.

During the work, Virginia would look over her shoulder to catch a glimpse of her husband inconspicuously peering at the work from the depot. Like a cat and mouse game, he would quickly retreat or turn in the other direction as if he were surveying the tracks before she could catch his eye.

The peas were sown and now the rest was up to Mother Nature. At harvest time, Martie, Bell, and Virginia went to find someone to harvest the peavine hay. The same farmer, who had laughed at the beginning of the season, was said to have nearly cried when the ladies refused to sell him the hay for his mules.

"There's something said for having the last laugh," Martie whispered to Bell.

No one was laughing during many fine dinners either. Kingston tables saw dishes of "hopping Johnny" field peas and rice with hog jowls served. Of course, many of the peas were snatched from the field when no one was looking. But, who cared, the scrumptious smell throughout the village was for all to enjoy. The park was beginning to yield its first harvest of years of enjoyment for Kingston residents.

Getting the peas ready for pickin' and the park ready for visitors had a price. Unlike in years past, the price of working together didn't come wrought with pain and suffering. It was a pleasant debt to pay.

"How about we make and sell sandwiches at the circus next week?" Martie surprised herself as she made this suggestion at the Kingston Woman's History Club afternoon tea and business meeting.

"That's not a bad idea," Virginia added. "We do need to pad the park fund a little. The sell of the hay was tremendous, but we have to plant the winter rye."

The room began to buzz with members exchanging favorite sandwich recipes and talk of who was going to furnish what ingredients.

"Ladies, ladies, please," Virginia half shouted above the dull roar. "Thank you. Now, I suggest we each choose an ingredient to furnish and decide when and exactly where we will serve the sandwiches."

From there, the discussion rolled on for about another thirty minutes. The ladies finally organized themselves and decided to serve a lunchtime sandwich meal. Their lunches were almost as big of success as the circus itself. Any time an event came to town, the ladies used their assembly line sandwich table to raise funds. And, for anyone who loved an excuse to eat, they also offered buckets of homemade ice cream.[1]

Martie always felt a little guilty thinking of her mother and all the original ladies who forged ahead during the hard times. She would work the booth, table, or tent serving food while having a good time. The Littons would patronize the club with their business, always leaving a generous tip. The best part of the days spent with the club having fun, raising funds, was to see her parents holding hands enjoying their later years. Even though her father walked with a cane, sporting his old war injury, he always had a kind smile on his face and a pocket of change for his grandchildren at circus time.

During the election year, the Kingston Woman's History Club cooked up another delicious idea. Politics, politics, everywhere they turned the women could not get away from the barber shop, drug store, local diner, arm chair election projections.

It wasn't long before a homespun, home-cooked idea hit the campaign trail in the village. A beautiful, fall Saturday afternoon just before the election, the ladies gathered downtown near the new park site. They set up their tables and began to transport wagonloads of homemade ice cream to the area. With signs in hand and ballots waiting, they rounded up anyone with a little pocket change to vote for their favorite freezes.

The entire afternoon was spent in a jovial mood watching people cast more than one ballot for their favorite cook's cold, homemade specialty.

The Littons, along with their children and grandchildren, went home that afternoon with no dinner as people in town could only talk about how much ice cream that bunch could put away.

Packing up that day changed Martie's life. As she was sloshing out another empty ice cream bucket near the well, she felt a small tug at her skirt and heard a very soft voice asking, "Do you have any more strawberry, lady?"

A surprised Martie quickly turned and nearly fell over a cherub-faced little girl.

"Well," she started. "I'm not sure if we do or not. I can certainly look."

"All I have is one penny," the little girl began, but Martie cut her off.

"Honey, you are too young to vote, and you can't anyway. I don't believe you get to cast a ballot in this election, so I can't charge you for any ice cream."

The little girl looked like her feelings were hurt, and tears welled up in her eyes. It occurred to Martie that she had unintentionally hurt the little girl's feelings. Immediately, she tried to rectify the situation.

"Sweetie, that's not what I mean," she started, but it was too late. The little girl began to run away. Unfortunately, she began to run toward the road where a wagon was just rolling through. Martie began to chase the little girl yelling for her to stop and come back.

Martie had just caught up to the child, who by now was perilously close to the wagon. The owner was pulling on the reigns of his team trying to stop them, but they were at a full trot and couldn't be halted in time.

She was reaching for the back of the child's dress when she looked up to see the child and herself in the path of the wagon. From nowhere, a gigantic force shoved Martie across the road and into a small gully at the edge of the park. She was face down in red mud, but that wasn't all. Something heavy had just fallen on top of her. Its weight was crushing. Martie thought she had reached the end, her breathing cut off, her legs paralyzed. Then, the something on top of her moved and began to talk. It even grabbed her by the shoulders and rolled her over. Still, she was paralyzed with fear and not sure of her breathing. The "it" wiped the mud from her eyes and said, "Can you move?"

Covered in mud, scared, and weak, Martie slowly took the hand of the most handsome man she had ever seen, and she allowed him to help her up.

"I see you can move," he said. "Are you able to speak?"

Now, embarrassed at her appearance, and still a little in shock, Martie could only nod a small "yes." By this time, several of the ladies had seen the near-accident and had joined the threesome at the edge of the park where they began to fuss over Martie. As they were ushering her off, she saw the wagon driver talking to the man and the little girl. The little girl-that thought snapped Martie out of her daze.

"Wait a minute," she shouted while sprinting back to the man and little girl. "This is all my fault. I'm so sorry."

The little girl, who was truly in tears, stepped behind the man and clung to the back of his shirt.

"Really, this is all my fault. She wanted some ice cream and told me she had a penny," Martie began. "I was teasing with her, telling her she was too young to vote and that I couldn't charge her for the ice cream. I think she misunderstood and thought I wasn't going to give her any."

By now, both the driver of the wagon and the man were just staring at a mud-covered Martie. The man was mildly amused. Martie continued out of breath.

"I wasn't going to charge her for the ice cream. I was just going to give it to her," she said winding down with slurred speech. "Honestly, I was just going to give her the ice cream."

Everyone was silent, and to Martie, a little distorted and fuzzy.

"I," was the last sound Martie uttered and even remembered before she hit the ground, again.[2]

Notes

1. *Lady Was Laughed At When She Mentioned Park For Kingston, Weekly Tribune News,* Bell Bayless, July 29, 1954, gives the story detailing quotations and in-depth details about the beginnings of the town's park.

2. Fictional incident surrounding the character of Martie is used for character purposes.

Good times roll on . . .

The next thing Martie saw was the ceiling in her father's office. Actually, it was the ceiling in her father and brother Ben's office. She was now clean, and it was dark outside. She rose up and saw the back of a woman. It was Bell.

"Bell. Bell. Is that you?"

Quickly, Bell turned around and smiled. "It sure is. You want me to get your mother?"

"No. What happened? Did I try to jump onto a train again?"

By now, Bell was really laughing which annoyed Martie because she knew that meant "nothing good" had actually occurred.

"No trains were involved in your latest stunt, I assure you," she snickered. "It was worse, oh, much worse. You chased down a little girl in the road, were pushed into a mud puddle, and then fainted in the puddle again."

Martie thought Bell should have gotten on the floor and rolled while laughing. By now, Martha, James, and Ben came into the room at the sound of Bell's laughter.

"I've got to go," she said, still giggling. "I'm just relieved to know you are fine."

She leaned down and gave Martie a hug and breezed out of the room.

Her parents and brother were trying hard to hide the same giggles as Bell, and Martie couldn't understand why. With a splitting headache, she added just one more to the other side of her head when the thought of why they were laughing hit her as hard as she had hit the ground. It was the man. She had obviously made a fool of herself, running back after him to explain herself and then fainting.

"Well, Sis," Ben began. "It looks like you just hyperventilated, fainted, and knocked out yourself. You don't have a concussion or any other injuries other than a bruised ego, maybe."

Then, Ben started laughing and so did James.

"Stop it you two," Martha scolded. "Get out, and let me have a moment with Martie."

Arms around each other in "good ole boy" fashion, both her father and brother left the room with pure amusement on their faces.

Martie began to tear up.

"Oh, stop that," Martha softly said. "It's going to be all right. I saw him, and if I were thirty years younger, I'd be blushing too."

"Was it written all over my face that I thought he was, well," Martie couldn't even finish her question.

"We all know you too well to know that you do not lose composure that easy," Martha said. "It was obvious you were a little smitten."

"What am I going to do? How will I ever face anyone again? I just wanted to explain about the little girl and the ice cream."

"Well, now's your chance to take care of all three of those issues," Martha said standing up.

"What?"

"You are going to talk to Michael Grady[1] by facing him right now because he has been in the waiting room ever since he carried you into this office about three hours ago," she said. "Now is your chance to explain whatever it was you were saying about ice cream to that nice young man. Plus, you have the chance to be formally introduced without horses, wagons, ice cream, and mud."

Martha turned to leave the room. As she put her hand on the doorknob, Martie screamed, "No!"

Martha stopped in her tracks, turned her head to look Martie in the eye, winked and whispered, "Yes."

When Martha opened the door to the office's waiting room that evening, she didn't just open it for a visitor. Martie had a feeling that God was opening that door to her future, and she was right.

Michael Grady appeared like an angel to Martie, and she knew she had the same dumbstruck look on her face as earlier in the afternoon. This time, she came to her senses and talked to the man. The two of them talked for at least an hour. She learned the little girl was Michael's daughter, Alice, and they were alone. He was a widower raising her by himself. Michael was working for the railroad and was sent to relocate in Kingston.

When Ben appeared in the room, Martie just wanted him to leave. She didn't want the evening to end, but Ben said she needed the rest. Michael agreed and was about to leave when he stopped short of the door and hurried back to Martie this time.

"Could we have lunch together?"

With that question began a long and happy relationship that led straight to the altar for Michael and Martie.

Martie recovered at home with her parents. Later, she learned they sealed her fate when they took in Alice, like she was their own granddaughter, that night. When Michael went to their house to take her home, Martha and James refused to wake her. They insisted she was too comfortable in a bed with about three other grandchildren. They told Michael that Alice was too happy and content to leave, and he could pick her up in the morning, or around lunch or dinner, just whenever he had the chance. They literally closed the door in his face and sent him on his way for the evening. Michael didn't mind. He also had a feeling he'd be related to these people soon, and Alice might as well learn to fit in with her new family.

Martie and Mike, as everyone called him, began a whirlwind courtship. Martie and Alice also began a courtship that included a formal "making up" with each other over a bowl of strawberry ice cream. Alice began addressing Martha and James as Granny and Pa just like the other grandchildren. This gave Martie and Mike no choice but to set a date. They had to hurry as Alice told Mike she was leaving him and moving in with Granny, Pa, and Mama M, a name she assigned to Martie. Strong-willed Alice packed her own little suitcase, loaded it in her little red wagon, and was a long-remembered sight walking along the crude sidewalk past every business in town just to make it to Pa and Uncle Ben's office where she knew one of them would take her to Granny's.

Alice did move in with Martie where they both lived with James and Martha the last two months before the wedding. Finally, the wedding day arrived, and all went well for the bride and groom. They were off to Atlanta for their honeymoon, leaving Alice where she was happiest with none other than Granny and Pa for the next week and a half.

Upon their return, Martie took her, now official, daughter with her to the next meeting of the Kingston Woman's History Club. She was proud to introduce her as a future member of the group. However, Martie got a surprise shower. Bell and Miss Leila Darden apologized for the delay of throwing the tea in her honor, but they had become preoccupied with the last-minute preparations for Confederate Memorial Day and had neglected to make arrangements for the party.

Years began to roll by. Martha and James got older and weaker. The grandchildren grew and learned to help take care of Granny and Pa. Martie and Mike added one more grandson to the family, Thomas.

During these years, the club pressed forward with their community service projects surrounding the school, the park, and the cemetery.

With the ongoing work in the park, the ladies began to assist with another project, replacing headstones in the Confederate Cemetery. In 1908, the club took on the responsibility of replacing the decaying wooden grave markers with new marble ones. At one particular club meeting, Bell and Virginia stood before the ladies who had just finished discussing the purchase of the markers.

"We'll order the headstones for the two Union soldiers," Bell said in a most serious and reverent voice.

There was silence from the members. Even Martie, Bell's best friend, had forgotten that Bell and Virginia were "Yanks."

Another quiet moment passed, and Martha took the lead. This was her first meeting in months. She attended because her input about the cemetery was needed. She now stood in front of the entire club to speak.

"No," she said firmly. "There was no blue or gray in the Wayside Home. There is no blue or gray in the cemetery. They are all our responsibility now. You both have worked too hard making this town beautiful again, and you raised money for our Southern men. We buy all markers equally."[2]

Martha had spoken, and all who were present knew about her trips to the corner of the cemetery where she still visited her Union friend. This was now a closed subject and a done deal. All were replaced with more permanent markers by the club.

Martie and Alice continued to work with the others to make the park a showplace. The torch had officially passed from Martha to Martie as the mother.

After the amusement of the men had quelled about the park and raising funds for its creation, the men weren't to be outdone by the women. At one point, the young men organized their own minstrel troupe and put on a show for fifteen cents admission. They entertained with songs, jokes, and some of them clog danced.[3]

Martie and the Littons claimed they would pay extra to see Mike clogging, but he always seemed to bring the house down with his sense of humor and jokes.

And now, the men made sure they were around when it came time to make some park improvements like "tree planting day." Wagonloads of saplings were brought in and the men were seen hard at work digging holes for the roots. Even before they had said, "I do," Mike took part in improving his new home. He joined the other men in digging and tramping dirt firmly around the trees.

The aging Captain Woolley planted young elms to shade the park's diagonal paths. The others pulled together choosing and planting their favorites like maple, sweet gum, redbud, oaks, sourwood, poplar, and other native Georgia trees.

The most usual site became a young pine tree pushing its top from the ground. Its life emerging from a long ago, buried pine cone.[4] Life in Kingston was growing as vibrant and alive as the town's park. Commerce continued to boom as the railroad thundered along the track daily.

The park project was a focal point for the town. Virginia wrote to Congressman Gordon Lee, and he had the Department of Agriculture send her seeds of blossoming shrubs and trees that were not native to the Georgia climate. Her project was to plant them in boxes at her home and tend to them until they could be planted in the park. They survived and became thriving additions to the land.

Everything began to thrive in the park's soil. Wildflowers, daisies, and even weeds began blooming. Of course, the crop rotations were tended each year, and Virginia had her very own last laugh.

The good times and laughter were well deserved by all. However, the old adage is true, "all good things must come to an end."

Notes

1. Michael Grady is a fictional character introduced as Martie's husband.

2. *God's Acre Reclaimed*, torn newspaper clipping about the Kingston Woman's History Club beginnings and civic works, Kingston Woman's History Club Museum scrapbook, no newspaper recorded, only handwritten date, 1909, is used as reference.

3. *History Of The Woman's History Club*, written by Mrs. Louise Pratt Hood, *Commemorative Program for 125th Confederate Memorial Service, April 23, 1989* is used as reference.

4. *Lady Was Laughed At When She Mentioned Park For Kingston, Weekly Tribune News,* Bell Bayless, July 29, 1954, story detailing quotations and in-depth details about the beginnings of the town's park is referenced.

Into ashes . . .

By 1911, life was a comfortable routine for everyone. Confederate Memorial Days continued to roll by with much fanfare. The Kingston Woman's History Club perpetuated their formal monthly teas and historical discussions. Commerce thrived inside the wooden stores of the downtown business district of Kingston. Trains thundered in and out of town, bringing passengers and goods to the small village.

Indeed, time was being gracious to Kingston. Of course, the usual life changes were met with joy and grief as young were born and old would die. Each woman worked in her own way to preserve as much of Kingston's history as she could by collecting letters, newspaper clippings, other family documents, and the list would go on. They each had a responsibility for their part in the records collection and retention project.

Everyone knew certain records existed but couldn't exactly put their hands on some of them. They were elusive and floated from person to person for several years. One set of such documents was the records of the Wayside Home, Doc Tippin's carefully and beautifully handwritten records. Kingston Woman's History Club charter member, Miss Leila Darden, would recall later in life having seen the remnants of the original grave-marking slabs as a child, but always said she was too young to remember anything on them.[1]

Seen or unseen, Martie was soon to learn history would write that those records, wherever they may have rested, could have perished on a windy March afternoon in 1911. School had just dismissed for the day. Alice and Thomas met Martie near the depot for a trek up the hill to visit Bell. Martie was carrying a batch of teacakes and fresh-fruited tea. Bell promised the kids she would try her hand at chocolate cake.

While Alice was to entertain Thomas, the ladies were going to collaborate on some of the town's history. They planned to put their heads together and document all of the ladies' history starting with the Civil War. Their inspiration had been the 1907 Confederate Memorial Day reading of Mrs. Evie White. She had detailed their role in those days, and with tears in her ever-aging eyes and the eyes of her still surviving sisters in arms, she silenced a crowd. For the first time ever, Martie had seen a spark of emotion on her father's face during the ceremony. As usual, her mother separated herself from the crowd where she spent several moments alone, talking to a corner grave. The younger generation now asked questions about why Martha would take off alone each year, and with as little explanation as possible, James would elaborate.

This was the year Martie and Bell began their very own separate "historical" committee to preserve as much in detail and as much on an accurate timeline as possible.

The past four years also led them on a quest for the elusive Doc Tippin's records. Rumors flew as to the whereabouts of the carefully collected Civil War treasure. Most everyone was in agreement the records should be turned over to the Kingston Woman's History Club for preservation. However, no one knew exactly where to locate them. Martie suspected that descendents of Doc had each been in possession of the records at one time, and through moves and passing them around, it was certain they were boxed up in a trunk or attic somewhere in Kingston, if not already lost forever.

Today was a typical March day. It was extremely windy. Skinny little Thomas was mildly struggling as he walked against the wind. Thoughts of those records raced through Martie's mind. What was the best way to find them? Who else could she and Bell query?

The threesome walked passed the wooden storefronts trying to stay close to the buildings to shield themselves from the wind until they hit the outskirts of town. Martie looked to the top of the buildings, wondering if anyone had stored the precious records somewhere inside. She looked past the depot to the other side of the village, picturing a complete handwritten Doc collection found buried inside one of the older homes. It would be like finding a pirate's treasure chest beneath the vast ocean's floor.

Martie snapped out of her thoughts just as little Steven Norris plowed into her legs nearly knocking her down.

"Sorry, Mrs. Grady," he shouted. "This wind really got a hold of my kite."

He was right. Martie saw his triangular-shaped creation flapping hard in the sky just above them. He could barely hold on to the string and handle. He was a small but stout child, and he was physically fighting the wind.

"It's okay, son," Martie replied. "Be careful. Looks like you could float away at any moment."

"Feels like it, ma'am," he shouted as he and his voice trailed off into the March tailspin.

The Grady family headed out of town and up the hill to the Bayless residence fighting the wind all the way. Small pine saplings were nearly broken along the trail. They were stretched and fully bended sideways. It looked as if a tornado had shoved them over.

Bell had been watching for her friends and trotted down the path to greet them. She took hold of Thomas' hand and helped Martie with the afternoon refreshments.

"How's the cake?" Martie had to raise her voice above the howling wind atop the hill.

"Not so good," Bell giggled. Never letting the train incident go, she added, "Looks like someone threw it against a slow moving train to Rome."

The ladies laughed and stepped onto the porch.

"Martie, I've had some ideas about Doc's records and whom we might talk to," she began. "Your mother would be a good place to start. If we can't find them, then we need to start talking to people like her who might recall some of what was in them."

Martie didn't hear the rest of what Bell was saying. Her voice was trailing in the wind. Martie was staring down at the village below. She could see little Steven had allowed his kite to go a little higher. It was now bobbing faster than a jack rabbit could hop and run. Martie's eyes followed the kite as it raced in the direction of the railroad tracks toward Rome.

"Martie, what's wrong?"

Martie didn't respond, she was hypnotized by fear and fixated on the moving kite. Its forward movement stopped and began to ascend, higher and higher. It was racing toward a clear blue sky, heading for a white puffy cloud. Little Steven must have lost control and let go of the toy. The kite was rising above an enormous cloud of smoke coming from the Kingston Inn. The child must have stopped to see what was going on.

"Fire, Bell, fire!" Martie was shouting and fighting the urge to run down the hill to help.

Shouts and screams could now be heard above the wind coming from the village below. Bell's knees went weak, and she dropped the pitcher of tea. The shatter of glass and trickle of thick liquid weren't heard as both women's eyes and ears were focused on the tragedy unfolding below them. The children stopped in their tracks just behind their mother. They too, watched in horror, as the smoke got thicker. Their horror turned into disbelief when piercing, orange flames appeared through the thick, black smoke.

The situation got worse as the wind picked up. The group on the hill, frozen in shock, watched as the wind carried the destructive flames from building to building, devouring the wooden structures. The noise from the villagers fighting the flames and fleeing from the heat roared above the howling wind.

Disbelief turned again to horror and fear when Martie came to her senses. On their walk up the hill, she remembered thinking how dry the ground had been. She recalled crunching some leftover fall foliage not yet soaked by spring rains and overtaken with fresh green growth.

"Bell," she turned grabbing her friend and running toward the Bayless well. "If that wind shifts, those flames are going to climb this hill faster than we can outrun them. We'll all burn with the house!"

Bell's eyes grew wide in sheer terror. She called for Alice and Thomas who galloped behind her to the well.

"This isn't much, but we need to start soaking the ground all around the house and then start throwing as much water on the house as we can," Martie ordered.

The four of them began a bucket brigade of their own to soak as much of the Bayless yard as they could. They had no help that day because Bell was home alone. Her family had gone on a two-day shopping jaunt to Rome.

For more than twenty minutes the two women and two children poured well water all around the property and doused the porch and front of the home as high as they could throw.

"Stop," Bell said touching Martie's sleeve after her last gallant toss onto the house. "Stop. The town is gone, and the wind is still blowing down the main street. I don't think it's going to spread up our way."

All four of them put down their buckets; little Thomas dropped his mother's other pitcher on the now mud-soaked ground. Even the tea had been sacrificed to help save the Bayless home.

Where the prosperous town of Kingston stood a half hour earlier, nothing but smoldering and flaming wreckage littered a street filled with onlookers covered in soot and smoke.

Surveying the damage from the hill, they watched the smoke diminish and billow away into the sunny, afternoon sky. Martie realized everything was gone, including her father's original doctor's office. She thought she could make out a blackened Ben administering first aid to the fire victims.

"We just walked by there," Martie tearfully whispered to Bell.

"It's all gone, isn't it?" Bell replied with her arm around Martie's shoulder.

From what they could see, several homes were gone too, and all but one brick building downtown had perished.

Martie was sure her parents' home had survived as they had moved several streets away from the downtown area when James retired. Now, the office and residence above it were Ben's loss.

Knowing the Bayless home was safe from the flames, Bell accompanied Martie and the children back into town to help render aid, but there was nothing anyone could do. Mike was out of town and would be in for the shock of his life upon his return in two days, as would the Bayless family.

As they crossed the railroad track, they heard a distant train whistle signaling the arrival of the afternoon mail train. Several men were helping move furniture from the railroad track. One desperate family had taken all of their possessions and furniture they could salvage from their home in the fire's destructive path and placed it on the railroad tracks. Now, safe from the fire, it was threatened by the just as devastating iron horse.

With nothing she could do for anyone in town, Bell invited Ben and his family to stay with her. Martie and the Littons also helped out by taking in refugees until better housing arrangements could be made.

Martie imagined Kingston now looked a lot like it did after the infamous, and in her opinion evil, Sherman left. The coming days were going to be hard and depressing for everyone.[2]

Notes

1. The personal writings of Miss Leila Darden, Kingston Woman's History Club charter member, and local historian, reveal information about the early days of Confederate Memorial Day celebrations, *History of Kingston Memorial Day.*

2. Fire details and story inspired by "Incidents From the Past," by Pauline Kennedy Martin, page 30, of *We Remember Kingston . . . Woman's History Club & Others*, Third Printing Courtesy of The Etowah Valley Historical Society, Cartersville, Georgia, May 1998.

Bricks, mortar, and beyond . . .

Mike and the Bayless family joined many others arriving in Kingston to a shocking scene. Passengers on the trains had no place to go when they arrived in the once thriving town. The looks on their faces as the trains lumbered into the village said it all. Word spread faster than the fire about Kingston's tragedy.

The one, small, brick building that survived became the busiest place in town. The merchants, who once competed with other shops, now had a difficult time filling orders and keeping up with the demands of the residents.

Life in Kingston evolved into yet another phase. One chapter's fiery end turned a page for a new story to be told. With a few less passengers arriving and only necessary commerce downtown, those who lost everything reassessed their positions and formed a new plan.

Bricks, lots and lots of bricks began arriving. Like a child who has to learn a stove is hot by touching it one time, the residents of Kingston unanimously agreed the new buildings would be constructed of these bricks.

A contractor began working with the shop owners to rebuild. The next years passed slowly as each brick was carefully placed. People adapted to the change in the way they had to do business. However, those ashes couldn't smother their determination to get back on their feet.

Seven years of construction and re-openings saw many small celebrations and victories. By 1918, the town had two banks, The Bartow Bank and The Bank of Kingston. The DeSoto Hotel was completed, and a drug store, pharmacy, and soda fountain were serving customers daily. A magazine and lending library opened, and the town had a telephone exchange office with both day and night operators on duty. Finally, the town was in full operation.[1]

Despite the years of rebuilding the physical structures of the town, the Woman's Club continued to flourish. Martie and Bell faced a harsh reality of their own. Doc Tippin's records were gone. Had they been anywhere in the downtown area the day of the 1911 fire, they perished with the buildings that may have housed them.

The search for them ended, and the ladies moved on. Now, the sheer ano-
nymity of the men buried in Kingston made them more precious and hard to
forget. Continuing the Confederate Memorial Day service became more important. More of the original members of the Soldiers' Aid Society were passing
away. Even Martha and James' deteriorating health continued to stress Ben and
Martie. William, or Bill as he was known to family, and his wife, Lydia, moved
into the Littons' house with Martha and James. William partnered with Ben in
the family's medical practice. He and his wife were now alone, as their children
had moved on with their lives. They began the round-the-clock care of Martha
and James.

Martie would visit her mother every other day keeping her informed on the
town's rebuilding progress, the club's latest news, and the antics of her own
children. Alice often came to visit Granny and Pa with Martie, who was now
just called "Mama." Thomas had grown into a fine, young ball player spending
most of his time on the diamond, and he didn't visit quite as often as his mother
and sister. Mike was busy most of his free time with his part-time job as a mason. He was considering leaving the railroad for construction work closer to
home and his family.

On one of her visits in 1916, Martie sat on the porch with her mother talking about the latest from the Kingston Woman's History Club. She could see the
cataracts were growing worse on her mother's soft blue eyes. Martha could no
longer read her Bible. Martie would sometimes read to her, as would Alice.

Later in life, Martie would be angry with herself for not writing down everything her mother began to ramble about with her scattered thoughts drifting
over the years. Her mother, who had only been fifteen at the Civil War's outbreak, was among the last left who could relate anything of a time the ladies
were so desperately trying to preserve.

"Mama," she began. "Is there anything you remember about Doc's records
that you could tell me?"

Martha took a deep sigh. "No, not really. Just one entry stands out in my
mind and that's my entry."

Martie knew exactly whom she was talking about. She was eluding to the
unknown Union soldier whose grave she used to visit weekly and then monthly
until she became too feeble to climb the hill at the cemetery.

"Doc wrote that no next of kin was known but that a friend was known,
Martha Malone," she said. "Those records are long gone, and it's a shame.
However, all of those men are known by our Creator and that's all that really
matters."

There was a long silence. The two women enjoyed the breeze blowing by
while they listened to the sound of a train whistle.

"Guess what, Mama?"

"What's that, Doodle Bug," Martha kidded. She hadn't called Martie "Doodle Bug" since she was a small child. Martie always hated that.

"We just got a letter from the state's Federation of Women's Clubs telling us that our suggestion of the Cherokee rose as the state's flower has been adopted, and a resolution is before the state legislature now to make it official."[2]

"You don't say," Martha sounded surprised.[3]

"It's going to be in the newspaper this week," Martie said. "Pretty much a sure thing from what I understand."

"Well, isn't that something," Martha retorted. "You gals are really doing something. I was just starting to think all you were good for was planting flowers, making ice cream, and sipping tea. Glad to hear ya'll are putting us on a map."

Martie kind of resented those statements, but understood that her mother's life had been a lot harder than hers. Her youth and young womanhood had been stolen and forced into a battle no young lady should ever have to fight. To keep herself from saying something she'd regret, she stood to go.

"I'll let Lydia know that I'm leaving," she said.

Martie had stood to walk inside the house when William's wife appeared at the screen door.

"Wait," Martha said. "I need to ask a favor."

"Granny, it's time to come inside," Lydia said. "You need to take a nap."

"Oh, go take a nap yourself, or better yet find James and get on his nerves, but go away," Martha snapped.

Martie felt bad for Lydia, but she was used to this treatment by now. She smiled at Martie, just shook her head, and closed the screen behind her. Martie heard her calling James, so it must have been time for his nap also.

"Take me to the cemetery," Martha demanded.

"Mama, I can't do that. Now? It's getting late."

"Please, Martie, I have to go today. It can't wait until tomorrow," she pleaded. "Tomorrow will be too late."

Knowing she probably couldn't get her mother there by herself, she told her she would go get Ben or William, but Martha said no.

"They won't let me go, and I have to go now."

Martha was in tears, and Martie's heart couldn't take it. She walked inside and told Lydia she was taking her mother for a short walk. Against a strange look from Lydia, Martie left with Martha's cane and shawl and escorted her off the porch. A half hour later, the slow-moving ladies emerged near the depot. It looked as if Thomas was already on the ball field, but a welcome site caught Martie's eye.

"Alice," she shouted.

She saw her daughter heading into the drug store for an afternoon treat with some friends.

"Mama," she waved, and her eyes lit up. "And, Granny!"

She ran across the street, nearly colliding with a horse and buggy. Martie's heart skipped a beat as the first day she met Alice crept into her thoughts.

"What's going on?"

"Can you help me get Granny to the cemetery?"

"Uh, yes ma'am," Alice was confused. "Don't you think we'll need a wagon or at least a horse?"

"No," Martha commanded. "I want to walk."

That settled it. In silence, the three generations of Kingston women began a final walk, for one, to the cemetery on the hill. It took about forty-five, agonizing minutes, but they finally made it.

"Stop," Martha whispered. "I know where I am now. You can let go."

Martie and Alice watched as Martha walked with confidence to the Confederate Memorial Monument. She caressed its side and leaned against it to rest. When she regained her strength, she continued to walk toward a familiar corner. Along the way, they saw her stoop down and pick a straggling wild flower from the hill. Martha stopped walking when she reached the grave of her unknown Union soldier. She carefully sat down on the ground in front of his small marker. Delicately, she placed the wild flower on his grave.

She was too far away for Martie and Alice to hear what she was saying to the grave, but Martie had a sickening feeling she was saying good-bye. Whatever she was saying, Martie knew it would be her last conversation with the soldier on this earth. It was Martie's prayer that her mother would be reunited with her silent friend in Heaven where they could make peace and finally know each other personally.

Alice could tell by the sky that the afternoon sun was giving way to early evening, and that the threesome should start their long journey back into town.

"Mama, shouldn't we go get her?"

"I don't want to, but I know we've got to get moving or we won't make it by sundown."

Just as Martie and Alice headed toward Martha, she stood on her own and then collapsed. Both women ran to her.

"Go, get one of your uncles and your dad, now," Martie shouted.

Alice ran as fast as a gazelle into the town and straight to her uncles' office. Ben grabbed a ride on a passing wagon whose speed picked up twice its normal pace as the driver cracked his whip on the poor horses.

Alice followed the construction trail to the DeSoto where she found Mike finishing his last brick for the day. The two of them raced to the cemetery on foot. Alice never realized her own exhaustion.

By the time they arrived, Martha was on the wagon and headed back to town. Alice and Martie rode on either side of Martha in the back of the wagon, holding her hands, just as they had walked her to the cemetery.

Notes

1. Fire details and story inspired by "Incidents From the Past," by Pauline Kennedy Martin, page 30, and "Mrs. Oletha Rogers Writes for Margie Hood," by Oletha Rogers, Page 18, of *We Remember Kingston . . . Woman's History Club & Others*, Third Printing Courtesy of The Etowah Valley Historical Society, Cartersville, Georgia, May 1998.

2. Joint Resolution No. 42 declared the Cherokee rose, adopted by the Georgia General Assembly, the state's flower at the request of the Georgia Federation of Women's Clubs, August 18, 1916.
www.netstate.com/states/symb/flowers/ga_cherokee_rose.htm (May 1, 2007)

3. Information located in *History Of The Woman's History Club*, written by Mrs. Louise Pratt Hood, *Commemorative Program for 125th Confederate Memorial Service, April 23, 1989.*

The true Cherokee rose . . .

By the time the wagon roared into town, Martha's breathing was labored, and her pulse was extremely weak. Both Ben and William worked to save their mother, but it was futile. Nothing could be done. Lydia and Thomas made their way into the office with James.

Ben took his dad to see Martha one last time. He closed the door and left them alone. No one ever knew what was said between the two of them. Those things are better left private between a husband and wife; especially these two childhood friends turned lifelong lovers.

Thirty minutes later, James emerged from the room and declared the time of death. He asked to sign the death certificate himself. Martha was the last patient he ever declared.

The next days were a time of mourning for a great many in Kingston. Martha touched many lives. For the Kingston Woman's History Club, her death was the ending of an era. The women all felt like orphans. The last of a kind had just passed away. This moved them all from the next generation of Kingston women to the oldest, most responsible group. The torch had officially passed to them.

The Malones had been buried on Myrtle Hill in Rome, and some speculated that Martha's body might be taken there.

"That's the most ridiculous thing I've ever heard," James bellowed. "She was born here, suffered here, lived here, and finally prospered here in Kingston. I'll shoot anybody who thinks they're taking my Martha to Rome. She'd haunt me for the rest of my life and make the afterlife hell on me if I put her body in any soil but Kingston's."

"Daddy, don't get so upset," Martie cajoled. "No one is saying we're going to do that. It was just a suggestion."

"And, a very bad one at that," he snapped.

With that said, gravediggers were sent immediately to the family plot in the Kingston cemetery to begin preparations for Martha's burial.

The Kingston Woman's History Club came through in their usual over-the-top style. Food and beverages of all kinds were brought to the Littons' home. There was too much food. Around-the-clock care was offered for James. He managed to insult and run off everyone except Lydia, Martie, and Alice who had to assume those duties in shifts.

On the day of the funeral, many conversations were disjointed and jumbled in Martie's thoughts. The happier conversations were overcome by grief. Mike, Alice, and Thomas headed to the Littons' house to join the family, but Martie wanted a few moments alone. She was sitting in the parlor of her home looking through a small box filled with little trinkets from her mother. She had taken the box last night out of fear it would get lost in the shuffle at the Littons'.

She was jingling a handful of dull buttons in her hand trying to hear her mother's voice talking about them and telling her the vivid story of how she got these Union souvenirs when there was a loud knock at the door.

Still clutching the buttons with her fist, Martie answered the knock with a "Come in."

Bell peered around the door with her usual smile. Martie was put off by this. How could she be smiling at a time like this? She took a seat beside Martie on the sofa in silence.

Finally, she spoke, "What are you doing?"

"Nothing really," Martie said. "I was just going through some of Mama's useless little keepsakes from the years. I took them last night. I didn't want them to get lost. I'm sure Daddy doesn't want them. All he's been looking for is his gun."

"His gun?" Bell was her usual self almost laughing.

"Yes, he's been threatening to shoot people for the past two days," Martie said. "We think he's serious. Mike and Thomas took both of his guns out of the house and they're upstairs in Thomas' room now."

Bell was really laughing now and annoying Martie.

"Oh, Martie, you have been so blessed," she said lightly. "Your parents were the best ever."

Bell continued, "Do you remember how mean you were as a child? It was entirely your mother's fault. You were the baby, and she babied you constantly. I didn't like you at all, at first. You would do the nastiest things, and then when your dad wanted to whoop you, your mother would let loose on him. I think he was afraid she would whip him."

Martie couldn't help but smile just a little, recalling at least one, clear incident from childhood where her mother had just laughed instead of punishing her.

One Confederate Memorial Day weekend, all the ladies were busy gathering wildflowers for the graves.[1] They each had several buckets they were trying to fill. Every time one lady would fill a bucket and get ready to take it to the entry of the cemetery, Martie would sneak up on them and steal that bucket of flowers. It would just disappear. In its place was another empty bucket.

Martie went all over yards and the hills doing this to each lady. She was so small and so fast that she didn't get caught until she ran right into James where she spilled an entire bucket of fresh cut flowers. He exploded. Martha came to her rescue as usual. The most punishment Martie received was having to retrieve all of the buckets she was hiding behind James' office and carry them to the cemetery by herself. After about four trips, Martha took pity on her and made William and Ben help.

The boys were not happy to be punished for their sister's crime since they had been nowhere around at the time of the infraction. This was a good memory, and it felt good to relive it.

"Oh, your dad could really whoop Bill and Ben, but I don't think you ever got one in your life," Bell laughed.

"By the way, it's not Bill or Billy anymore," Martie said in a very snooty voice. "Bill did not return from Atlanta, William did. It's Dr. William now. The socialite, Lydia, insisted he use his formal name."

"You're kidding, right?" an amused Bell said with a frozen smirk.

Now laughing, Martie said, "I wonder what would happen if Daddy suddenly found one of those guns? Do you think he'd clean house with the Dr. William and Dame Lydia?"

Laughter mingled with tears was cleansing for both ladies in the Grady parlor.

"Martie, we better head to the church now," Bell's voice got low and serious.

"I know," Martie said standing and wrapping herself in a black shawl.

She was glad Bell had stopped by the house. She had brought Martie back to earth and focused her thoughts where they needed to be, on the happy times.

Martie joined her family. At the church, instead of crying, Martie smiled because her mother's casket was covered with a beautiful, white Cherokee rose pall.

She recalled the last conversation the pair had on the Littons' porch just days earlier. In fact, today's paper was running the very article about the club's state flower selection that Martie had planned to read to Martha.

At the cemetery, each lady from the club placed a red rose on Martha's casket before it was lowered into her home soil. James picked up several of the roses and headed toward the Confederate Cemetery. Martie joined him.

"Hey, Sweetie, I just feel I have to do this for Martha," he said. "I know why she had to come here. She knew it was her time, and it just meant a lot to her. I don't blame you for bringing her. I'd blame you if you hadn't."

James knelt as best he could and placed the roses on the Union soldier's grave.

"You know I dug this grave with your Uncle Will," he said. "I was home on leave, and I helped with his funeral and burial. Of course, it wasn't a very good funeral. None of us knew him. To be unknown and related to no one here, this man has had more flowers and visits than many of Kingston's beloved, thanks to your silly and sentimental mother."

Martie knew that visit was hard on her father, but he had to do it for her mother.

The town's progress continued, and life got back to normal. Martie was a little lost without having someone to talk to about what was happening on the main street. James didn't really care like Martha, especially about club business. He literally entertained himself by running Lydia ragged and ordering her around. Martie wondered sometimes why she just didn't knock him on the head really hard and get it over. She had a new respect for the debutante who hung in there with the old man, but she still didn't like her very much.

On August 18, 1916, the state legislature officially declared the Cherokee rose as the state's flower. Martie took two of them to the cemetery and told Martha all about it while placing a single rose on her grave, and then she walked to the Confederate portion and placed the other on the grave of Martha's friend, visualizing they were talking in person now.

Martha died one year too early to see the next generation of ladies in their full, wartime action. Just before Confederate Memorial Day on April 6, 1917, the United States entered World War I, and the ladies sprung into action.[2]

The club president wrote a letter to the Red Cross Headquarters in Washington, D.C., requesting instructions on how they could help. When the instructions arrived, the ladies assembled themselves and dug into the trenches to do their duty, again.[3]

Notes

1. As of April 2007, club members continued the tradition of providing cut flowers from their yards or gardens for the Confederate Memorial Day services.

2. The U.S. entered World War I on April 6, 1917.

www.americaslibrary.gov (June 4, 2007)

3. *History Of The Woman's History Club*, written by Mrs. Louise Pratt Hood, *Commemorative Program for 125th Confederate Memorial Service, April 23, 1989*, provides information concerning the women's service projects.

World War I . . .

By the end of April 1917, Confederate Memorial Day was behind them, and the next generation of ladies found themselves focused on a new war being fought on foreign soil. This time, the nation was bonded together as one instead of divided against itself. Young men began to enlist in the United States Army and Navy. They were off to fight for their country.

Orders from the Red Cross in Washington arrived late in the month, and a special meeting of the Kingston Woman's History Club was called to order.

Like the ladies of the original Soldiers' Aid Society, Martie called these ladies together in one of the town's churches. She had carefully reviewed all of the instructions and had prepared several lists for the women.

"The Red Cross has specific directions for us to make bandages," she began. "I have a diagram of exactly how to roll muslin for them. I'll need two committees. One will be to collect the muslin and the other to roll."

Hands began flying in the air, and soon two committees formed.

"Thank you all for your enthusiasm, but I have quite a few more needs," she continued. "In addition to the bandages, the hospitals need nightshirts, other specialized bandages, and wash cloths. Muslin is the preferred textile for these things. Does anyone know exactly how much we have?"

A newer member, Mrs. Sarah Parker, offered her hand to the now silent room.[1]

"Muslin isn't going to get any cheaper with the war coming," she said. "My husband and I just purchased the dry goods store downtown, and I know we don't have much of it in stock. I cannot completely speak for my husband, but you are welcome to all we have now. I can prepare an order for more this afternoon, and if you can pay cost for it, I'll let you have it for that price. No profit for us."

The ladies all agreed this was great news, but where would they get the money?

"You know we're well known for our parties and fund-raisers?" Bell was speaking now. "Why not fall back on what we do best?"

Bell's two simple questions sparked another explosion of ideas and eventually weeks of planning for fund-raising plays and teas. It was a patriotic duty for Kingston residents to attend these events.

The ladies met regularly in homes throughout Kingston where they could be found hard at work rolling bandages. This was just the first committee. The "acquisitions" committee stayed busy, placing muslin orders and planning and setting dates for fund-raisers. When they had enough money, they purchased two Liberty bonds.[2]

The months of preparations flew by like a whirlwind, just like the budding, young romance of Alice Grady and Bruce Parker. Bruce was the son of the newly arrived Parkers who were supplying the muslin. Bruce had signed up for Naval service. One week before he was to deploy, he surprised everyone by proposing to Alice. Martie and Mike were not happy when the young man arrived on their doorstep with flowers and asked Mike for Alice's hand in marriage.

"Son, I think you're moving too fast, and I think you both are too young," Mike started his fatherly speech, but something snapped in Martie's head, and she quickly silenced Mike by grabbing his arm.

"You two just have a seat on the porch, and we'll be right out," she said as she motioned them out the screen door. She closed the second door behind them.

"What are you doing, Martie?"

"Well, it just hit me that he might not be coming back. And, who are we to actually say they are rushing things?"

"Have you lost your mind?" Mike was in shock.

"I think about my parents and what they went through. They were just fifteen when he left, and look at how that turned out?"

"I know, but they waited until your dad returned and actually finished medical school."

"That's true," she said. "But, they could have handled it. What if my dad had never returned?"

"For starters, we wouldn't be having this asinine conversation right now."

Martie gasped in disbelief that Mike could be so callous.

"Mike," she said, as calmly as possible, through her mounting anger, "Alice and Bruce aren't children. They are several years older than my parents were when the War Between the States broke out. Why are you so against this?"

"I guess it's hard to let go," he said. "I just thought circumstances would be different. Time would be more on our side, on her side."

"Life isn't always neat," Martie responded. "I believe we make our own time, and sometimes we have to run a race to keep up. But still, we have the choice and the power to make the most of the time we have."

"So, what do we go out there and tell those two?" Mike was wearing down.

"We go out there and give them our blessing. And, I lay my hands on someone's old wedding dress and alter it for Alice. Then, I get with Mrs. Parker, and we start planning a wedding."

Just as Mike and Martie finished giving the young couple their blessing, Thomas rounded the corner of the house out of breath. Instead of hello or any other civil greeting, he began with "Hey, Dad, can I . . ."

Mike cut him off before he could finish. "Whatever it is, the answer is no." And then, he walked in the house leaving everyone to go about his or her business without him.

Mike might have been scarce for the next two days, but Martie managed to get him to the church in time to walk his daughter down the aisle. Martie cried when she saw how beautiful Alice looked in Martha's altered wedding gown.

"I've seen that dress somewhere before." James half shouted to Lydia as Alice walked by him on her way to the altar.

Whispering, Lydia tried to silence the elderly, hard-of-hearing James. "That's Martha's wedding dress. Shh."

"Don't shush me. Who is that wearing it? Why is she wearing it?"

Both William and Lydia just patted the old man between them and did their best to keep him quiet. Thomas began to giggle at the circus next to him. Bell leaned forward and gave the snickering boy a swift smack on the back of the head.

Aware of the commotion behind her, Martie laughed a little too. In her head she thought, "Do you see this, Mother? See how we miss your presence. We've no one left in charge."

Despite the lack of planning time, the wedding was beautiful and uneventful except for the ever-confused James, who everyone eventually either ignored or just went along with whatever he said. The young couple boarded the afternoon train to Rome for a brief honeymoon. From Rome, Bruce would take a train to Atlanta to deploy from there. Alice would say good-bye in Rome and return to Kingston by the end of the week. The Parkers had offered her a room with them, but she declined and chose to stay with Martie and Mike until Bruce's return.

This slight diversion in war-preparation plans only affected the Grady and Parker families. All the other ladies continued the Red Cross work.

Alice threw herself into working with the ladies just to keep her mind off of Bruce. Letters began coming from him. The family knew he had arrived aboard a Navy ship somewhere off the coast of Europe, but details and locations were not specified or given.

The ladies relocated their operations and designated an official Red Cross site for their work. A store building was used as the Red Cross room. Located next to the post office, everyone in town knew patriotic works were taking place inside the building.

Soon, the "acquisitions" committee came up with another form of fund-raising for the ladies' work. Unlike the Civil War, where shots were fired all around Kingston and news was sparse and broken, this war and its news were brought directly to residents through photographs. The ladies began having "picture evenings" in the lobbies of the town's hotels. They turned rooms into virtual art galleries of war zone images. They displayed pictures of foreign lands and other interesting places.

Alice attended every picture evening offered. She would frantically search the faces of American soldiers for anyone she recognized. Every time a photo of a Navy ship came to town, she would look into each face in the image hoping to see Bruce.

Then, there were the devastating images. No one liked looking at these. Mothers and wives would turn their heads and hurry past them as if not looking made them not exist. However, these images only reinforced the work of the Kingston Woman's History Club. They knew they were helping win the war by providing what little they could.

When the final tally was taken of their work, one hundred and fifty-five yards of muslin was used making hospital nightshirts, triangular bandages, abdominal bandages, and more. Washcloths were even knitted.

During this time, a large quantity of gray yarn was donated to the club. Members who could knit were called to action for making sweaters, long mufflers, helmets, and wristlets.

Hospitals needed more supplies that only American women were experts at making. They needed quilts. During the summer, the ladies stepped up the sewing duties to three afternoons a week at the Red Cross room. It became a rare sight not to see the small building manned with busy women.

They each gave quilt tops, as well as cotton and lining to finish them off. Kingston had its own service flag. Train passengers could see Kingston's patriotic storefronts with Old Glory waving up and down the street. The store owners proudly displayed the service flag alongside the American flag.[3]

During this time, letters came from Bruce on a regular basis. This put Alice's mind at ease. And then, on November 11, 1918, it all ended.[4] The war was over. Men began to arrive home slowly and steadily. The war took its toll on all towns across America, including Kingston. They mourned their dead heroes and welcomed home the rest.

Alice met Bruce's train in Atlanta. His mother had wanted to be the one to greet her son, but conceded to her daughter-in-law. A huge family party was held at the Parkers' store just days before Christmas to welcome home a war veteran. Christmas was good to the families that year, but it wasn't to last.

They had become well liked in the Kingston community, and everyone thought they had decided to make it their home. However, Mrs. Parker's mother fell ill in South Carolina and needed her help. The family decided to sell the store and move. Mike and Martie assumed Bruce might take over the business and stay with Alice, but he surprised them when he decided to leave. Alice was heart broken, but decided her place was with her husband. On February 24, 1919, the Parker's left Kingston. Martie went into a deep depression for several months. Finally, she was drawn out of her personal tragedy by another Kingston devastation.

Notes

1. Mrs. Sarah Parker is in no way based on an actual person, nor is the surname, Parker, used in any reference to an actual person. She is a fictional character.

2. Information taken from *History Of The Woman's History Club*, written by Mrs. Louise Pratt Hood, *Commemorative Program for 125th Confederate Memorial Service, April 23, 1989.*

3. Information taken from *History Of The Woman's History Club*, written by Mrs. Louise Pratt Hood, *Commemorative Program for 125th Confederate Memorial Service, April 23, 1989.*

4. "The Allied powers signed a cease-fire agreement with Germany at Rethondes, France on November 11, 1918, bringing World War I to a close." http://memory.loc.gov/ammem/today/nov11.html (Library of Congress) (June 4, 2007)

Rising from ashes . . .

Just as the most of the town was continuing to recover from the great fire of 1911 and completing the construction of the last buildings, the school burned. Bells began ringing throughout Kingston, and shouts in the streets awakened all who lived within earshot of the village.

"What's going on?" A sleepy Mike rolled out of bed and stumbled to the window.

"Oh my God!" he exclaimed. "The school's burning."

Mike was eyeing the bright flames flashing against the night sky, billowing in the direction of the school.

Martie sprang to her feet and located her robe. Mike and Thomas threw on their pants and grabbed the first shirts they could find. Hopping out of the house while trying to put on shoes, the two of them ran to the aid of the school. Martie hastily dressed and ran down the street behind them.

A bucket brigade was already in place when they arrived. Mike and Thomas joined one of the lines, but it was too late. The wooden structure was completely engulfed. The fire was too intense and too much for small buckets of water. The flames were destructively burning faster than water could be drawn, passed, and thrown. Within minutes, the well-loved structure would completely collapse.

All of the hard work that went into furnishing the school was going up in flames. Memories of the great fire struck cords of sadness in everyone's hearts. The only thing they could do was to watch their school burning.

Martie noticed several men had left the bucket brigade and walked to a dusty, dirt patch next to the school. She eased up behind them to see what they were doing. By the light of the fire, they donned sticks and were sketching something in the dirt. They were making plans for a new school.

One of them was busy making a sketch of the layout of the current building now moaning and writhing in the hot flames. He had drawn the two-story, frame structure with its two large classrooms downstairs and the large auditorium, library, and music teacher's room upstairs. He had even included the stage.

The man kneeling next to him was making revisions and improvements to the current design. He was sketching in additional classrooms. Martie was impressed and shaken from her shell to see this. They weren't giving up. The flames torturing the school were not going to snuff out, in its leftover ashes, the drive and determination of this town. Life was going to go on. The school would be rebuilt. The silhouettes of those men in the light of the fire gave Martie a new direction and new hope. She was going to be needed, again.

As soon as daylight broke, many returned to the smoldering ruins of the school. Nothing was left. All of the books and furnishings were now ashes.

Quietly, Martie walked to the side of the school where she had stood as a silent observer the night before. The hastily drawn plans for the new school were still in the dirt. They were just waiting to take form on this very spot.

Within days, Martie was back to herself. She opened the doors of her home and used her parlor as a classroom. She took one small class of children, as did many other ladies of the town. She picked up with their lessons just where they had left off. The regular teachers, who did not have homes in Kingston, used places like the Masonic Hall and churches. The children of the town did not go without a classroom education for lack of a building.

Mike and Thomas both helped clear the rubble from the site as soon as it was cool enough to be moved and disposed. Martie and Bell attended a town meeting where it was decided the town should sell bonds to raise funds for the new school, a two-story, brick structure built on the same design as the one they lost. The builder was put to work immediately on the new building.

Martie spent her days happier now because she was needed, and she was contributing to the needs of a town she so dearly loved. She followed the school building's progress with great interest. Its rise from the rubble symbolized her rise from her personal devastation.

Then, came news. Alice was having a baby. Letters and telegrams filtered into Martie and Mike's hands over the next six months, and eventually the one she had waited for arrived. One month before the baby's due date, Alice sent a telegram to her mother saying she needed her.

Martie took charge of the situation and ordered Mike to make travel arrangements for a two-month visit to South Carolina. One week of preparations went into packing and deciding what to do with Thomas, who refused to go. William and Lydia promised to feed him and keep him out of as much trouble as possible. Bell volunteered to take over Martie's small class, so all was set for the trip.

Mike and Martie left Kingston for their extended visit. Although Mike had traveled with the railroad, this was Martie's first trip out of the state. She was excited and apprehensive. The train ride was very enjoyable for the couple, and they had a great time being alone for what seemed like the first time ever. Their extended stay was very pleasant. They resided for two months with Bruce and Alice. Steady telegrams from both Lydia and Bell reassured Martie that her class was excelling under Bell's tutelage and that Thomas was staying out of major trouble.

In fact, the most trouble he was causing was for his grandfather, James. Lydia reported in an actual letter that Thomas would aggravate Pa by sneaking up to the front window of the house and peering inside at the cataract-laden James. James would holler at Lydia that someone was trying to get him or break in, and when Lydia would investigate, Thomas would be long gone. William finally caught the naughty, young man on his way home for lunch one day and put a stop to his behavior. Martie read all about this incident in letters from her sister-in-law. She just sighed to herself and thought, "It's a good thing we hid those guns."

A month after the birth of their grandson, Michael Bruce Parker or Mikey, it was time for Mike and Martie to return to Kingston. Although she would sorely miss her daughter and new grandchild, Martie longed for the sights and sounds of the only place on earth she knew she loved. The trip home seemed to go a lot faster than the one to South Carolina. Mike and Martie arrived on the evening train. Greeted by Ben and Thomas, they all took a stroll to see the last couple of months' progress at the school. It was really looking good. It wouldn't be long before the children of Kingston had a central place to learn, once again.[1]

Notes

1. "Notes On School," *We Remember Kingston . . . Woman's History Club & Others*, Third Printing Courtesy of The Etowah Valley Historical Society, Cartersville, Georgia, May 1998; page 2, gives details of the school fire.

Swing batter, batter, oops!

The 1920s would garner the name "The Roaring Twenties," but for Martie, life in Kingston just went on status quo. Music drifted over the airwaves and from homes with phonograph players throughout the small town, bringing the sounds of the larger cities to the small village. Residents continued to enjoy their slower pace of life. An ice cream at the local soda fountain was entertainment enough. A trip to Rome or Cartersville to see a moving picture show could top off a month nicely.

Visitors passing through brought some of the latest dances like the Charleston. Other part-time residents like traveling salesmen and mysterious women made some of the local hotels their home during the week.[1] They caught on to the easier, lighter side of life in Kingston. On weekends, they would leave to live their faster-paced lives somewhere else. Then, Sunday evenings would find them home, again. The halls of the hotels were filled with strange smells of jasmine perfume. The women who passed through town brought newer fashions with them. The skirts were a lot shorter and their hair was bobbed. Their jewelry sparkled in the sunlight and twinkled by candlelight. The men all donned fancier suits than most of the Kingston women's dresses. Times and styles were changing rapidly.

One day, Martie noticed Bell had shortened her skirt quite a bit.

"What are you wearing?" Martie was gasping in a semi-shocked way. Then, she giggled. "I see your ankles and stockings."

"That's right. I'm changing with the times," Bell replied.

"Where did you get that dress?" Martie was curious now.

"I ordered it from a catalog."

"Well, I like it," Martie said. "Do you still have the catalog?"

Bell had beaten Martie to the punch. She knew her friend still had a little childhood spark in her. She produced the small catalog from her bag and relinquished it to Martie.

"What do you think Mike will say if I order one of those dresses?"

"Honestly, I'm not sure he will notice," Bell said. "I truly believe that the only fashion change he'd notice on you would be if you put on Thomas' baseball uniform, cut off all your hair, and began chewing tobacco and swinging a bat."

"Oh, Bell, that's not fair to Mike," Martie said. "He still thinks I'm beautiful. I think? Maybe a new dress would shake things up a bit in this house."

"Perhaps you're right," Bell conceded. "But just to make sure things go your way, be sure to carry your son's baseball bat when you model the new dress for him."

"What for?"

"Sweetie, if you can't figure that one out, then I wouldn't order the dress." This was Bell's final word of advice on the subject.

Baseball truly was a huge pastime for everyone. The World Series was a must hear by all males who had learned to walk. Holding a bat wasn't required, just the ability to stand and listen.

Martie thought Thomas was one of the best baseball players in Kingston. He was an outstanding catcher. If you got to cross home plate past Thomas Grady, then you were an all-star player yourself. Thomas had gone to work in the nearby saltpeter mine and continued to play for Kingston. Mike finally retired from masonry work when the school was completed. He continued to work part-time on odd jobs around Kingston, so the two of them spent a lot of time together at the field.

Martie kept up with her work for the Kingston Woman's History Club. The school was back in operation, and Martie's temporary teaching services were no longer needed. However, the women answered the call for help again by assisting with books, furnishings, and any other needs of the school taking up much of Martie's free time.

As always, the club continued to assist with Confederate Memorial Day services. Miss Bell Darden eventually took over the committee and most of the preparations for the service.[2] Leila Darden and Bell Bayless also took on new roles for the town. They researched history thoroughly and wrote many papers and articles about Kingston.[3]

Martie was very proud of her friend, Bell, who had numerous articles published in the newspaper. These articles, along with many other family papers and historical documents began to mount into piles of scattered paper throughout the homes of club members. The need to organize them, collect, and preserve them became a task.

The club began throwing around the idea of building its own clubhouse. This would be an even larger task than creating the park. Where would they build? Who would run it? Would anyone be interested? All of these questions and their answers overwhelmed the ladies. This discussion and the continual collection of artifacts would continue for decades.

But, for the 1920s, the issue was tabled. Afternoon teas, changing fashions, growing children and grandchildren were all pleasant conversation for their monthly afternoon visits. Even the ladies would venture out to the ball field with their umbrellas drawn for an afternoon game.

One particular game stood out in Martie's mind, and in later years, she was glad she witnessed it. This one incident became legendary in the minds of many who became "oletimers" at baseball.

Little Steven Norris, the child who had run over Martie in 1911 while flying his kite the day of the great fire, was now "Big Steven," and he was stepping up to the plate just as a passing train blew its whistle signaling its intentions to pass through Kingston versus stopping. Martie hated it when this happened because the rumble of the tracks always shook the ground and drowned out the calls from the umpire. She always thought the game should kind of pause while the trains went through town. However, baseball in Kingston stopped neither for man nor machine.

"Batter up," was the last call heard from the umpire as Steven took a strong batting stance. The first pitch was hurled across the plate, and he took a powerful swing. The cracking of the bat against the ball was like an ignition spark against a firecracker when the ball changed directions with the swinging of the bat and took flight. The train whistle wailed one last time and was silenced as the train began to edge up on the ball field. The crowd's cheers were music to the Kingston team's ears as they saw a homerun in the making. Suddenly, the cheering stopped, and a pin drop could be heard on the ball field when Steven's homerun ball went straight down the smokestack of the passing train.

Martie would not have believed the story except that the ball flew over her own head as it went out of the ball park. She had turned to follow it just as it shot straight down the pipe.

The ball was gone, the crowd silent, and it appeared to Martie that for the first time in Kingston's ball history, the game was stopped. Obviously, you can't play ball without a ball. After the teams and the crowd watched the train trek on out of town, the laughter began. Several members of the Kingston team had an idea. Thomas, along with his teammates, jumped on the backs of the nearest horses and flew out of town, faster than a gang of bandits.

"Where are they going?" Martie was asking Mike, but he was still laughing.

The umpire was at a loss. The ball was gone, and half of the home team had fled town. He was now trying to call a little order to the crowd.

"Mike," Martie shouted. "Where did they go?"

Wiping tears of laughter from his face, Mike responded, "I think they are going to try to cut off the train at Hall's Station and get that darn ball."

Sure enough, about an hour later, the small band of baseball thugs returned to the field victorious. They had beaten the train, stopped it, and fished the ball out of its smokestack.

Martie and some of the other ladies had returned to the ball field in time for the gang's arrival with homemade lemonade and cookies. Both teams enjoyed the refreshments before resuming the game with a new ball. Steven's ball was immediately retired and became a prize possession of his. When the game resumed, he was once again at bat. This time the count was one and zero. More celebrations followed when Kingston won the game.

Kingston was a very good team. They faced mill village teams like Lindale and Shannon. They also played Atco, Sugar Valley, and Anchor Rome.[4]

Notes

1 Stories in this chapter concerning the atmosphere and activities of the town inspired by an article, *Old Hotel Full of Surprises, Dateline Georgia* by Bob Harrell. No publication or date preserved on copy. However, it was handwritten as article #2 on the copy. Article probably originated from *The Atlanta Constitution*, circa 1977 (A #1 was placed on another copy of a clipping found with the one above.)

2 Personal writings of Miss Leila Darden, Kingston Woman's History Club charter member, and local historian, reveal information about the early days of Confederate Memorial Day celebrations, *History of Kingston Memorial Day*.

3 Many personal papers and letters are on file with the Kingston Woman's History Club Museum belonging to Miss Leila Darden. Miss Bell Bayless wrote many newspaper articles, several of which are used in this book.

4 Game and incident details retold in this chapter were inspired by "Oletimers" by Cliff E. Johnson, Jr., page 29 of *We Remember Kingston . . . Woman's History Club & Others*, Third Printing Courtesy of The Etowah Valley Historical Society, Cartersville, Georgia, May 1998.

Progress?

Martie hated to admit it, but Bell was right about one thing. She needed to have a bat handy when she tried to model her new dress for Mike. She had worn it off and on for more than two months before Mike even noticed. What made matters worse was who noticed it first, her father.

One Sunday afternoon, Mike and Martie had relieved William and Lydia of their duties. Martie was preparing the table for Sunday dinner when she breezed by James.

"Isn't that new dress a little indecent for church or anything else for that matter?" James was eyeballing Martie's appearance with his good eye.

This caught Mike's attention with a strange look.

"I asked you a question," James almost barked as he swung his cane at her skirt.

"Um, no," was all she could muster.

"No what?" James was enjoying himself now. "The dress is not new, or it's not too indecent for Sunday services."

"Actually, Dad, it's no to both. I've been wearing this dress for two months, and no one has noticed it. So, I conclude that it's perfectly fine," she said. Martie had regained her stern and confident voice, as well as her spunk. Mike had yet to open his mouth. Actually, he had yet to close it.

"I'm not sure what this world is coming to. Women showing their legs in public, cutting their hair, looking like men. I can't tell the girls from the boys from the neck up any more," he was now babbling.

Sunday supper was quiet save for the occasional rambling from James. Later at home, Mike finally regained his voice and only complimented Martie on how nice she looked in the dress. She ordered two more from Bell's latest catalog on Monday.

New people and new fashions weren't the only strange sights in Kingston. One day, one of the railroad's luxurious passenger trains rolled into town right on time. There was nothing unusual about that. What was unusual was the open freight car right behind the private dining car. Securely affixed to this freight car was something large and covered with a huge canvas tarp. Everyone either stopped where they stood on the street, or they at least slowed down to peek at the strange sight.

A very well-dressed gentleman stepped off the private car followed by a man in an unusual suit and hat. Rail hands began to uncover the large object on the car while the two men supervised. When the tarp was removed, pulleys and levers began to slowly and carefully lower the machine to the ground.

It was a Ford Model T car. The man overseeing the entire operation was none other than Henry Ford, and the strangely dressed gentleman was his driver.[1] Yes, this scene was a show stopper for the daily routine of Kingston.

Martie and Bell were just two of the witnesses that afternoon.

"My goodness," exclaimed Martie. "Have you ever seen anything quite like that?"

"Yes, Martie," Bell said mockingly. "That's not the first car we've ever seen you know. Several people around here have them."

"I know, but I've never seen one so clean or shiny," Martie said. "That must be brand new. I don't think it's ever been driven. Do you?"

"Probably not," Bell responded. "If I were Henry Ford, I'd probably drive a new car everywhere too."

The excitement over for Bell, she nudged Martie and motioned for her to join her on her way to the meeting.

"I'll be there in a minute," Martie said.

She hadn't realized who the man was until Bell pointed it out, and she was in no hurry to join Bell. She was enjoying the show. Several people did have cars, including her brothers William and Ben. The vehicles made travel around the countryside seeing patients a little easier and more convenient for the patients. Of course, their cars weren't new. They had much older "Tin Lizzies" than Henry Ford's bright new shiny one now on the street.

She watched as Mr. Ford seated himself in the passenger side while his driver shooed all the children away from the front of the car while he cranked it. They were off. Following the road to Rome along the railroad tracks, they should be there in say an hour or more.

Martie knew where he was going. He was going to visit Miss Martha Berry, who had started a school mainly for the underprivileged that had no access or means for an education. Martie had been told Henry Ford and his wife were impressed by her tenacity and her work. They were helping financially with her school.[2] Several from Kingston had taken advantage of Miss Berry's work and education opportunities. They had moved on to larger cities and better jobs than could be found at home. Martie and Mike had encouraged Thomas to do the same, but he was now a supervisor at the mine and enjoyed the slower pace of life in Kingston. He had found a girlfriend in Cartersville whom he enjoyed dating. Martie didn't like it, but Thomas would borrow one of his uncles' cars just to go see her every Saturday. He had the money for the gas and the date, so she couldn't stop him.

Martie watched the spectacle as Henry Ford waved his hat and said, "Good day, all," and rumbled out of town in his new Model T.

She began walking in the direction of the meeting while thinking to herself how unsettling this scene had been to her. Martie didn't like cars. She was slightly afraid of them, which was strange considering her daring younger self, seeing as how she had once tried to board a moving train. Reports of tragic accidents where cars stalled on railroad tracks and people being killed by oncoming trains disturbed her greatly. Besides, cars made funny noises to Martie. They were very loud and shaky. She didn't like to be bounced around. She kind of got sick to her stomach every time she would go for a ride. She constantly worried about her brothers and Thomas.

Bell would always laugh at her and say, "But, Martie, trains are louder and when they derail, it's ten times worse than one small car accident. I'm surprised at you. I thought you would like being in control. On a train, someone else is in charge of making it move."

Bell's mocking words left her mind, and she returned to her own private thoughts on cars. If more people begin to purchase them, what will that do to the railroad and all the business that Kingston gets from it? Of course, Kingston was a stop for gas for those rich enough to own a car or just daring enough to invest in an old one. It was comforting to know that the gas still had to be brought to Kingston on the rail line for the few cars in and around the town. Martie relaxed a little as three wagons passed her on the way to the Kingston Woman's History Club meeting that day. It'll be a while before they completely take over, she laughed to herself.

And, Martie was half right about the train versus car discussion. While the cities were becoming traffic jams, Kingston's rail travel continued to bring commerce to the small village. In 1924, a new coal chute was built. Construction of any type was exciting. For Martie, this new chute was confirmation enough that her way of life wasn't going to drastically change any time soon. However, she did enjoy the newer fashions, but that was on a personal level, not a global one she thought.

Children were impressed at the chute's size and how it seemed to tower high above the town. The smaller the child, the more it reached to the clouds. Out-of-town workers labored on its construction. One day as Martie and Thomas were coming by the new chute, almost complete, there was a gasp from the usual audience. Martie and Thomas turned to see the commotion just in time to see a man falling from the top of the towering structure.[3]

Martie dropped her sack of groceries, as did Thomas, who began to rush to the scene. Tears welled in Martie's eyes. She couldn't bear the thoughts of what was happening. She was frozen.

She watched as Thomas ran to get a doctor. He returned with William, who now just covered the man with a blanket brought from a nearby home. The man had fallen to his death.

Her fresh eggs splattered on the ground at her feet, and Martie knelt to clean the mess and pick up what hadn't broken from her bag. Thomas joined his mother and began to comfort her.

Martie didn't feel much like cooking that evening. Instead of cooking dinner, Mike and Thomas offered to take the downtrodden lady out for the evening. Although it was a nice gesture, Martie just couldn't eat much. The image of the poor man falling to the hard ground haunted her for a long time.

Notes

1. An instance of Henry Ford unloading his car in Kingston is found in an article, *Old Hotel Full of Surprises, Dateline Georgia* by Bob Harrell, no publication or date preserved on copy. However, it was handwritten as article #2 on the copy. Article probably originated from *The Atlanta Constitution*, circa 1977 (A #1 was placed on another copy of a clipping found with the one above.)

2. The New Georgia Encyclopedia, online at www.georgiaencyclopedia.org; Berry College entry notes Henry Ford's substantial donations. (May 1, 2007)

3. The tragic incident in this chapter was inspired by "Some of the Remembrances of my Old HomeTown" by Earl M. Hood, Page 26 of *We Remember Kingston . . . Woman's History Club & Others*, Third Printing Courtesy of The Etowah Valley Historical Society, Cartersville, Georgia, May 1998.

The interview . . .

Not long after the coal chute incident, Thomas proposed to his girlfriend in Cartersville, married her and brought her home to Kingston. Martie didn't care for Vera at first, but after a few months, began to like her without letting anyone know. Bell noticed it right away and pointed it out to Martie.[1]

"You are going to have to get along with Vera," she said. "I know you, and I know you just say and act like you don't like her because she married your baby. By the way, I think it's because she's just like you. She's opinionated, set in her own ways, knows who she is and where she's going with her life."

Vera was more than just a homemaker. She was a bookkeeper at the mine where Thomas had been working. Thomas was trying to talk her into quitting, but he had not yet succeeded.

"Maybe you're right," Martie conceded. "But giving her a chance doesn't mean I'm going to ever like her."

"I never said you had to like her," Bell insisted. "I just said get along with her, for Thomas' sake."

Martie hated it when Bell would come over to walk with her to the meetings, and then set her straight on issues.

"Hey, I have an idea," Bell's voice was one Martie knew well and didn't like. "Why don't you invite Vera to one of our meetings? If it goes well, then you can present her for membership. Lots of family connections exist in the club."

This made Martie long for Alice, even though letters and telegrams were steady. Alice now had two children, Mikey, and a daughter named, Edith. Mike and Martie's last trip to South Carolina had been just after Edith's arrival. She treasured the few and far between photos that arrived. She wished she were inviting Alice to the meeting instead of Vera.

As if it weren't bad enough, Bell had gone and invited Lydia to a meeting and presented her for membership. Martie tolerated Lydia, but the snooty air about her really got under Martie's skin. She was just hoping Lydia had gotten tied up with James this afternoon and couldn't make it.

"Have you heard a word I've been saying?" Bell asked, stopping in her tracks.

"Yes, I have and I'm choosing to ignore you right now," Martie responded. "I'll ask, but I'll bet she's working."

"No, you hope she's working," Bell added.

The pair arrived at the meeting in time to be greeted by Lydia, who was bubbling with excitement. She was presenting the program. Martie's stomach did a few flips of nausea while Bell's demeanor changed from jest to plain snooty in playful mocking of Lydia.

At the conclusion of Lydia's presentation about medical aid rendered in Kingston during the Civil War, she added an announcement.

"I am pleased to announce that a reporter from the Cartersville paper will be in town on Tuesday to meet with my father-in-law, Dr. James Litton," she positively bubbled the words.

Martie was stunned that she didn't know. Shock evolved into pure anger. Knowing her friend well, Bell reached over to hold her hand in an attempt to calm her.

"He came by William's office last week to talk about doing a piece on one of the area's Civil War heroes. They aren't getting any younger, you know," she continued. "William sent him to the house, but Papa James wasn't feeling well at the time, so I made arrangements for next week."

All the ladies clapped with delight. Bell let go of Martie's hand just long enough to allow her to show a little phony support for her sister-in-law.

"I'm going to give her a big piece of my mind," Martie snapped at Bell in a whisper.

"I agree, but not here," she whispered back. "This is not the place nor the time for a family squabble."

"Well, if I hold it in until I can get her alone, I might just slap that uppity look off her face." Martie was now fighting mad, and Bell's grip on her wrist was cutting off her circulation.

To make matters worse, Lydia sauntered toward Bell and Martie. Bell's heart was pounding with fear for Lydia. The unaware Lydia gave Martie a sisterly-like hug.

"Can you believe it? The Cartersville paper wants to do a story on Dad," she said.

"No, I can't," retorted a solemn Martie. "And, what I can't believe is that you didn't have the decency to tell me before you announced it to the entire club. You must realize that he's my flesh and blood, not yours."

"Oh, Lord help us," Bell softly whispered to herself while letting go of Martie's hand in sick anticipation of it flying toward Lydia's face.

"Well, if you would come around a little more often, you might stay abreast of family business," Lydia replied without missing a beat. "If you choose not to visit, then you can just learn our good news with the rest of the ladies."

Lydia sauntered away from them undaunted, just as she had come toward them. Martie made a lunge in her direction, but she was cut short by Bell who had regained her own senses by this time.

"Fine, I missed two Sunday suppers," Martie admitted. "I had Vera and Thomas over to our house after church. I'm trying to like her. I confess."

"It's going to be all right," Bell comforted her. "Just haul yourself over there this weekend and take charge of the situation. That should make you feel better. He's your father."

Martie took Bell's advice and joined the rest of the Litton family for Sunday supper, even taking food and her new daughter-in-law along for the ride. She was able to get the upper hand on Lydia when she offered to take James to her house for the interview. Lydia was livid at this suggestion. To prevent the two of them from having a fight, William suggested that Martie be present at the Litton house since James was growing a little too frail for many trips out a week.

So, Martie moved herself into the number one spot in charge of the interview, and Lydia kept control of the location. They would just have to live with it.

Tuesday afternoon arrived, and both Martie and Lydia remained calm as they communicated with each other. Bell was present in case an umpire were to be needed.

There was a knock at the door, and Lydia turned on the Southern charm when she allowed the reporter to come in and be seated across from James.

"Dr. Litton, it's good to meet you," he said. "How are you feeling today?"

"I'm older than dirt. I can barely hear you. I haven't walked straight since I was eighteen," he complained. "How do you think I feel?"

A very bewildered gentleman looked to Martie and Lydia for support. Both women just smiled and gave a gentle nod toward James.

"Dad," Martie began. "This man is here to talk to you for the newspaper. He wants you to tell him about your service in the Confederate Army."

There was a long pause while James' face softened. He looked twenty years younger as he began to speak about a time in his life he had never really talked to anyone about. It was a time he'd tried hard to forget but couldn't.

"No one's asked me anything about those years since long before your mother died," he said.

"I know, Dad," Martie continued. "Mama always said you didn't like to talk about it. It hurt too much."

Turning to the reporter, Martie said, "His brother died next to him at Peachtree Creek. He had him buried but never found his grave."

The reporter looked down solemnly in reverence. This was about all Martie could tell the man. Martha never recounted much for her either. Both of her parents kept this part of their lives silent.

"I can speak for myself," James was now talking. "I'm not a child. However, I was a child then."

That was all it took. For the first time since he returned to his mother's kitchen in 1865, he told the complete story of his war-time service. He shed tears while he talked about his brother, Brad, and the way he died. He recounted all of the battles he took part in, and he even told the complete story of his trip around Georgia while recovering. Martie wasn't sure her if mother ever knew this whole story. To the best of her knowledge, the two of them just never talked about it.[2]

The tears are what broke down both Martie and Lydia. Neither of them had ever seen him cry. In all the years of Confederate Memorial Day services he attended, he was solemn and quiet. Looking at his face was like looking at a stone wall carved with bitterness. Now, this man who had been the strength of the world to his wife, his children, and his entire family was crying like a baby.

Neither Martie nor Lydia knew what to do. Bell didn't move, as it wasn't her place. From the shadows of the room, Ben's wife came forward and put her arms around her father-in-law. To Bell's surprise, Martie and Lydia reached for each other in comfort.

Ben's wife was the living ghost of the family. She was rarely seen, and sometimes, even the family didn't know she was in the room. She would frighten them as she floated by. Ben had married a full-blooded Cherokee woman. Her English-speaking name was Ann.[3] Everyone in the family liked Ann, but they never talked about her in public. As with the family, she was rarely seen by anyone in town. Many times, Martie had wished Ann was a club member with her rather than Lydia, but Ann never expressed any interest.

Ben and Ann had two children, who had married and moved away from home just like William and Lydia's.

Like usual, Martie hadn't realized that Ann was in the room, but she was thankful that she was that day. Still wearing her dark, silky hair in two braids down either side of her head and soft leather shoes, she was a welcome sight kneeling and comforting her father-in-law until his tears subsided.

Of all the bad things James could say in his later years about his entire family, Martie never recalled hearing one bad word against Ann. As soon as his tears stopped, Ann relinquished her grip on James and once again disappeared into the woodwork.

James stopped talking and sat like an Egyptian Sphinx, perched and solemn in his chair. The reporter finally stopped taking notes and closed his tablet. As soon as Martie and Lydia realized they were clutching each other, they separated with a jerk.

Quietly, and without fanfare, the emotionally shaken reporter stood and took his coat and hat from Ann, who had reappeared.

"Look for this story in next week's issue," was all he said as he walked out the door.

His emotions wouldn't even allow him a good-bye to the women and James. The four women left in the room didn't know what to say to each other or to the now silent elderly man sitting in the chair.

Finally, James broke the heavy silence, "Has anyone seen my gun?"

Laughter and tears roared in the parlor. The family had decided that James' unstable condition, since Martha's death, would not allow firearms to return to the house. The poor old man had been looking for at least one of his guns since 1917.

Martie was the first to ask, "Why do you need your gun?"

"Because those damn Yankees might be coming back, you know," he said. "I forgot all about them until you all made me talk to that man. I thought you gals were smarter than that. I'll bet they're looking for me now. They want to put me in jail. I bet that feller was a Yankee spy."

"How about we just put you in bed for a nap?" Lydia almost couldn't stop laughing and enjoying herself with Martie.

Notes

1. Vera is in no way a portrayal of any real person. Her character is fictional.

2. Stories retold to a local newspaper by Dr. John D. Goodwin, dated August 20, 1925, in article titled, *Dr. John D. Goodwin Tells War-Time Stories of Past.* Article archived in Kingston Woman's History Club Museum, Scrapbook 1, are used for this chapter. No newspaper source was saved or cited in the scrapbook files.

3. Ann is in no way a portrayal of any real person. Her character is fictional.

Ending with a crash . . .

Martie may have been mad at Lydia about the set up of the interview, but after it was published, the anger and resentment disappeared. Martie now had in her hands the answers to many questions from her parents' past. She read the article more than once. In fact, she almost had every word memorized. It spoke volumes to her that her father never could. She treasured the words on the newspaper page as if they were golden. This article and the words written about him became a fitting, final chapter and tribute to a great man.

James' health continued a slow and steady decline with his mind lapsing into long periods of dementia. On February 18, 1929, the legendary Confederate soldier drew his last breaths. His family surrounded his bed. Together, William and Ben pronounced the Southern hero dead. The controversial interview of a few years earlier now seemed trivial to Martie, and she was thankful and grateful to Lydia for arranging it. She had some of her father's final coherent words as a tribute and keepsake forever.

A hand-sewn Confederate flag draped his coffin and was presented to Martie. Mike made a special shadowbox for it. He carefully enclosed the flag in beveled glass and mounted it on the parlor wall. James was laid to rest next to his beloved Martha on the cemetery hill in Kingston.

The year 1929 roared on like the entire decade. William retired and Ben passed away shortly after James when he suffered a massive heart attack. William and Lydia invited the reclusive Ann to live with them. Many in town never recalled seeing her after Ben's death and only remembered her when they read her obituary years later.

With two deaths of beloved family members, this year was one Martie couldn't wait to see end. By fall, she was already planning a small family gathering to ring in the New Year and a brighter decade.

Reflecting on the 1920s one afternoon, Martie and Bell decided to document some of the club's work and service during the past nine years. Bell had realized the repercussions of such grief for Martie. She had been trying to lift her spirits with weekly visits where they were keeping a journal of the club's activities. These journals were for personal use, and were more like diaries for the two of them.

"Hey, Martie," she began. "Do you remember about fifteen years ago when a lot of women descended on Kingston for the state's Federation of Women's Clubs annual meeting?"[1]

Martie began to laugh. "Why, of course I do. I've never seen so many scared and shaking men in my life. They thought it was some kind of warring, women's tribe coming to take over the town."

"Yeah," Bell added. "As if we aren't bad enough, running around and getting into something all the time. You know, I think we really make the men around here nervous."

"No," replied Martie. "I think we keep them entertained when baseball season ends."

It felt good to have Bell around during these times.

"Hey, how are Vera and Thomas?" Bell knew how to get Martie to talking. She and Vera were always at each other about family matters. Martie had followed Bell's advice, once again, and presented Vera for membership into the club. Vera had stopped working after she and Thomas had their twin daughters Jeannie and Josie.[2]

"Oh, please, don't get me started," Martie squawked. "That girl wouldn't know what a broom was if one rose from the floor and smacked her square on the behind."

Vera was not known as a housekeeper or cook for that matter, but she was a very talented bookkeeper. She had promptly begun to serve as recording secretary for the ladies.

"And, I think those two girls are sick all the time because she's slowly poisoning them with her cooking," Martie continued as Bell remained amused. "You know, I had a case of, well, you know runny movements after Sunday supper at their place last week."

By now, Bell was laughing loudly.

The ladies calmed down a bit as they continued to recall numerous service projects and meetings throughout the decade.

"By the way," Bell said. "I forgot to ask you if you need me to bring anything for the meeting tomorrow."

It was Martie's turn to host. She could see a conniving wheel turning in Bell's mind.

"I've known you long enough to know that you are about to suggest I ask Vera to bring some refreshments," Martie retorted. "You better not even think about going over to her place telling her I need help."

"Now, why would I do that?" Bell was holding back some more giggles.

"Because, you just would. I think you like to hear me fuss about anything," Martie said. "And, by the way, I've had some of your cooking too. Just bring yourself tomorrow."

With that, Bell jumped with the chiming of the clock in the hall and was off for the evening. Mike and Martie took a crisp, fall walk to William and Lydia's for a light supper. This was one unusual evening when Ann decided to appear from the woodwork and join the crowd. Being forced to deal with the rest of her immediate family brought her out of her hiding. Of course, this was limited to conversations with Martie and Lydia. Mike was semi-fascinated by Ann and a little scared of her for some reason. Everyone picked up on it and teased him about it. At one point, he finally worked up enough guts to ask Martie a very important question about Ann.

"Does she ever speak?" he whispered.

"I don't know," she said. "Why don't you ask her?"

Turning in Ann's direction with Mike trying to restrain her, Martie raised her voice and said, "Hey, Ann, Mike wants to ask you a question."

Having never said a word to his sister-in-law before tonight, Mike was speechless.

"Go ahead, Honey, you have her attention," Martie was amusing herself with this situation.

Ann was silent and slightly amused too. She was never brought to the center of attention. She sat motionless, staring at Mike. Mike was turning red and sweating slightly.

"Uh, I was just wondering," he said in a nervous voice.

The rest of the family stopped eating and began to snicker. Forever the out-doorsman and baseball fanatic, Mike spent very little time around the family during social hours. He showed up for meals. Sometimes, this annoyed Martie. Tonight, she saw her chance to get under his skin.

"Well, I was just wondering if you talk at all?" There he had said it. He breathed a huge sigh of relief.

William, Martie, and Lydia had gotten acquainted with Ann well enough to know how she would react. She didn't like to be ridiculed or insulted. She was stern and quiet, and Ann spoke only when she had something to contribute to a conversation. They knew she would see Mike's question as an insult.

Calmly and with reserve, she put down her fork, folded her napkin and stood up. Mike was slightly scared. The others were controlling fits of giggles. At the top of her lungs, Ann said something in the Cherokee language, pushed her chair up to the table and left.

"I guess you got your answer," William said to a red-faced Mike.

Lydia and Martie apologized to Ann for the entire scene explaining they knew she would scare Mike, and they all thought he had it coming. Ann calmed down and saw the humor in it. Until her death, she enjoyed sneaking up on him and scaring him with strange, Cherokee words. Little did he know some of them were words of love and blessing.

The next day, Mike still wasn't speaking to anyone in the family. Today, he was too busy getting out of the house. He knew a buzzing queen bee party was about to converge on his castle. Unless he wanted to be "stung" some more by these busy bees, he knew he had to make an exit. He decided to spend the afternoon with William at the drug store over a cigar and lunch. They could hear a little news on the radio and enjoy the company of some of the other retired husbands escaping their "queen-free" hives for the afternoon.

Just into the social hour of the meeting, the ladies were interrupted by a commotion in the downtown area near the Bank of Kingston. From Martie's front porch, the ladies had a clear view of Main Street. Shouting and what looked like rioting was taking place in front of the bank's front entrance.

"What in the world?" one shocked lady gasped.

Bell told the ladies to stay put. She was going to investigate. Not to be outdone in any way of daring, Vera volunteered to accompany her.

The ladies watched as the two women blended into the gathered crowd. Ten minutes later, they both returned, pale and out of breath.

"We better all go back inside and sit down," Bell urged.

Martie's heart sank. Was the country at war again? What was going on? News filtered in constantly via radios from stations in the larger cities.

"The stock market has crashed," Bell began.

One of the older ladies meekly raised her hand and asked, "What is a stock market? How bad was the crash? Was anyone hurt?"

Vera, a former bookkeeper stepped in.

"The stock market is where men invest or buy stocks in a company. They literally purchase a little piece of ownership in a business," she could see no understanding on the ladies' bewildered faces.

"In other words, the stock market has lost its value, or money," she continued. "The radio is reporting that some investors have killed themselves because of the massive amounts of money they will lose. They are speculating that people are going broke."

"But our money is safe in the Bank of Kingston," one lady spoke up.

"Well, that's not exactly how the financial exchange works," Vera smiled in an understanding tone.

Bell took over by saying, "Ladies, maybe this is not for us to worry about. Let's get all the facts before we march on the bank ourselves."

Immediately following refreshments, the ladies dismissed early. Leftovers were sent home with Vera. It was Martie's opinion that Vera's family should have decent food for one evening.

Mike was extremely worried about what became known as Black Thursday, October 24, 1929. Most of the couple's money was nestled in the Bank of Kingston. Only about a thousand that they had saved, over many years, was tucked safely under their mattress.

By the end of the month and two disastrous days on the market the following Monday and Tuesday, the start of the Great Depression began trickling into Kingston. Martie's hopes for a brighter decade in the 1930s came crashing down around her with the failing economy.[3]

Notes

1. Information taken from *History Of The Woman's History Club*, written by Mrs. Louise Pratt Hood, *Commemorative Program for 125th Confederate Memorial Service, April 23, 1989.*

2. Jeannie and Josie are in no way formed or inspired by actual people.

3. *The Great Depression: A Brief Overview, No job, no hope* contains historical facts, dates, and information that was obtained from the Website, www.todaysteacher.com/TheGreatDepressionWebQuest/BriefOverview.htm (June 3, 2007)

Bright lights, small town . . .

The new decade didn't drift into town any better than the last one had "roared" out for Martie and Mike as they received tragic news from South Carolina. Like a nightmare's premonition come true, Martie's fear of cars was confirmed when Bruce was killed and Alice severely injured when a train struck their car. Alice's left arm had to be amputated at the elbow after the accident. Both of their children were safe at home with Mrs. Parker when the accident occurred.

Alice could no longer care for the children alone. Her father-in-law had passed away two years earlier, and her mother-in-law was too arthritic to aid in any way. Vera and Thomas left the twins with Mike and Martie and boarded a train to South Carolina to retrieve Alice and her children. She needed help packing and selling what furniture she could.

Plans were to have Alice and the children live with Martie and Mike. An unusual surprise offer came from Lydia and William a week before Alice and the children arrived in Kingston.

"Lydia and I have been talking about our living arrangements," William began a speech to Mike and Martie. "It's just the three of us wandering around in that big house about two streets over. You are going to more than double your household next week. Why don't we trade houses?"

Martie and Mike were stunned. This was the house they had raised their children in. This was their first and only home all these years.

"Seriously, Martie," Lydia said. "That big house is just as much yours as it is ours. You all need it much more than we do. Please trade with us. Mike and William can work out the deed transfer, or we can retain ownership of our current homes. Either way you look at it, we will all benefit."

"How will I benefit by losing my home," Martie retorted.

"Don't look at it like you are losing your home, Sis," William said. "This house will remain in the family, just like Mom and Dad's. You will benefit by exchanging residences with us because you need more room."

Lydia assumed the conversation from here. "And, we will benefit by moving into a smaller home where the three of us have a lot less to take care of. You know, we aren't getting any younger ourselves."

Martie knew they were right. The small, two-bedroom home where she and Mike had raised their two children was going to be too crowded for all of them.

Gently taking her hand, Mike said, "Martie, this is a good thing. We will have plenty of room for everyone. And, if you don't want to legally trade, we won't. We'll just shake on this as family."

Martie decided it was good enough to just shake on the whole deal. William's children and Ben's children would never be interested in the old home place.

When William, Lydia, and Ann's time would come, either Martie or Thomas would inherit the house. Martie's wheels were turning. This way, if she and Mike occupied the home, Vera couldn't get her hands on it while there was still a breath in Martie.

A few young men were hired the next day to help the families exchange homes. The wayward South Carolina group arrived two days later to the surprise turnover in residences.

"Wow!" Vera's exclaiming tone spoke loads to Martie. "What a surprise! When did ya'll decide this?"

"We had a family meeting after you left and decided this was best for everyone," Martie said. She had no other intentions of expanding on the subject.

Alice was grateful to see home. As soon as her children were tucked in, she fell into the arms of her parents and cried herself to sleep. As frail and thin as she had become, Mike had no problem carrying her up the steps and to her room. Even tiny Martie was able to dress her for bed. She stayed with her precious Alice until morning.

"Mama," whispered Alice to the sleeping Martie. "Mama, wake up."

"Oh dear," she replied grabbing at her stiff neck.

"Did you sleep in that chair all night?"

"I guess I did," Martie said smiling. "I just didn't want to leave you last night. I thought you might need me."

"I'm going to be fine now that I'm home," Alice said. "I just can't believe you and Dad have moved into Granny and Pa's house."

"Me neither," Martie said. "You know, this is going to be great. We have a lot of room. The entire family is together."

Alice smiled and interjected, "Yeah, all of your favorites in one central location."

Martie rose, made a mocking smack at Alice's hair and said, "Get dressed. I think you need to make breakfast today."

Alice was proving herself quite a cook despite her one-arm infirmity. Many times, Bell would hear Martie brag about Alice's superb domestic capabilities compared to those of Vera's.

Martie was delighted at the very next meeting to present Alice for membership into the Kingston Woman's History Club. Martha would be proud to know that four of her descendents, a daughter, daughter-in-law, granddaughter, and granddaughter-in-law, had all taken a keen interest in the social and civic affairs of her hometown.

Despite an ever-growing concern over the worsening economy, Kingston did have a bright spot in 1930, literally. Georgia Power brought service to the town.[1] Businesses and homes began to burn brightly, deep into the night.

Of course, there was the matter of pole rent that continued for many years, but electricity began to change the way people lived.

Having moved two streets over from the downtown area, Martie was a little miffed that Lydia and William had power before she did. What made it worse, and gave Bell a good laugh, was that it was run to Martie's house first. Lydia made sure she told Martie all about the wonders of having power in her home. She invited Mike and Martie for an inspection of the new wiring, and Mike enjoyed the tour. He was getting ideas about the wiring of their "new" residence the entire time. Martie was less enthusiastic and skipped the impromptu inspection. She decided to wait for the Georgia Power men to come to her house.

One bright Thursday morning late in the year, they arrived at Martie's. Bell, who lived on the hill and wasn't privy to power yet, came for the big event. The two ladies stood in awe on the porch as men began to dig large holes in the ground. Enormous, tall poles were taken off of wagon-like trucks and carefully set into the ground.

The men took a lunch break and headed downtown to eat. Martie and Bell cautiously walked toward the poles. They each had to touch them.

"These must weigh a ton," Martie said. "How do you suppose these poles carry the electricity?"

"Oh, Honey," Bell replied. "You've seen it downtown. They are going to come back and run the wires across the tops and then one to your house."

"You know, that's kind of ugly isn't it?" Martie was in one of her pondering moods again. "It's unnatural to have a wooden pole sticking out of the ground without bark, pretty leaves, and blossoms on it, don't you think?"

"Well, it's called progress," Bell answered. "If you want to keep up with the times, you have to adapt to them. It's just like riding in a car or you shortening your skirt."

"I still think it's ugly."

"Yeah, well, so are your chicken legs, but I never said anything about it to you when you moved into this century with your new wardrobe," Bell said, rapidly moving out of Martie's reach.

Chicken legs. Martie was too stunned to reply. She barely spoke to her friend over lunch on the porch that afternoon.

"Martie, come on," Bell said. "What good is life and friendship if you can't have a good laugh once in a while, even at each other?"

Bell was right. Martie was very skinny, and her legs did resemble those of a skinny, sickly chicken. She was about to respond when the Georgia Power crew returned to the house.

'Look at that!" Martie exclaimed. She pointed to a man climbing one of the poles. He had what appeared to be a long silver rope in his hand.

"Well, there you go," Bell said. "That looks pretty natural to me. That's an overgrown, human monkey climbing a fabricated, transplanted tree in Kingston."

The women continued to watch, as men would climb the poles all up and down the street. They were running wires along the poles. It took several days to complete the task, and Martie and Bell just couldn't help themselves. They had to see the whole thing.

Mike made sure he was home when it came time to run the final wires to the old Litton house. For now, Mike had one "outlet" run to the parlor. He said he might have more made and connected later. He was anxious to try it out before he committed completely.

Martie wasn't sure how much more "committed" Mike could be when the very next week he came home with an electric lamp and an electric radio.

"Now that's going a little too far," Martie said. "We have a perfectly good battery operated radio right here on the table."

"I know, but just think of the money we'll save on batteries if all we have to do is just plug in the radio and it keeps on going, night after night," Mike argued.

"What is this?" Martie had just picked up a small box with a glass bulb inside it. It contained a series of small wires and was tapped off at the base by metal.

"This, my dear, is our first light bulb," he said.

Alice had joined her parents in the parlor.

"Wow, Dad," she added. "I saw one of these one time when we went to Charlotte, North Carolina. It was in a large hotel a few years ago. There were no smells of kerosene or coal oil lamps. And, they burned brighter than anything I've ever seen in a building."

"Well, as soon as the sun goes down ladies, we are going to fire these babies up," Mike said.

Martie just left the room. Like cars, she didn't trust anything new that seemed remotely dangerous.

Darkness fell on Kingston, and lights went on all over town, including those on one more street that night. By the light of an old Rayo lamp, Mike plugged in the new electric one, and the entire room was illuminated. Cheers from Alice and her children resonated throughout the house. Mike smiled as he picked up the second cord to his new RCA radio.

A soft glow emitted from the numbers on the front of the cabinet. The children inched closer to the new object. Mike gently turned the knobs. Soon, a voice could be heard. Then, music drifted softly into the brightly lit room.

Mike caught Martie's eye. "May I have this dance?"

Martie hated to admit the new electricity amused her. She waved him off despite his caressing her arms and trying to sway her to the music. Alice and the children were smiling.

"Well," he said in mock agitation. "If one of you beautiful ladies won't dance with me, then I know the other one will."

Mike took Alice by her right hand and they danced until the music faded. The children joined in on more upbeat songs. They were a sight to see, Martie thought.

After about an hour of entertainment and being a slight "sour puss," Martie drifted up the stairs and to her bedroom where she read her Bible by the light of her trusty coal lamp.

Notes

1. The date and details of power coming to Kingston are inspired by the article in "Kingston Remembered" by Mattie Belle Malone, page 22 of *We Remember Kingston . . . Woman's History Club & Others*, Third Printing Courtesy of The Etowah Valley Historical Society, Cartersville, Georgia, May 1998.

The Depression . . .

If modern terms for people could have been applied to Mike, he would have made his mark on Kingston's history as their first official "couch potato." Each night after dinner, he fell into a routine of pulling his easy chair next to the radio and listening for hours. He kept up with all the news from around the country and the world. He was fascinated by the hoards of information he could obtain from the wooden box.

Once he had heard the news, he would then read his newspaper by the light of his prized electric lamp while smoking his pipe. The site of Granddaddy, as they all called him, nestled in his chair with the sweet smell of his tobacco bouncing around the room comforted his grandchildren. They each took their turns sitting on his lap while listening to the soft tones emitting from the radio. News of the Depression disturbed all who listened to the saddening reports making their way into town.

All who had money nestled in the Bank of Kingston lost it, and Martie and Mike took a mild financial loss.[1] However, they managed to continue their lifestyle with the money tucked under their bed. Alice had an insurance settlement from Bruce and a small inheritance for the children.

Thomas was one of the lucky ones to remain employed. Lydia's family in Atlanta had lost everything with the crash in 1929. All she had left was the money William had made as a physician, which wasn't much at all. Just like other residents, the majority of William's money was lost in the Bank of Kingston. Ann didn't trust institutions of any kind. Like Mike and Martie had done with a portion of their money, all of hers had been stuffed in old hat and cigar boxes and under her mattress. Through Ann, the three of them were actually living off of Ben's portion of the practice.

Stories of fortunes made and lost spread throughout the nation. Kingston never missed a beat, now that they were connected to the rest of the world. Knowing there was a national Depression happening and actually feeling it were two different things. Money had been lost, but to Martie, not the town's way of life. Many were farmers or tradesmen. Their goods and services were still needed and traded.

Throughout the years of the Depression, good times continued. Alice's children, Mikey and Edith, didn't know they were actually poor. There was too much fun to be had. Kingston was fortunate enough to continue having school. Schools in parts of the neighboring state had closed. New children from as far away as Alabama were moving to the area. Their families were looking for better living. New friends made life more interesting since they brought with them stories of different places.

The little things in life would later resonate of good times and major events. Taking the once-a-week, Saturday night bath always started with Mike bringing in the old tub. Martie and Alice would warm the water on the wood-burning stove, and each child would have a turn splashing in the kitchen.

For food, the entire family contributed. Martie found Vera to be a very capable gardener. She and Thomas were responsible for vegetables, spices, and herbs. Of course, the other ladies took over once the veggies left the dirt. Canning was a very important task for the remaining four. Ann and Lydia raised a few chickens for fresh eggs and poultry. Mike and Marty kept a cow and shared the milk. They would have one of the children take bottles into town to Vera and Lydia. The milk was kept cool in the cellar and placed in the well behind Lydia and William's in town.

At hog killing time, the men got together and purchased about three hogs a year. The children couldn't wait to taste the first, fresh sausage fried in the old Litton kitchen. Seasoning was very important, and Martie had the knack for this.

The children enjoyed taking hot water up the hill behind the old home place so the men could clean the chittlins. Their reward was a large stick and the pig bladder. To them, it resembled a balloon from the circus.

All of this good food might have been one reason the children didn't notice they were poor. Alice perfected her own cooking style using her one arm. Martie shared the beloved teacake recipe that originated with the late Camille with Alice who enjoyed making them for the children. She would tie them up and store them in a flour sack in the corner of the kitchen. Alice also had savory sweet potatoes waiting for the children after school.[2]

Before time for the radio came around, late afternoons brought live entertainment for the children. While eating sweet potatoes or teacakes, Mikey and Edith, along with the twins, would sit on the front porch with their Uncle William. Calling him Uncle William reminded Martie too much of her late uncle, so it wasn't long until she convinced them to call him "Uncle Bill," much to the distaste of Lydia.

Afternoons on the porch were spent watching the passenger train, "The Dixie Flyer," come through town. The crowd enjoyed watching the people eating lavish meals in the dining car. It was obvious to the children that these people didn't know there was a Depression from the way they were dressed. The men all wore expensive suits, and the women were wrapped in furs or wearing dresses that showed off their jewelry.

Even the dogs of the town knew the sound of the "Dixie Flyer's" whistle as it approached. They had learned that the cooks would be tossing buckets of leftovers and scraps from the dining car.[3]

However peaceful these years may have been for many in Kingston, Martie once again, endured another loss. In 1932, the Depression kicked in full-swing and even Kingston's commerce took a hit. It seemed to Martie that some of the passenger trains cut back on a few of their runs. Mike began to tighten the purse strings a little, but no one went hungry thanks to efforts of the entire family.

They were all enjoying good health and peaceful times when tragedy struck Bell's family as the Bayless home burned that year.[4] Martie was happy that her mother wasn't alive to see another beautiful home burn to the ground on land that had once belonged to her family. Unfortunately, many of the carefully handwritten books of notes Martie and Bell had entertained themselves with on countless afternoons were lost.

Martie was also thankful that Bell wasn't around to see it burn. She had moved to Brownsville, Texas, where she had been living with her brother. It wouldn't be until 1938 that Bell would return to see the empty lot where her home once stood.[5] Martie sorely missed her friend during her absent years from Kingston, but she understood what it meant to be near your family.

When she returned, it was the first time in their forty-year friendship that Martie saw Bell cry. She was thankful that she was there for her friend this time. Martie just held Bell while she wept.

"My home is gone," Bell said weeping.

"No, Bell," Martie answered. "Your house is gone. Kingston is your home, and this town is still here. Any place you decide to live in this town will be your home."

Bell cried some more. "I'm so sorry that I lost all of the books we were working on."

"Hey," Martie said while wiping tears from her friend's face. "We didn't lose anything. We're both still here, and everything that was in those books is right here. And, here."

Martie was pointing to her head and her heart while comforting Bell.

"You're right." Bell perked up. "You are absolutely right. I'm alive, and everything we know is still with me. A building is just that, a building."

Bell went to live with her sister, Virginia. Now, she was closer than the hill where the Bayless home had stood, and Martie and the children enjoyed more visits from their precious friend.

Notes

1. The losses suffered by the characters in this book are inspired by "Some of the Remembrances of my Old HomeTown" by Earl M. Hood, page 26 of *We Remember Kingston . . . Woman's History Club & Others*, Third Printing Courtesy of The Etowah Valley Historical Society, Cartersville, Georgia, May 1998. The writer recalls his grandfather losing all of his money in the Bank of Kingston in 1929.

2. The description and events of life during the depression are taken from a story written by Hazel Litton, "Kitchen Memories," page 14 of *We Remember Kingston . . . Woman's History Club & Others*, Third Printing Courtesy of The Etowah Valley Historical Society, Cartersville, Georgia, May 1998.

3. Notes on "Railroad Memories" prepared by Sara Johnson for a Kingston Woman's History Club Meeting, February 28, 1991, provide the story of the "Dixie Flyer," and her family's memories for this portion of the chapter; page 36, *We Remember Kingston . . . Woman's History Club & Others*, Third Printing Courtesy of The Etowah Valley Historical Society, Cartersville, Georgia, May 1998.

4. Photograph and caption of the Bayless home states the structure burned in 1932, page 72, *We Remember Kingston . . . Woman's History Club & Others*, Third Printing Courtesy of The Etowah Valley Historical Society, Cartersville, Georgia, May 1998.

5. *Bell Bayless Buried Sunday At Kingston, The Weekly Tribune News*, Cartersville, circa March 1955, provides information about her absence from Kingston for this section.

Not so new . . .

Bell's extended visit to Texas had been hard on Martie, but it now gave her and Bell a few months of afternoon "catch-up" sessions to enjoy. Bell would visit the Grady house often. She and Martie would talk while cooking breakfast, lunch, and dinner together some days. They would sit and discuss historical topics over afternoon tea. In fact, Mike applied for a job at the mine, not only for money, but to escape the continual "hen" party in his home.

Evenings were filled with news, information, and entertainment. Bell would linger after dinner to hear the news and have discussions about politics and the ongoing unrest and war in Europe. As soon as she and Martie would wind down their conversations, Mike would drive Bell home for the night.

Mike wasn't the only one enjoying his radio. Martie and Bell found themselves laughing out loud at the antics of the late afternoon adventures of *Little Orphan Annie* with the children.

Bell would joke, "Why do we need to listen to this when you have a real life orphan in your own home most afternoons?"

Then, she would begin to tell stories of Kingston to the four siblings and cousins gathered at her feet. Unknown to them, Bell was giving them a wonderful, historical education they would come to treasure in future years.

Monthly meetings of the Woman's Club continued to travel from house to house, and Bell rejoined the group. But, not before Martie could catch her up on what she missed, mainly a gallant effort in preservation by Miss Leila.

She told Bell that the ladies had done their best to identify people they could help. What donations they could make to the school continued to flow from their thinning pockets. However, one item of business couldn't be ignored, she told Bell. The Confederate Cemetery was slowly washing away.

She recounted the story of how Miss Leila Darden, and her sister, Bell Darden, had assumed many of the planning responsibilities for the annual Confederate Memorial Day. Despite the dwindling female forces of the Ladies' Memorial Association, the community and the Kingston Woman's History Club, who still

shared members with the Memorial Association, carried on with the obser-
vances.

During the June 1936 meeting, Miss Leila was leading the program. She
began an elaborate history of Confederate Memorial Day. Many of the older
ladies wondered why she was recapping history they had lived. Then, they
caught on to her plan. She was trying to rally the troops of the club into action to
save the cemetery and Confederate Memorial Day.

"Throughout all these years," she began, "the entire cemetery grounds,
both soldiers and citizens, were set in order and Confederate Memorial Day fit-
tingly observed with plenty of flowers for each grave."

All of the ladies were nodding and sipping tea as if to give their approval to
the speaker just firing up her words.

"Such orators as General W. F. Wofford, who often with his beautiful little
daughter, known as 'the Sweetheart of the Confederacy,' came to add her
greetings of love and cheer to the wonderful address of her father and other no-
tables," Miss Leila proclaimed. "These ladies of the Memorial Association had
the cooperation and support of all patriotic citizens within a radius of five miles.
The ceremonies were attended by all sections of Georgia."

Just like the shouts of "Amen" begin at camp meeting revivals, the ladies
began to lift their teacups and politely pronounce, "yes ma'am," in Miss Leila's
direction. Miss Leila was just getting started. Today, the lady who would earn
the title, "The Gallant Little Rebel," showed her fellow club members why she
deserved the name. The passion in her eyes for the cause was shining brightly
now. Her words flowed with force as she spoke. No one dared to interrupt. Her
fists were clenched and rising.

"I remember the gallant Capt. A. F. Woolley would mount his old war horse
steed, dressed in full Confederate uniform, followed by hundreds of old Confederate soldiers and lead the parade to the cemetery," she said.

Miss Leila was now delivering an inspirational sermon.

"Among these soldiers was my beloved father who volunteered before he
was fifteen years of age. They kept perfect step to the horn as it played *Dixie*."

Miss Leila now paused to touch her sister, Bell Darden's, shoulder. They
each had tears in their eyes. Martie also caught her breath as she remembered
her father who marched away from home at age fifteen.

Regaining her composure and momentum, Miss Leila resumed her preach-
ing. She gave a brief history of the monument built in 1874 that was sponsored
by the ladies. She was now recapping the history of the burials from the Wayside Home for those who remembered and teaching a new lesson for those who
had just joined the club. Discussing the wooden slabs that were replaced with
marble markers in 1908 by the Kingston Woman's History Club, she once again
began to get emotional. The ladies clutched their teacups tightly, preparing to
raise them in reverent toasts to Miss Leila's speech.

"Yes, all of the records have disappeared," she said. "They have perished in
the flames that have so cruelly attempted to take our town from us. By the loving grace of God, we have survived. I do remember seeing slabs, or fragments of

those old slabs, in my early recollection, but not enough to give us any information. Sadly, as the years have marched on, the noble ladies, one by one have either passed away or become inactive."

A silent moment was observed in honor of their fallen and bedridden sisters.

Miss Leila concluded with a plea. "Our help is needed to preserve this cemetery and our traditions. On behalf of my sister, Bell, and the memories of those before us, let us take charge of the cemetery preservation. We have kept alive their memories and their honor. It is our duty to retain their hallowed sleeping grounds."

Promptly, Miss Leila was appointed by the Kingston Woman's History Club to apply for a Federal grant to preserve the cemetery, as well as, placing in permanent fashion, the old Confederate Monument that was now rapidly crumbling to pieces.

Martie offered her assistance in this massive undertaking. Their first appeal was a letter to the Bartow County Commissioner. They asked for assistance from the Cartersville S.C.S. Camp 13. The ladies' plea for help was heard, and by November 17, 1936, the monument had been stabilized and was rededicated. The markers were reset in permanent concrete in straight lines, uniform distances and heights. A large diversion channel was constructed around the cemetery that would carry water off the grounds.

By Confederate Memorial Day 1937, even the citizens' cemetery had completed a conservation project.[1] The ladies were proud of the entire area. Their months of hard work, letters, and meetings asking for assistance had paid off.

Arms around each other overlooking the graves from the monument, Martie said to Miss Leila, "We've done our parents proud today."

In silence, the two ladies took deep breaths and just looked around at what, mainly, Miss Leila had accomplished. Bell told Martie she was impressed by the work of the ladies and was pleased to rejoin the group.

For Martie, completing this project injected fresh life into the club. Their group had started out of necessity during the Civil War and remained together through wars, devastation, and now a Depression. They felt as if they could accomplish anything as long as they put their minds to it and their hearts in it.

By 1939, their imaginations were sparked by the release of the film *Gone With The Wind*, inspired by the book of the same name written by Atlanta journalist, Margaret Mitchell.

Out of curiosity and anticipation, several of the ladies, including Martie and Bell, took an overnight trip to Atlanta to see the motion picture in color.

It was Martie's first trip away from Mike, and her first time to see a color movie. Needless to say, Martie was unimpressed.

"What do you mean you didn't like it?" Bell gasped on the train ride home.

"The movie seemed a little too bright, cheerful, and unreal to me in places," Martie replied.

"How can you say that? Didn't you read the book?"

"Of course, I read the book, and I liked it very much," Martie said. "But, I also feel kind of like I lived that time too. You don't know the details Mama gave me about the days of the war."

"What do you mean?"

"No one was that rich around here. Maybe some were in other places, but there was a lot of suffering in and around Kingston," Martie continued. "My mother and her family didn't have bright parties. I guess the color on that screen just didn't coincide with the darkness in my mother's voice when she was describing the long hours she spent in the Wayside Home.

"It didn't capture, for me, the actual pain felt by my family when Sherman burned most of our town. It didn't accurately capture the degradation slicing through Kingston's souls when the church pews were thrown in the yard where horses could eat from them."

Bell was silent now.

Martie continued, "I never knew Mama, or any of the ladies I remember from the original group, to throw a 'hissy' fit like the character, Scarlett, swing themselves around with perfect hair and clothing, and say something like, 'Well, I'll think about that tomorrow'."

Bell still had no reply. For the first time in their years of friendship, Martie silenced her friend.

"I remember war-toughened, veteran women who remained soft and gentle to their families and others," she said. "Their only choice was to make tomorrow a better day than the current one they were living. They didn't have the luxury of thinking about it. They had to act. To me, those dark days brightened by women like my mother and the others are what are real. When I want to think about the War Between the States, I'll remember my parents and their lives."

"I suppose you are right," Bell conceded.

"I guess we have to take it with a grain of salt that what we saw is just Hollywood entertainment and not every word Miss Mitchell captured about the South in her book," Martie said. "It was fun escaping into that glamour though, wasn't it?"

"Perhaps, for a few hours," Bell smiled and closed her eyes. She napped the remainder of the train ride home.

Martie didn't sleep. She turned to look out the window where she enjoyed the Georgia scenery and countryside as the train sped through it. She imagined her father, just a boy, loaded with a haversack and his gun, trampling through the untamed land of North Georgia. He was defending his family and home. Then, she imagined her mother looking down on her beloved Kingston from the hill where both her home and Bell's house once stood. She could feel the tears run down her mother's cheeks while she thought about her father and James.

A live broadcast of the Oscars filtered into the Grady home. Mike couldn't miss any type of radio show. Martie had to smile when *Gone With The Wind* swept the awards in record-setting style.[2]

Notes

1. Personal writings of Miss Leila Darden, Kingston Woman's History Club charter member, and local historian, reveal information about the early days of Confederate Memorial Day celebrations, *History of Kingston Memorial Day.*

2. *Gone With The Wind* facts, htp://ourgeorgiahistory.com/chronpop/836 (June 3, 2007)

More farewells . . .

As for the end of the 1930s, Martie wasn't planning a send-off like that of 1929. The Thirties had not been that bad, but this time she quietly hoped for better days. In 1939, some interesting people came to Kingston. Several businesses had fallen victim to the Depression, and buildings were up for sale or lease. By July, another family named "Malone" had moved to town. They, along with some partners, purchased a couple of buildings and established the Kingston Chenille Company.[1]

Martie was one of the first to welcome the ladies of the family by inviting them to a Kingston Woman's History Club meeting. As it turned out, the Malones from Sugar Valley near Calhoun were of no relation to Martie's mother's family, of the late 1800s.

With the opening of the chenille bedspread factory, it looked like business might perk up a little in the next decade. Martie thought that President Franklin D. Roosevelt's "Fireside Chats," piped through the radio, had brought some comfort to the nation. However, the actual opening of a new business that would employ local residents injected new hope into the town.

The year 1940 ushered Kingston into the next decade, and life continued at a comfortable pace once again. Tensions were growing throughout the world as Hitler continued on the aggressive. The Japanese were beginning to pose a threat to the United States, and the news of political unrest made Martie a little uncomfortable. Then, as 1941 came to a close, a nation froze in its tracks. The Japanese launched a full-blown attack on a sleeping Pearl Harbor in Hawaii, where most of America's Naval fleet had been at anchor.

Like the rest of America, no one in Kingston traveled out of earshot of a radio. With the rest of a grieving nation, they heard President Roosevelt declare Sunday, December 7, 1941, as "a date which will live in infamy." Those powerful words led America into war, again.

Faster than American troops could mobilize, the Kingston Woman's History Club sprang into action. This was not their first time in the role of "combat support." They had perfected their assembly line processes of Red Cross work during World War I. Knitters and seamstresses divided themselves into committees that promptly began work on sweaters, scarves, and garments.[2]

Many Kingston boys evacuated their homes, trading their warm beds for military barracks, cots, and tents. With sad and happy remembrances of World War I, Alice had to say good-bye to another loved one. Mikey celebrated his eighteenth birthday in 1943 by enlisting in the U.S. Army. A heartbroken Alice waved good-bye to her only son with a scary premonition that this would not end well.

Sixteen-year-old Edith had fallen in love with a sailor from neighboring Adairsville. Martie would just chuckle to herself while listening to many mother and daughter talks. All Edith wanted to do was get married.

One evening, after listening as long as she could without butting into the conversation, Martie walked through the parlor to give the latest on the two girls to Mike. She noticed he looked a little pale while he was sleeping, so she dared not wake him. He hadn't been feeling well lately, and Martie had encouraged him to see a doctor. He hadn't trusted doctors since William had retired, therefore he hadn't seen one.

About an hour later, Martie called everyone for dinner. Alice and Edith arrived in solemn moods with each other. Martie smiled because she was just thinking that Alice was getting what she deserved. Martie couldn't wait to share this with Mike. She walked into the parlor to find him still in his chair, in the same position as an hour earlier.

"Honey," she said touching him. Then, she realized, Mike had passed away in his sleep. She took hold of his now cold hand, and she touched his ashen face. She just wanted a moment with him before she called the girls into the room.

"There's so much I wanted to say to you before you left me," she said. "I love you for one. Also, thank you for making my time on this earth a happier life. It was good before you pushed me into a mud puddle, but you made it a little better and brighter after that."

She paused for just a moment to wipe away some tears before she continued.

"You've made me laugh along the way, too. You were the best father and husband anyone could ever have. No man on this earth today will ever take your place."

By this time, both Alice and Edith had entered the room. They realized what had happened. The head of their family, their rock and foundation, had passed quietly from this earth while sitting in his favorite chair by his trusty radio.

Alice motioned to Edith who knew she needed to get help. Alice knelt on the opposite side of her father and placed her head on his shoulder. Then, she and Martie just held each other's hands forming a circle with Mike while they waited in silence for help to come.

The Kingston Woman's History Club came through in their usual "over-the-top" fashion. From the overflowing food brought into the Grady home, no

one would ever have known there was a war going on with strict food and supply rations.

Martie was grateful to have Bell and Lydia around for the next few days.
They each brought words of comfort and hope during the darkest times. Mikey
was overseas when his grandfather had passed away, so the only comfort Martie
received from her grandson was a letter several months later.

Instead of feeling sorry for herself, Martie rejoined the living about a week
after the funeral. She aided with all of the war effort. Her favorite part was
writing letters to the soldiers. She and Bell had that department covered. Lifting
someone else's morale kept Martie going. As Christmas approached, the need
for sending gifts to the troops took the forefront.

Knowing it would be a sad Christmas without Mike, Martie organized a
weekly group to wrap and prepare the gifts at her home. Lydia was faithful in
her attendance, and she appeared to be a lot less snooty in her golden years. In
fact, Lydia had just about replaced the more absent and aging Bell as Martie's
sidekick.

However, nothing Lydia could ever do would replace Bell in Martie's heart
as her life-long, best friend. Martie was proud of Bell. She was a correspondent
for the weekly newspaper in Cartersville. She had a lot less time to spend so-
cializing. But, that was just fine by Martie, she had plenty to do with the Christmas project, and she still saw Bell once a week during their letter writing
campaign.

Sunday suppers were a favorite time for Martie. They rotated between her
home and Lydia's. Vera and Thomas were always there because poor Thomas
constantly longed for a home-cooked meal. Vera had promptly started working
again at the chenille company when it opened. Thomas was disqualified from
military service. In addition to his age, he was diagnosed with asthma.

Ironically, Ann had died just before Mike. And, like her "favorite" brother-
in-law, she too passed quietly and peacefully. Martie figured they were having
fun about now laughing at the rest of the family. Alice and Edith were back at
each other's throats like a mother and daughter should be when it came to boys.
Everything was back to normal.

The war entered 1944 still in full swing. The ladies continued their diligent
war-time service. Even with a gas ration, people seemed to prefer traveling by
car rather than by train. By the mid-forties, all was becoming quiet on the railroad, which distressed Martie.[3]

In June of that year, the war took a dramatic turn, and it looked as though it
would be over soon. America took part in storming the beaches of Normandy,
France. As soon as Alice heard the news on the radio, she became sick.

"I can't explain it, Mama," she told Martie. "I just feel sick all over. I'm un-
settled and nervous. I can't eat or sleep."

By Independence Day, Alice had lost fifteen pounds, and then a telegram
arrived for her. It began with the usual regrets to inform her. Her only son had
given his life for his country. There was no body to send home. He rested in a
military cemetery in Normandy. Alice, Edith, Thomas, Martie, and Lydia at-

tended a ceremony in Atlanta a few months later where Alice was presented with a posthumous Purple Heart for Mikey.

Life moved too fast for Martie during those first five years of the Forties. She lost her husband and grandson. For Martie, the world and Kingston were never going to be the same after this war.

Notes

1. The date and details of the Kingston Chenille Company coming to Kingston are taken from the article in "Kingston Remembered" by Mattie Belle Malone, page 22 of *We Remember Kingston . . . Woman's History Club & Others*, Third Printing Courtesy of The Etowah Valley Historical Society, Cartersville, Georgia, May 1998.

2. Information taken from *History Of The Woman's History Club*, written by Mrs. Louise Pratt Hood, *Commemorative Program for 125th Confederate Memorial Service, April 23, 1989*.

3. The time frame and conclusions about transportation in Kingston inspired by "The Railroads and Kingston" by Mamie Jo Gallagher Hood, pages 32-33 of *We Remember Kingston . . . Woman's History Club & Others*, Third Printing Courtesy of The Etowah Valley Historical Society, Cartersville, Georgia, May 1998.

Transitions . . .

May 1945 saw the end of the war with celebrations breaking out nation-wide. Kingston held its own small, town party. Martie and Bell attended to-gether.

"It's been a while since we've 'painted the town'," Bell said.

"I'm getting a little too old for this," Martie nodded and peered over her glasses.

"Oh, you're only as old as you feel," Bell jabbed at her friend. "I'm a lot older than you are, and I feel a celebration coming on."

"Bell," Martie began. "I've lost so much over the past five years. Where do I go from here? This feels like a new beginning. Actually, if feels like the beginning of the end for me."

"Martie, please don't talk like that," Bell winced at her friend. "You've still got a lot of living to do. From what I hear, you've got three granddaughters that could be married by Christmas, and this time next year, you could be a great-grandmother."

"Since you put it that way," Martie said as she began to stand up from the bench the two had been sitting on, "I think I'll just go ahead and have myself carted on up to the cemetery tonight."

Both Martie and Bell were right, times did start changing drastically. By 1948, Martie would be a great-grandmother four times over.

After spending a decade in the Depression and the first five years of a new one at war, the United States was in need of great changes and progress. With the war over, surplus barracks were brought into Kingston just to accommodate the booming population of school children. It was clear the town would soon need a new school.[1] Martie would just shake her head and reflect on the night she saw the school burning, while townsmen etched the plans for a new one in the dust. She was saddened by the state in which the school now looked. It just wasn't large enough, and the poor facility was too outdated to handle the changing world.

Both Martie and Bell decided to take a step back in the late Forties and let the younger generation ease their way into the club's leadership. They saw each other less as Bell's health began a steady decline. She continued her position as a newspaper correspondent for *The Tribune News* in Cartersville as best she could. She had been their North Bartow reporter for years, covering Kingston and Adairsville events.[2] Martie always looked forward to reading Bell's stories. Times were definitely changing.

However, one thing that didn't change was Confederate Memorial Day and the work of the Kingston Woman's History Club. By now, the ceremony was evolving into a little more formal event than in the past when everyone went straight to the cemetery for speeches and testimonials.

Martie saw each year as a transition in the ceremony as the ladies began to sponsor an afternoon church service with a guest speaker and special music. The Carl Boyd Post 42 American Legion had taken charge of the cemetery service including taps and a gun salute in 1937.[3] Kingston children continued the duties of placing flowers on all the graves. The entire town still turned out in force to honor the military dead.

After World War II, the meaning behind a memorial day took on new sentiment. Everyone in the town was touched in some way by a war. Despite the rest of the country's days of memoriam, Kingston continued to cherish its own celebration.

In 1947, Martie's life took one more sad turn as William died. Lydia was now alone, but so was Martie. Both of her siblings had preceded her in death, as well as her husband. On a visit to Bell's home one day, Bell came through with another one of her great ideas.

"Why don't you move in with Lydia?" Bell had announced this as an inquisitive statement rather than posed it as a question.

"What did you say?" Martie was in shock with Bell, as usual.

"I said, why don't you move in with Lydia?"

"I think you need some rest my friend," Martie said. "You know how miserable I would be."

"Knock it off, Martie," Bell sounded irritated for the first time ever. "I've put up with your attitude of your family for years. You know you need each other. Why, I don't know what I would do without my sister. I'm thankful every day to live with her and be with my family."

"But, Lydia isn't my sister," Martie said. "She's just my sister-in-law."

Bell cut off Martie before she had a chance to respond. "She's the closest thing you have. You know, your attitude at times reminds me of why I never really liked you when you were a child."

Martie was flabbergasted at her friend's candor. Her eyes began to tear up. "You don't like me?"

"I love you as much as a sister, now," Bell said. "But, you were spoiled and hard to handle when you were growing up. The reason I always tried to talk you into anything that would get you in trouble was because I didn't like you. Then,

I got to know you on the inside, and I liked what was there. But, I continued to goad you just because it was fun and easy to do."

Martie was speechless as Bell continued to talk.

"I got to thinking about how much I enjoyed having a sister, and I thought you could use one considering all you had were two brothers. I guess I made you into my little sister. In fact, I love you so much that I'd invite you to live with us, but you are needed elsewhere."

Still unable to speak, Martie realized Bell was right, once again.

"You love Lydia like a sister, just like you have grown to love Vera as a daughter. I know you, and you have a good heart. You can comfort Lydia right now like no one else can. Plus, I don't think you are going to kick her out of your house, are you?"

"No," Martie said remembering that William and Mike never recorded a transfer of deeds. Lydia was living in Martie's house. "But, I could charge her rent."

Both women began to laugh. Their humor was back.

Thomas and his sons-in-law moved Martie's belongings into her old house. She had to admit; it felt good to be home. As she was moving out, Alice only asked for two things, Mike's first, old electric lamp and radio.

"They belong in this house," Martie said as she walked out the door and into her new life with her sister-in-law.

In her own golden years, keeping a record of all she had experienced became important to Martie. She spent many of her days writing memories and compiling scrapbooks of special photos and clippings. She wasn't the only one who saw the importance in this task. Many of the club's older women began the same project. The afternoons were peaceful and enjoyable as Lydia joined Martie, some of the time.

Notes

1. Information taken from "Notes On School," *We Remember Kingston . . . Woman's History Club & Others*, Third Printing Courtesy of The Etowah Valley Historical Society, Cartersville, Georgia, May 1998, page 2.

2. *Bell Bayless Buried Sunday At Kingston*, *The Weekly Tribune News*, Cartersville, circa March, 1955, provides information about Miss Bayless' career.

3. Personal writings of Miss Leila Darden, Kingston Woman's History Club charter member, and local historian, reveal information about the early days of Confederate Memorial Day celebrations, *History of Kingston Memorial Day.*

Ring, ring, the future's calling . . .

Something was a "buzzin" in Kingston.

It seemed everyone was excited about something new, the telephone. For the past two decades, Martie had wanted to send off the bad and ring in the new in style. Now, she had her chance to see the decade go with a bang, literally. The town was planning a celebration complete with fireworks. Southern Bell was building a telephone system in Kingston. Martie gasped at how much it cost, $25,000.[1]

"Where does money like that come from?" She was reading the newspaper in a loud voice to the hard-of-hearing Lydia.

"Did you say $25,000?" Lydia shouted back.

"Yes! And, the paper says nearly everyone in town from the mayor and city council to the school's PTA is involved in kicking off this system," Martie continued to disseminate information. "There's going to be a barbecue and fireworks."

Folding the paper, she placed it on the table beside her with her glasses on top and shouted across the room at a nearly napping Lydia.

"You know, this town is almost getting out of hand. Fireworks. Of all the silly things the town could waste good fireworks on. Why would you go to a little booth or pick up a 'thing' in your house to talk to someone in Rome or Cartersville?"

"Well, don't you think it will be kind of fun?" Lydia was now awake.

"I've seen those little booths downtown," Martie said. "Why would someone want to stand in a small little room built for one and talk to someone they can't see? Why not just hop aboard a train? There sure are a lot more interesting things to look at from a moving train than in a tiny little room."

"Martie, I think you are getting forgetful," Lydia responded. "The Rome passenger train hasn't run since October of 1944."[2]

Disgusted with her sister-in-law who had dozed back off with her head askew, Martie got up and walked across the room to put a pillow under her neck.

Talking to the snoring Lydia, Martie toned down her voice and said, "You can't remember what we had for breakfast, but you know the exact date of something that happened five years ago."

Walking out onto the porch of her first home as a married woman, Martie sat in the little swing to enjoy the chilly, December wind. She watched the cars go by in disgust. The Forties were going to end with a bang whether or not she liked it. Her visions of the car taking over had come into full focus. Those passenger trains were much fewer and far between. Even the coal chute was getting less use as the new diesels powered over the tracks. No, Martie didn't care much for the changes, but she had to accept them.

Sure enough, 1949 ended with a huge celebration as one hundred and ten customers went on-line with telephone service. Kingston was now connected to the rest of the world. Thomas made sure Martie and Lydia had phone service.

"What's wrong with you?" Martie interrupted Thomas while he was explaining how to use the phone to a belligerent mother and senile aunt.

"Nothing," he said without missing a beat of instruction.

Martie wasn't listening and cut him short again. "Are you too lazy to walk two streets over to talk to me? Or, has that fabulous car of yours quit working? It would serve you right if it did. God gave you two good legs to carry you anywhere you need to go."

Thomas realized the lesson for the day was a lost cause. Martie also began to see that she was acting more and more like her father, James, and she was too young, she thought, to become a mean, old person. She stopped herself short and tried to make a joke when she looked at Thomas and asked, "Where's Pa's guns?"

Thomas gave up for the time being and decided to check on them personally until they accepted the phone. Eventually, they both caught on to the party line system and discovered new ways of getting town news, information, and gossip. Once in a while, they would be discovered and instead of being conspicuous and quiet, they would make sure the offended knew who was listening as they slammed down the phone receiver.

The year 1950 proved to open new doors for the younger generation and close yesterday's to the older. The chenille company folded, and Vera officially retired. She and Alice picked up the pace of care for Martie and Lydia. They made sure the pair never missed a Kingston Woman's History Club meeting. A call on the telephone was worth picking up on meeting days. They loved their afternoon meetings at the hotel managed by Mrs. Margie Roberts. She gave the club a home base of operations.[3]

The club's age wasn't getting any younger. Those doors opened after World War II led the way for some ladies to become "working mothers" and "career women." Having run the country from manufacturing to professional jobs, some of these women refused to go "back home to the kitchens." This was just one more trend Martie disliked. Vera seemed to contribute to it as she encouraged her daughters to focus more on themselves and building careers. Martie believed they needed to be involved with the club and the business of making the town a little better, raising funds for the school, and supporting commerce and history.

What Martie never realized was that she, her mother, and all the women of the club were responsible for the positive changes she considered to be "bad." The women gathered at the hotel were all pioneers in their own way, bringing about the changes that made the town great in its day. Bell, Martie, Bell's sister, Virginia, the Darden sisters, and the countless others had all been the driving force behind Kingston's progress. They were laborers behind the scenes, the keepers of the precious past, and the providers of the future.

On one of Martie's visits to her ever-ailing friend Bell, she expressed her distaste for society's future, and how there might not be anyone around to carry on the club unless some of these younger women quit messing around in places they didn't belong. She told Bell they needed to go home to take care of the important things.

"Here we go again, huh," Bell said. "How hard did you really hit your head on that train all those years ago?"

"Explain, please," Martie sighed and sat back for the lecture to follow.

"You almost became stuffy. I think your sense of adventure got knocked out of you that day. You reflect too much on the past and how things have always been done. It's important to preserve, but life moves forward. People change, life changes, the way we do things changes. It's not all bad you know."

Their conversations were getting more somber and serious around 1951. Martie didn't like them sometimes.

"Oh, Martie, you just have to live life as it comes. You can't fight it, and you can only control so much of it. You've always been this way, and I've always been there to give you a pep talk, to put you back in the game. I guess you could say that. Well, here's my advice. You are either going to have to stay on the bench, or get off your behind and bat. Life's umpire is still calling 'batter up' to you."

Because of their friendship, and because Bell never acted her age, she was forever young. Everyone seemed to forget that Martie was more than a decade younger than her lifelong friend. Even Martie forgot it most of the time, until today. This was the day she realized she would soon be on her own, truly. Where was she going to go for advice and pep talks to keep her moving? As a grandmother and great-grandmother, Martie realized she finally had to grow up.

Notes

1. "First Day of Telephone Service and Mrs. Roberts at the Hotel" by Mrs. C.V. (Mary Lee) Harper, page 31, *We Remember Kingston . . . Woman's History Club & Others*, Third Printing Courtesy of The Etowah Valley Historical Society, Cartersville, Georgia, May 1998 is used as reference information.

2. The time frame and conclusions about transportation in Kingston inspired by "The Railroads and Kingston" by Mamie Jo Gallagher Hood, page 32 of *We Remember Kingston . . . Woman's History Club & Others*, Third Printing Courtesy of The Etowah Valley Historical Society, Cartersville, Georgia, May 1998.

3. "First Day of Telephone Service and Mrs. Roberts at the Hotel" by Mrs. C.V. (Mary Lee) Harper, Page 31, *We Remember Kingston . . . Woman's History Club & Others*, Third Printing Courtesy of The Etowah Valley Historical Society, Cartersville, Georgia, May 1998 provides details of events for this chapter.

Honor the past, move onward . . .

Martie made a change in her life, and just like most of the positive changes, she credited Bell with the attitude adjustment. She cast her inhibitions and thirty-year fear of cars to the wind and allowed the younger men of the family to drive her wherever she needed to go. She made sure she took care of Lydia and enjoyed afternoons with the great-grandchildren underfoot after school. Martie even let go of resentments that her granddaughters decided to work instead of "properly" raise their children.

Martie decided her life was in the "seventh-inning stretch." She might have been one of the oldest members of the club, but she made sure she was the most active of the oldest. In the fall of 1951, just as the new school on the hill was being completed, the past rose from the grave once again.[1]

Of all the years they had been honoring the heroes on the hill, the women of the club had allowed one courageous hero to be forgotten, including Martie. She knew Martha would have been ashamed. William "Doc" Tippin, the driving force and original angel of mercy behind the Wayside Home, had slept in an unmarked grave for eighty-eight years.

Time had marched all around his resting place, unnoticed and untouched. Sadly, Doc's family had moved away after his death. This true Confederate hero who gave his life for his country, not in battle but in kindness and peace, had never been properly honored.

Miss Leila, who continued her historical documentation, began efforts to secure a marker for his grave. She made sure his actions and his place in history were properly recorded. Martie had the utmost respect for this little dynamo. In addition to the aging Bell, Martie looked at Miss Leila as another inspiration to stay in the game.

Finally, on Sunday, October 21, 1951, Doc's grave marker was dedicated in a ceremony held by the Daughters of the Confederacy. The speaker that day, Tom Linder, Commissioner of Agriculture in Georgia and the Georgia State Commander of the Sons of Confederate Veterans, wrote in an editorial, "The fact that this Confederate hero was buried in an unmarked grave is mute testimony to the poverty in which the people of the South was left after Appomattox."

Reading these words in the *Georgia Farmers' Market Bulletin,* Martie thought of the stories her mother told about Doc.[2] She remembered how her mother said the ladies had no time to properly mourn him or even place a marker at his grave. A quiet man of simple means and good heart had finally come into his proper recognition.

Whenever she could, and all the Confederate Memorial Days to come, Martie made sure that Doc's grave was cleaned and had fresh flowers on top.

Thomas, Vera, and Alice urged her to slow down a little. She volunteered to help set up classrooms in the new school at the end of 1951. Undaunted and stronger than ever, Martie joined her family on the first day of school in January 1952 when the children moved into their new state-of-the-art facility.

A few sad notes resounded in her heart as the old building was abandoned. She waited alone at the old school until everyone was gone with the last of the supplies. The cold, December chill kept her alert as she closed her eyes and stood in front of the school. She could feel the enormous warmth of the fire that destroyed the wooden school giving birth to the glorious, new brick structure. She could still see the dirt drawings of the plans for this building.

She recalled a young Thomas and a strong, vibrant Mike assisting the others carrying off the rubble. Martie thought about bringing lunch to her husband who would take a break from his masonry work at the new school to head off to a picnic with Martie in the park. She could still smell the fresh paint inside the classrooms, now abandoned before her.

Today, she was saying good-bye to an old friend and just another part of her past. But, it wasn't going to get her down. Bell's words of wisdom echoed in her mind. She had to keep on living. She smiled and thought about what kind of pitch she would get next. Little did she know it would be a tricky curve ball.

Many afternoon visits and a couple of years later, Martie picked up the phone and felt as though she had been hit in the stomach with the curve ball. Bell had fallen and fractured her hip.[3]

Martie immediately called Thomas to take her to the hospital in Rome. When they arrived, a sedated Bell weakly looked at Martie and took her hand. There was no need for any words to be spoken between them. Through the years they had said enough to each other. Now, it was time for Martie to give back to her friend. She just held her hand until she fell asleep.

Bell's health slightly improved, but she had to be confined to a nursing home in Dalton.

"That damned place might as well be a thousand miles from here," Martie shouted at Lydia over breakfast.

"Did you just curse at me?" Lydia was getting more sensitive the older she got.

"No," Martie replied. "I'm just mad that Bell is so far away. I apologize for the strong language. It was not necessary."

"Are you going to go see her today?"

"As soon as Thomas gets here, I am," a frustrated and rushed Martie said. "That boy has lost all sense of time these days."

She heard a car drive up. When Martie got to the door, she had a surprise greet her. Instead of Thomas coming to pick her up, Vera was driving the car, and Alice was getting out of the passenger side.

"What's going on here, girls?"

"Mother Martie," Vera said, "I got my driver's license yesterday. I'm going to take you to see Miss Bell. Thomas has started building another room onto our house and doesn't have time. Alice is going to stay with Aunt Lydia until we get home."

Vera sounded as though these were the final words on the subject, but Martie decided to circumvent the woman and go straight to the top. She was going to call Thomas. She quietly walked to the phone she had refused to look at years earlier and picked it up to call her son. Alice took the receiver from her hand and placed it back in its cradle.

"If you want to see Bell, then you get in the car with Vera and just go."

Alice had never talked to her mother in such a tone. Martie opened her mouth to lash out at the two insolent girls and then realized that they were now in charge. She picked up her purse, coat, and hat and walked out the door without an argument or scene. Martie didn't consider this a "lost battle" in the war in the years to come with her family, she just thought of it as "picking her battles." She still got what she wanted, a chance to visit Bell, just as long as Vera didn't kill her on the way.

Martie found over time that her rides to visit Bell were enjoyable except when Vera, who thought it was chic to smoke, would light up one of her long cigarettes and swerve going down the road as she tried to smoke them and look elegant. This disgusted Martie, but "it's just another adaptation," Bell would tell her.

Notes

1. Information pertaining to the new school found in an article by Vera E. Lee, "The 'New School'-1951," page 5, *We Remember Kingston . . . Woman's History Club & Others*, Third Printing Courtesy of The Etowah Valley Historical Society, Cartersville, Georgia, May 1998.

2. *Georgia Farmers' Market Bulletin, Confederate Marker*, editorial by Tom Linder, October 24, 1951 contains details of erecting a marker.

3. *Bell Bayless Buried Sunday At Kingston, The Weekly Tribune News*, Cartersville, circa March 1955 contains information pertaining to Miss Bayless' injury.

Double our devastation . . .

It wasn't long until Bell's health began to deteriorate to the point that Martie's visits became shorter and less often. From her hospital bed, she wrote about everything she remembered and continued to be published.[1] Martie would save every tear-stained newspaper clipping she got her hands on. She would try to hold back her emotions, but thinking of Bell telling her to be strong would just turn on the waterworks more.

Further reminders of Bell were all over her house. Bell had possessed another talent. She was a very gifted artist. She had the ability to draw and paint.[2] In addition to her writings, Martie had several of her friend's paintings hanging on the walls of her home, each one signed and dated. Just touching them made her feel closer to her friend.

Even without Bell's presence, the club knew time was going to have to march onward. Despite the sickness of the older members of the club and the infirmities of the citizens who helped out, clean up week for the cemetery arrived. Miss Leila's brother, Marcellus Darden, was recovering from pneumonia. He had been instrumental for the past fifty years in helping the ladies prepare for Confederate Memorial Day. This year, Miss Leila had restricted his activities in hopes his health would improve. Unfortunately, he did not listen to his sister's protests.

On Wednesday, March 9, 1955, he saw a few wild fires burning on the surrounding hills. Soon, he realized the wind was beginning to pick up fiercely, and that the fires would soon reach the cemetery where they would destroy a small church as well as a neighbor's timber.

Without Miss Leila's knowledge, he crept out the back door of their home and began to brave the violent wind as he climbed the hill to the cemetery. He was out of breath from the climb and weak from illness when he began to hold off some of the fires. Too weak to fight anymore, Marcellus' clothes caught fire and he couldn't extinguish them.

Miss Leila discovered he was missing when she went to check on him. She looked out the window in the direction of the cemetery knowing exactly where he had gone when she saw the smoke. By the time she arrived with help, it was too late.

After surviving two, agonizing hours, Marcellus told both of his grieving sisters that he was ready to go, and he wanted them to meet him in Heaven. The doctors told Miss Leila that on top of his weakness, he had suffered a heart attack from overexertion.[3]

The club grieved alongside the Darden sisters, and a portion of Confederate Memorial Day in 1955 was devoted to his memory.

Still reeling from the tragic and devastating loss of Marcellus, the ladies were dealt another fatal blow just ten days later.

On March 19, 1955, Bell died.[4]

Martie knew exactly what Thomas was coming to tell her when she saw him standing at the screen door. He took off his hat and came into the room where he sat beside his mother on the parlor sofa. Lydia was napping as usual. Martie would just break the news to her later.

"Mama," he began, "she just couldn't get over the pneumonia. It was too much for her frail body."

Crying now, Martie said, "I think it all began with that fall."

Normally, Bell would be sitting beside her on the sofa, giving comfort in a time like this. When Mike and Mikey died, she was there. When both James and Martha, and her brothers passed away, Bell had been there. She had made her reflect and laugh to get through those tough times.

"I'm okay," she told Thomas. "I'd prefer to be alone right now."

"Are you sure?"

"Sure, I'm sure," she said. "When Lydia wakes up I'll tell her, and she might surprise me. We share a lot of memories of Bell that you just don't know about. I probably need her more than you right now."

Sure enough, Martie was right. When Lydia woke up, she was like a rock for Martie. Together, they recalled many of the good times. Martie was able to talk about that first meeting at the Bayless home before Lydia came to town.

"So, that's a true story," Lydia said. "Goober hulls. That sounds like our Bell. Always pulling something."

"Well, it had significance," Martie said. "They certainly got our attention, I'll tell you that."

"Yes, that's one thing Bell was good at wasn't it?" Lydia was smiling too. "She could get attention."

Turning to face Lydia's good ear, Martie said, "She saved your life too, you know?"

"What do you mean?"

"Well, there were times that I just didn't like you very much, and Bell always restrained me, once physically."

A not-so-shocked Lydia replied, "I know."

"How did you know?" Martie was the one surprised this time.

"Bell told me," she said. "You were very mad that I made an interview appointment with that reporter and your father. When Bell put it in perspective, I completely understood. I was jealous of you because you always had it together, and you had friends like Bell. Until the day she visited, I never knew how lucky I was to have you as a sister-in-law and Bell as my friend too."

Now, they sat in silence with a new understanding of each other. All these years of tension that had eased with time were unnecessary.

"I wish we had had this conversation about thirty years ago," Martie said.

"Bell told me I should talk to you that day she visited," Lydia responded. "But, I was a little too proud and selfish. I eased up a little, but I still had fun yanking your chain. It's not that hard to do."

Martie began to laugh as she recalled a very similar conversation with Bell a few years earlier. It was at that moment she realized Bell's final deed for her just came from this conversation. Bell had passed the torch from herself to Lydia.

Lydia was staring straight into Martie's eyes by now.

"I'm going to tell you something I should have a long time ago," Martie said. "I love you."

"I love you too, Sister." Lydia rose slowly from the sofa and kissed Martie on the head and left the room.

The sisters-in-law had spent the evening going through scrapbooks of Bell's writings, personal letters, and other historical documentation compiled by Martie and Bell through the years. It was late into the night when they finally had their defining conversation, and then one after the other drifted off to bed.

As she fell asleep, Martie's thoughts were on Bell and one of their many conversations about Lydia.

Martie whispered toward the ceiling as though she were looking to Heaven, "You were right, Bell, she's not that bad. Thanks for making the difference in my life and leaving me with so much. You are just another reason life was better for me and so many more on this earth. Tomorrow is better because of you."

The funeral was held at Virginia Irby's home, Bell's sister with whom she had resided after her house burned. The ladies of the club took her passing very hard, but in her honor, they forged ahead.[5]

Notes

1. "Bell Bayless, Well Known Citizen, Recounts Things She Remembers," article taken from the Bartow Herald, Cartersville, Georgia, Thursday, April 29, 1954, an editor's note states she was confined to a hospital at this time, Page 42, *We Remember Kingston . . . Woman's History Club & Others,* Third Printing Courtesy of The Etowah Valley Historical Society, Cartersville, Georgia, May 1998.

2. Artwork by Miss Bell Bayless is on display in the Kingston Woman's History Club Museum Martha Mulinix Annex, Kingston, Georgia.

3. Personal writings of Miss Leila Darden, Kingston Woman's History Club charter member, and local historian, reveal information about the early days of Confederate Memorial Day celebrations, *History of Kingston Memorial Day.*

4. Death date is recorded in Kingston Cemetery Records, online at http://www.gabartow.org/cem/cem.KingstonCity.shtml. (June 3, 2007)

5. *Bell Bayless Buried Sunday At Kingston, The Weekly Tribune News,* Cartersville, circa March, 1955 gives details of Miss Bayless' funeral.

Back to the park . . .

Life did go on, and younger members came. Vera and Alice continued to take Martie and Lydia to as many meetings as they could attend. The ladies had adopted the hotel as a kind of temporary clubhouse, but soon discovered they needed a more permanent home.[1] They had people just itching to donate all kinds of historical records and artifacts that belonged in a museum.

An ongoing discussion began about how to raise funds and complete a facility. While one group discussed how and how big, another group began discussing location, location.

As the ladies discussed the future of their club and its activities, the town around them began to slowly die and disappear into history. Trains didn't stop anymore. All of the little coal engines had given way to massive diesels transporting freight and zooming through Kingston with no regard for its former years as a type of resort stop. Even the coal chute had died. Martie was saddened by its passing in 1952.[2]

Finally in 1958, one train carrying household goods did stop in Kingston, or right outside the town to be exact. Martie, and even poor, deaf Lydia, heard the ruckus as the train hit the bridge outside town, derailing and completely destroying it. Onlookers watched from their houses for months as the massive cleanup and rebuilding of the bridge took place.

"It's amazing to me how people like to look at the strangest things," Martie was telling Lydia over dinner. "A train wreck, of all things, is not entertainment."

"Sure it is," Lydia said. "What else is there to do here?"

Sadly, Lydia was right. Martie knew that friends and neighbors were dying, and many of their children weren't making Kingston their home. They were leaving for larger towns like Cartersville and Rome. Those who did stay only used Kingston as a stopover at night and on weekends. They worked, shopped, and sought entertainment elsewhere. So yes, a train wreck would be entertainment.[3]

The Fifties ended with more devastating blows for the ladies of the club as they lost Miss Leila on July 2, 1959, and her sister, Bell, on December 8, 1959.[4] However, a few dreams of the club that would honor the memories of Miss Bell Bayless and the Misses Leila and Bell Darden came true that year.

Several panels were put on display in the lobby of the hotel where the ladies held club meetings. These panels depicted the history of Kingston from its settlement through the Civil War. Plans were to take these further, but time and room constraints prevented much of it.

The panels just perpetuated the dream of the group to build their museum, and in 1960, a little more excitement rocked the town when a bill was proposed to deed an acre of land to the city for a Confederate Memorial Museum. The state of Georgia had owned this land and leased it to the L&N Railroad. Since the railroad had no use for it any longer, the state gave it to the city.[5] This was the same land where the ladies had sought permission to make the town's park. Now more than half a century later, the Kingston Woman's History Club was going to have their long-awaited museum.

After the announcement, Martie asked Vera and Alice to go to the park with her. She and her girls, as she called them, sat together in the pavilion built by the club around 1909. It was located near the site of the future museum.[6]

"Girls, I'm so proud of you both," she began. "Thank you for all of the work you are doing to keep this club and this town's history alive. I was afraid everything was going to disappear."

"Where are you going with this, Mama?" Alice asked.

"No place special," she said. "I just wanted to sit here with you both and enjoy just a few, fleeting moments in this park. You know how ironic it is that the museum is going here? This must be hallowed ground of some kind.

"Sherman began his march right here. He tried to crush this town. Then, Bell's sister, Virginia, made her visions of a park come true in this very spot, right down to this haven of shade where we sit. And now, ya'll building a museum. It's almost more than I can take."

Words just couldn't express how emotional Martie became when she thought about everything that had happened around this little park. And, what was about to happen to it.

The three women rested together in quiet meditation for more than an hour. They could see the pine pollen swirling in the air and smell the new blossoms of spring. Gentle breezes wafted through the pavilion. They watched cars and trucks pass around them, and occasionally a train would fly by the park at breakneck speeds.

The silence between them meant something different for each. Martie was reflecting on everything she'd seen in this town, especially from this park. From the time the first seeds were planted here to the time Mike shoved her in the mud, the park had been a part of her life.

Alice was thinking about the first time she met Martie. Alice had never known her birth mother as she died when she was born. Martie came into Alice's life and took over as the only mother she had ever known or needed. Their first meeting over strawberry ice cream hadn't gone too well. Alice hadn't thought about that in years, but it happened right here at a Kingston Woman's History Club ice cream fund-raiser.

For Vera, the pavilion was special too. It was here that Thomas proposed after a Fourth of July picnic. Finally, Thomas drove to the edge of the park in his new truck. This contraption was funnier looking than any car Martie had ever seen. Cars still got to her.

"What are you three doing?"

"Sitting in the park," Martie said. "What's it to you?"

"Nothing to me, just wondering what was up?" he smiled at them as he honked his horn and drove off.

"Girls, I guess we better go," Martie said. "I think we've said enough to ourselves."

Martie had gotten her point across to the girls that day. She was coming to the end of the line with her service. The two women needed to focus on what was important to them and what would be important to the preservation of their way of life. With silence, she taught them one of the greatest lessons of their lives.

Notes

1. "Kingston Business Establishments 1939-1973 As I Recall," Part of History Club Program, February 1973 by Mrs. Lois Malone, page 3, states that Mrs. Roberts "allowed the Kingston History Club (to) start their Museum in the hotel."

2. "On August 20, 1952 the chute was gently reduced to rubble and became another page in the railroad memory book." Quote from "The Railroads and Kingston" by Mamie Jo Gallagher Hood, page 33 of *We Remember Kingston . . . Woman's History Club & Others*, Third Printing Courtesy of The Etowah Valley Historical Society, Cartersville, Georgia, May 1998.

3. Storyline inspired by "The Big Train Wreck" by Sara Johnson, page 35 of *We Remember Kingston . . . Woman's History Club & Others*, Third Printing Courtesy of The Etowah Valley Historical Society, Cartersville, Georgia, May 1998.

4. Death dates for the Darden sisters found in Kingston Cemetery records online at www.gabartow.org/cem/cem.KingstonCity.shtml. (June 3, 2007)

5. Information gathered from *Kingston's History Club Sponsors Museum Building*, March 31, 1961 (date written on article), newspaper clipping, no source available, archived in the Kingston Woman's History Club Museum scrapbooks.

6. Photograph information of old, cedar log pavilion places its construction around 1909. Photo located in the Kingston Woman's History Club Museum scrapbook collection.

Fire, again . . .

"Something's burning," Martie said to herself. She could smell bacon mixed with the stench of charring wood. She rushed to the kitchen in time to see flames shooting from the stove toward the ceiling. A grease fire on the stove was leaping from its surface to the wall as the flames climbed higher and higher.

Martie couldn't see as well as she used to, and the smoke was getting too thick to navigate. She knew Lydia had been trying to make breakfast, and her only thought was to find her sister-in-law. She began calling her name while her lungs filled with the thick, gray smoke. Martie felt light headed and sank to her knees. She felt something in her leg crack, and she was scared. Pain shot up and down her side, and Martie couldn't move.

"Lydia, Lydia," she called over and over. The fire was spreading throughout the kitchen, and Martie couldn't stand up to search for her almost completely deaf companion.

Martie felt herself begin to lose consciousness when someone started dragging her across the parlor floor toward the now open door. The fresh air revived the faint Martie. She looked up to see her one-armed daughter was stronger than she ever imagined. Alice had managed to pull her from the burning home.

"Aunt Lydia is in that kitchen," Martie screamed in a panic.

Alice held her down and calmly said, "No she's not. Look over there."

Edith's son, Daniel, who was Martie's great-grandson, was carrying the limp, lifeless body of his great-great aunt from the side of the house. Alice and Daniel had been on their way to Rome when they passed the house to see the flames shooting from the side.

By now, a local physician was on the scene as well as many neighbors tossing large buckets of water on the burning kitchen. The fire had not been as bad as it appeared from inside the home. The only loss was the kitchen. The rest of the structure could be aired out and repainted, but the kitchen was totally destroyed.

Both Lydia and Martie recovered with lots of fresh air and a couple of nights in a Rome hospital. But, it was time to make some tough decisions about the elderly ladies. The crack Martie had heard and felt in her leg wasn't actually in her leg but in her hip. She had broken it. After two surgeries, she was unable to care for the poor, deaf Lydia. Alice and Thomas had the house repaired, but they all feared the two elderly women couldn't live in it alone any longer. A meeting between Alice, Thomas, and two of Lydia's children gave way to the only decision they could make, a nursing home for the pair.

Lydia and Martie were able to share a room in a Rome facility. Lydia didn't notice as much as Martie, but deep down, Martie felt a little betrayed by her children. She felt as though they had ripped her from her home. Her mind was still sharp, but her body just wouldn't allow her to do the things she wanted and needed to do daily.

Martie finally adjusted to nursing home living and was talked into staying. However, her children broke the news to her that she would have to sell her home to pay for the nursing home arrangements. She didn't like this idea, but what use would she ever have for the place? She was a little relieved to know that Alice was going to buy it and live there with her new husband. After more than thirty years as a widow, Alice had met a World War I veteran and widower who had moved to Kingston from Adairsville. They tied the knot in a small, church ceremony and combined their retirement money to purchase and renovate Martie's home. This made the sale so much easier. Somewhere in the back of her mind, Martie pictured herself going home to live with Alice and her new son-in-law, George Smalley.[1]

In honor of their absent loved ones, Alice and Vera became exceptionally active in the affairs of the Kingston Woman's History Club museum project. They made regular visits to the Rome nursing home to keep Lydia and Martie updated on the progress.

"We are planning fund-raisers like you wouldn't believe," Alice said. "There is so much to be done."

Before she spoke, Martie turned to a snoring Lydia and shouted, "Hush up, or at least close your mouth. The girls are here."

Now, turning back to Alice and Vera, "Yes, I know. Don't forget, I've been through enough of them myself."

"We miss you, Mama Martie," Vera said. "Do you have any suggestions?"

"There's nothing I can advise ya'll on anymore," she said. "My day is done. Times and people have changed. Ice cream socials just don't cut it anymore."

"Well, suppers do," Alice said. "We have a few things up our sleeves. We are planning turkey dinners, spaghetti suppers, and bake sales. We're planning just about anything we can cook and sell."

"Wait a minute there, Alice," Martie said as her face illuminated with an idea. "You of all people should remember a great fund-raiser from World War I."

"What are you talking about, Mama?" Alice looked confused.

"Do you remember all those old photographs we put on display? We hung them on the walls like an art gallery, and then we charged admission to raise money for the Red Cross."

"Hey, I do," she said. "I remember looking at every picture, especially those of Navy ships, just hoping to catch a glimpse of Bruce's face."

Alice was smiling and remembering the happy times mingled with the sad ones. While Alice was skipping down memory lane, the wheels inside Vera's brain began churning out the possibilities. Their visit ended that day with the two younger sisters-in-law taking a fresh, new idea for a fund-raiser from the memories of the former generation.[2]

Once they left, Martie turned on her television. She could only laugh as she thought about how much Mike would have enjoyed seeing a picture that could go along with the sounds from his radio. She turned up the volume just a little to drown out Lydia's snores. On the road home, Alice and Vera held their own two-person committee meeting about an idea sure to be pleasing and profitable to the club. Out of the memory files of an elder emerged a fresh, recycled idea.

Notes

1. George Smalley is entirely a fictional character in no way related or based on anyone in Kingston or Adairsville, Georgia.

2. Information about the museum and its funding taken from *Club's project nears completion*, *The North Bartow News*, Adairsville, Georgia, page 10, Thursday, October 29, 1970.

Revival and home . . .

Alice and Vera were prepared for the next club meeting. Just like the Darden sisters, who preceded them with motivational speeches on Confederate Memorial Day, the two "girls" recalled the days of socials, food, and fun that were now a rich part of the club's and town's history.

Alice was wrapping up her part of the sell to the ladies. "So, in conclusion, I say we gather all the old, historical photos we can find, and we shoot some footage of the town today. Let's bring a World War I idea into the Sixties with a slide-show feature during our fund-raising dinners."

Smiles crossed the faces of the ladies like a tidal wave. The idea was a smashing hit. Soon, a committee formed and the first of several fund-raising evenings were held.[1] Alice jokingly called it Kingston's version of the dinner theatre. People laughed and enjoyed the home cooking of the ladies, just as they had a half of a century earlier.

Alice and Vera continued their trips to the nursing home on a regular basis throughout the Sixties. Martie enjoyed comparing the ever-changing fashions of her girls to those on the television. They would entertain Martie with the latest club news and town gossip. In addition to all the planning and fund-raising going on with the club, they managed to continue festive and celebratory Confederate Memorial Days. And, in 1964, the ladies wholly commandeered the event.[2]

"Well, that's no surprise," Martie mumbled. "Should have happened years ago."

Then, Martie would want to start talking too. She would tell them all about the brewing war in Vietnam and the Women's Lib Movement. Martie loved to catch them up on whatever soap opera she was watching at the time, and she would complain about the nursing home food and compare it to Vera's cooking.

She couldn't help herself when she asked Vera if any of her granddaughters had joined the Women's Lib Movement, yet? To her surprise, two of them had, and she was pleased to know it embarrassed Vera a little because she considered them slightly militant in their techniques.

Through these afternoon discussions, Lydia continued to snore. And, then, one day in 1968, there was no more snoring. Like a bad dream relived, Martie went to wake her golden-years companion for supper, and she discovered Lydia was gone. She had been through this before, so she just held her hand and said her good-byes uninterrupted by the people in white who would soon come to whisk her away and out of Martie's life.

Alice and George picked up Martie from the nursing home two days later for the funeral. She was pleased with what the pair had done to her home. Fresh paint and wallpaper gave the place a whole new look. The newly rebuilt, modern kitchen now included a dishwasher. They had completely torn out the original water closet and replaced it with a new, pink bathroom.

Martie was prepared to return to the nursing home after the funeral, but the pair surprised her. They wanted her to live with them.

"Mama, you would be too lonely over there without Aunt Lydia," Alice said. "So for one month, you will stay here. I'll help you fix up your room in our house. And, next month, you will stay with Thomas and Vera."

"I like the sound of it so far, but what will I eat next month?" Martie said. "That woman still can't cook."

"Well, we'll just cross that bridge when we get there," Alice said.

Her days were pleasant with her children. She got to know George and liked him very much. He took her anywhere she wanted to go. During her stays with Vera, she would con George into picking her up on a daily basis and driving her to the nearest hamburger joint in Rome or Cartersville. In fact, for the first time in her life, Martie gained a little weight.

She longed to go to the club meetings, but Vera and Alice insisted the business end was long and drawn out, and it would be too much for Martie to sit through. So, they just summarized the proceedings for her.

According to Alice, things weren't going too well. Time was closing in on the ladies.

"What do you mean time is running out?" Martie was just trying to understand the panic of the situation.

"Well, when we got the land for the museum, there was one stipulation," Alice said. "We were only given ten years to build the museum on it, or the land reverts back to previous ownership."[3]

"Wow," Martie said.

"Yeah, I know. It's sad that this idea has been kicked around for all these years, and it's going to come down to the fact that we just might not be able to pull it off."

"No, that's not what I'm 'wowing' about," Martie said. "I'm in shock that a modern group of educated women like ya'll can't build one small museum in ten years."

Alice didn't know what to say.

"In my day, we watched our entire town burn, and a few years later we saw the school go up in flames," Martie said. "We rebuilt an entire town and a school in less than ten years. You all sound like a fleeting flock of whimpering chickadees. What in the world have you all been doing?"

Alice thought a moment and responded to Martie's question as best she could, "Well, Mama, I guess according to you, not a lot, huh? It's just things aren't as simple as they were in your day. We have construction costs, labor fees to consider, and . . ."

Martie cut her off. "Hogwash. If you want something done, then you just do it. Nothing but the Good Lord can stand in your way. And, if you do it putting Him and the goodness of the project first, then it can be done."

With those words, Alice was not only embarrassed but also spurred into action with a renewed sense of purpose. The ladies were getting too bogged down in business affairs. Alice thought that some days it seemed they had lost sight of the purpose and plan that had been placed before them.

Just the thoughts of their predecessors like her grandmother, the Soldiers' Aid Society, the Ladies' Memorial Association, the Darden sisters, Miss Bell, and Mrs. Irby brought waves of guilt to Alice. These ladies would never give up. They were all the reasons why this project was important now.

The world was changing faster than ever. Time was moving at supersonic speed, just like the trains that no longer acknowledged Kingston. Businesses were leaving town for the larger markets. The small, once bustling town was fading into the cracked streets and deteriorating buildings of its once-great self. Time was taking its toll, and Kingston was falling victim to what all small towns were facing, eradication.

If history ever needed to repeat itself, it was now. It was the women who had stepped forward in loyalty and service to Kingston since 1861. If this group let go of the rope now, then all would be lost. They could not let this happen.

And, they didn't. During the last years of the 1960s, the museum project took off like a rocket. Fund-raisers continued to pad the building account, and activity began in the park.

Alice and Vera would drive Martie by the construction site on a weekly basis for her inspection and approval.

"That's kind of small, isn't it?" She'd ask the same question every time they had their drive by.

Finally, Vera asked, "Why do you keep saying that, Mama Martie?"

"Well, you've got more than a hundred years of history you have to put in there, and that's if you just started with the War Between the States," she said.

"Well, it is a Civil War museum," Alice responded.

"Yeah, but don't you want to include a little more about how the town was founded? Who was here first, like Aunt Ann's people? A little about industry, the land, businesses?"

Both Vera and Alice took a deep breath knowing full well that Martie was right. The Kingston Woman's History Club would outgrow their new museum before they even moved into it.

"You younger girls just amaze me," Martie was mumbling from the back seat. "Don't know anything about how to get things done, and done right."

Vera lit up a cigarette as Alice drove off.

Notes

1. *Club's project nears completion, The North Bartow News,* Adairsville, Georgia, page 10, Thursday, October 29, 1970, provides information about fund-raising and construction of the museum.

2. *North West Georgia Historical and Genealogical Society,* Volume 2, October, 1970, Number 4, "Kingston Woman's History Club," by Martha H. Mulinix, 1970, page 11, provides information about the club's takeover of the Confederate Memorial Day services.

3. *Club's project nears completion, The North Bartow News,* Adairsville, Georgia, page 10, Thursday, October 29, 1970, provides additional information about fund-raising and construction of the museum.

A place of their own . . .

As 1969 gave way to the dawn of 1970, Martie watched America on her television struggling, once again, in a state of political unrest. Martie, whose mind was slowly fading, continued to watch every moment of news coverage she could. Most of her days were spent watching television. Her favorites were soap operas and the news. Game shows slightly interested her, but she claimed they required too much thinking to enjoy.

One day, George walked into the den where Martie was just finishing her soap opera, and he cut off the television and pulled up a chair beside her.

"Hey, what'd you do that for?"

"Mama," he said, "I need to show you something and have a little talk with you."

Becoming as cantankerous as James had been before he died, she got a little smart with George, "Am I in trouble? What're you gonna do? Send me to my room without supper? Ha, just send me back to Vera's if you're gonna do that. That's torture enough, don't you think?"

"Calm down," he said. "I just wanted to read something to you."

George pulled a copy of *The North Bartow News* out of his back pocket and began to unfold it to a large story about the museum.[1]

Martie interrupted to ask why he felt it was necessary to read this to her. The girls were keeping her updated weekly, sometimes daily.

"I'm reading you this because you have been a little too hard on Alice and Vera," George said. "I just wanted you to hear how well the entire club is doing. It doesn't help for you to keep talking about how much faster and better your generation did things."

Martie did feel a little guilty. Although her mind was starting to wander and her personality beginning to be gruff, she still had most of her wits.

"Listen to this," he kept reading the article, which detailed how members had donated their time and labor to save money.

"You know what else?" George continued by explaining that the husbands had joined the efforts with these cost-savings, labor exploits. "You'll also be happy to know the ladies contributed their own funds to this building. Instead of giving each other Christmas presents at their annual parties, they put the money they would have spent on a gift into the building fund.

"They also took prize money they won with their fair exhibitions and used it to complete the building."

Martie reached up and touched George's arm. "I'm so sorry. I guess I'm looking at a little too much television. I'm glad to know the girls I love aren't the selfish people who only care about profit and themselves, like the ones I see on that box."

"No, they're not," he replied. "None of them are. That's why, just like always, we men have been there to help them. I think if you just gave them a chance, they would please you."

Alice had stepped into the room toward the end of this conversation.

"Well, why didn't Alice and Vera ever tell me all this?"

Alice now took over the conversation. "We have tried to tell you. But, all you want to do is fuss and talk about the way things used to be. Mama, those days are gone. We're working on preservation, but we are also planning for the future."

George stood up from the chair and motioned for Alice to take his seat. She took Martie's hand and started talking.

"We're hoping to have the museum open for Confederate Memorial Day next spring," Alice said. "We have the panel exhibits ready to go, and they follow your advice."

"Really," Martie said. "What are they called?"

"Cotton Kingdom, War Comes to Kingston, Kingston Responds, and Memorial Days," she said. "Those are just the first exhibits. We have other plans for the museum. We are going to open it up for the school children to visit. One of our members, a teacher, Mrs. Martha Mulinix, is planning an entire program for the children."

Martie's mind wandered, "Did you know my mother's name was Martha? And, mine too?"

Alice knew she was off again, reliving her past. She stood and gently kissed her mother on the head. She turned on the television on her way out the door.

Martie's health continued on a rapid decline as spring 1971 approached. George and Thomas took turns staying with her while Vera and Alice worked long hours alongside the other club members finishing the displays and preparing the new museum for its debut on Confederate Memorial Day.

Finally, the spring weekend arrived. A very weak Martie had to be assisted by her girls just to get dressed. Thomas and George made sure she was comfortable in the front seat of the car as they headed to the services. George secured a wheelchair so that Martie could enjoy the museum.

After the group gathered in front of the museum for the annual tea and the usual cleanup began, Martie asked to be wheeled into the building. It was a small, white, concrete-block structure. Freshly painted and furnished, it smelled clean and new. However, it held a flood of memories for Martie.

Thomas took over the wheelchair duties from George who assisted in moving tables and chairs. Martie asked to stop at every exhibit. The words her eyes wouldn't allow her to make out, Thomas read to her. Pride welled up inside as she saw what had been accomplished by the women of Kingston, past and present. She felt secure knowing that women of the future would soon be here to perpetuate the memories, spirits, and mission of this special group.

Despite a dwindling business district, no more railroad commerce, and no younger generation willing to stay put for long, Martie knew Kingston was going to survive because there was a school and now, a museum. No one would forget his or her past. Its mistakes would not be repeated because of this club.

Making a full circle through the exhibits, Martie emerged from the building to a group of women who saluted their eldest member with a rousing round of applause. Vera and Alice stepped from the crowd of ladies and finished pushing Martie to the car. Martie waved to the group knowing it would be her final farewell. She could go home and rest in the knowledge she had seen the goal met. Discussions of their own home had been ongoing since before World War I, but something always took precedent. There had always been something to do. Now, the job was done.

Two weeks later, George and Alice were awakened by a gasping sound coming from Martie's room. She was having a stroke. Alice called Vera and Thomas who joined them in rushing their mother to the hospital. Martie couldn't recover. She was paralyzed down her right side and her mouth was too drawn to speak clearly.

Her four closest family members, who had been responsible for her care, kept a bedside vigil in pairs. Grandchildren, great-grandchildren, and even a couple of great-great grandchildren paraded in and out, a few at a time. But when her time came, her beloved Alice, and now Vera, surrounded her on either side. She began speaking in her broken and slurred voice.

"My best friend, Bell, once told me that life is a game, and you need to play it with all you have until the end. I think she was referring to baseball. We both liked to watch it out in town."

She paused to catch her breath and try to lick her dry lips. Each woman took her by a hand as tears began to well in their eyes.

"Girls, it's the bottom of the ninth and I'm at bat. I feel like I have one more swing left in me, so here goes. Stick together. Don't give up on anything. Finish what you start. Don't let anyone forget what has happened in Kingston. It's important not to lose your past. I spent too long living there, so don't make my mistakes, please move on with things. Teach the next generation that it's up to them to carry the torch."

She closed her eyes, and both women hung their heads and waited. But, Martie wasn't ready to go. She had one more zinger for the pair.

"Thank you both, and thank the ladies of the club for everything. My family and the friends I made through the club have made this life worth living and playing in. Oh, I just hit a homerun. Alice, do you think I won the game?"

With that, Martie was gone. Alice leaned in to kiss the top of her mother's head like she had so many times in the past.

"Yes, Mama, you just hit a grand slam."

Notes

1. *Club's project nears completion*, *The North Bartow News*, Adairsville, Georgia, page 10, Thursday, October 29, 1970, gives details of the museum's construction and funding.

Frozen and lost in time . . .

The woman who had said so many good-byes to her loved ones through the years had to bid farewell herself. The last of a special kind of lady left the earth that year but didn't take with her the impact she made on the next generation of women.

It appeared to Alice that people began to scatter after the completion of the museum in 1971, and the town seemed even quieter. It was almost eerie at night. Distant train whistles could be heard, and the rumble of a freight train plowing through the night could be felt. But, something was always missing. The ladies continued to meet in each other's homes where they would hold their afternoon teas, complete with historic programs and delicious food.

The school program took off also. The members had fun filling their afternoons with volunteer work and preparing the museum for the next group of elementary school children. Each one loved to talk to the eager students as they passed the exhibits, wide-eyed and curious about each Civil War relic and black and white photograph.

Finally, the town agreed on something, the depot. The town's last remaining piece of railroad history was in danger of disappearing. The Louisville and Nashville Railroad was leasing the building from the state. They were using it to store grease. Now, they feared it was a safety and traffic hazard, and they wanted it removed from the track. [1]

Residents banded together to save the historic building. This depot was an exact replica, built in 1900, of the one constructed after the Civil War in 1870. The original depot was just another victim of the violent War Between the States. Now, the town that once thrived on railroad commerce was about to lose the last shred of its glorious past identity.

Alice and Vera joined the local residents in their petitions and letters to the state about saving the beloved depot. They won approval from the State Properties Commission to have the building relocated to a nearby state-owned park.

Even Governor Jimmy Carter agreed to donate $2,000 from his emergency fund for the efforts.

Alice felt like a new breath of life was flowing into the dying town. Once again, they had a common goal and were working together to make it all happen. Then, in July 1974, the town awoke to a desolate and crushing scene. The depot had burned in the night. All that was left of the historic, little relic was its chimney. Reduced to smoldering rubble and ashes, their dreams of saving this last piece of their railroad history drifted away with the last puffs of smoke.[2]

Alice couldn't help herself. She could see the burned-out, smoking patch beside the railroad tracks from her front porch. She sat and cried. George heard her whimpers from the kitchen and slowly walked to the porch with a fresh cup of coffee for her.

"I know, Sweetie," he stroked her hair. "It's hard to let go sometimes."

"This is terrible, George," she said. "What is happening here? Why is this happening to this town? This used to be the greatest place on earth. There was nowhere else I would rather be than at home, here in Kingston."

"Unfortunately, it's called progress," he said. "You and I are relics ourselves now. We just seem to care about different things than the young people today care about."

"Do you think somebody did this to us on purpose?" Alice was thinking hard about that question. "Why would someone want to hurt us? What have we ever done to anyone?"

"I don't know. That place was so old, it was probably a fire trap to begin with," he said. "I don't think anyone would do this on purpose. I have a feeling that no one is going to care that it's gone except us old timers. And, that's a shame."

"People just don't see the beauty in old towns like ours anymore, do they?" Alice was becoming more despondent.

"No, they don't, dear," George replied while leaning back on the swing next to Alice. He put his arm around her shoulders and rocked the swing for both of them.

"I'm so glad that Mama isn't here to see this day," Alice said. Then, she took a long sip of coffee. "So, so glad."

"Oh, she sees," George answered. "She sees, and the next time it rains, those are her tears shed for Kingston. I'm sure of it."

From that day forward, Alice couldn't look at the rain without thinking of her mother and how sad she would be if she knew what was happening to her beloved town.

The ladies continued their work with education, historic preservation, and the operations of the museum. Both Alice and Vera donated scrapbooks found in Martie's personal belongings. They knew it would be what she wanted.

The ladies took apart some of these donated articles and began formal club scrapbooks that eventually comprised a tale of their history. Although the town around them was dying, the ladies continued to boom inside the small, concrete building in the park. However diligent the ladies' work was, it wasn't enough this time. Unlike in years past when Kingston picked herself up and came back bigger and better, she surrendered to the changes that were aiming to crush her.

Eventually, nearly all of Martha and James' descendents passed away or moved away. Every now and then, one might wander into town for Confederate Memorial Day services. They were well advertised each year by the local newspapers. The efforts of the ladies in preserving such an important piece of the past didn't go unrecognized. The speakers from all walks of political and educational importance paraded in and out of Kingston.

This practice continued to take place through the Seventies and Eighties. Not a year went by since 1865 when a service wasn't held. Wars, the Depression, the lean years, and the booming years didn't stop this practice.

During the 1980s, several sad things took place. Some of the buildings in the downtown district were condemned and torn down. Others were in repairable states and would eventually get the attention they deserved. But, that didn't slow down the decay. Nothing changed. Those twenty years after the museum's construction saw little Kingston go down far enough until there was only one place left to go, back up.[3]

And, that's just where she decided to go.

Notes

1. Information about the depot fire found in *Fire Destroys Kingston Depot,* (handwritten date July 26, 1974); no newspaper source identified, clipping archived in Kingston Woman's History Club Museum scrapbook.

2. According to "The Railroads and Kingston" by Mamie Jo Gallagher Hood, page 33 of *We Remember Kingston . . . Woman's History Club & Others,* Third Printing Courtesy of The Etowah Valley Historical Society, Cartersville, Georgia, May 1998, the Kingston Depot burned in the early-morning hours of Friday, July 26, 1974.

3. The information concerning the bypass of travel to Kingston, Georgia, after the railroads were no longer a primary mode of travel was obtained online at www.notatlanta.org/kingston.html. (June 3, 2007)

The not-so-nice girl...

Sitting quietly, baking in the afternoon sun, breezes drifting through like the trains of her glorious past, Kingston lay in wait. The poor, little, innocent town that bore witness to so much activity and history was now asleep. Broken windows along the remaining downtown buildings stared at the mostly deserted railroad tracks. The cracks in their glass resembled the tear-filled eyes of a child whose heart was broken from abandonment by her best friend.

The stronger, afternoon Georgia winds could awaken the buildings with empty moaning, begging people to stop and listen to their tales. Many days of stories were just waiting to be re-told about these old friends of Kingston. However, no one seemed to care much anymore.

"What in the hell kind of a sick joke is this?"

A young reporter from *The Daily Tribune News* in Cartersville was approaching the little town for the first time. Growing up in neighboring Floyd County, she had heard about Kingston all her life but never actually visited the place. Now, she knew why.

Munching on her favorite snack, a peanut and caramel-filled, chocolate candy bar and a diet cola, she barely caught the speed limit sign and hit the brakes when she "hit" the city limits.

"Okay," she said out loud, "let us rephrase that rhetorical question. Where in the hell am I? Better yet, how in the hell do I get out of here?"

She had thundered into town in her prized Ford Probe, complete with a ground effects package, sunroof, and custom stereo system that she now adjusted the volume down by about five decibels.

A fresh graduate of the University of Georgia, she had been assigned to cover the North Bartow County area, which included Kingston. She was arriving for her first city council meeting.

A student of a political journalism program conducted at Georgetown University in Washington, D.C., she was now highly insulted to be assigned to such a small, undetectable place like Kingston, Georgia. What a waste of her time!

"I'd rather be selling makeup in the mall," she thought. "This is ridiculous! I'll just have to have a word with someone about this tomorrow. This has to be some kind of test."

She killed the rumbling engine on her shiny, red car that looked out of place and opened the door. Gathering her notebook, micro-cassette recorder, and purse, she got out and walked to the door of city hall. When she opened the door, her life changed.

Already inside was one face she recognized, another reporter from a local Cartersville television station. Instead of feeling the competition, Dana felt reassured she was going to survive her first, and only she hoped, trip to Kingston.

Hard stares came from the council members seated at the table in the front of the room. It was obvious they were cautious of strangers, especially "the media."

"They don't know who they're dealing with," she thought. "I don't want to know them any more than they obviously don't want to know me."

Unbelievably, she survived that first city council meeting, and over the next few years, countless more. Those stone-hard faces she met the first night she arrived in town changed and softened as she got to know each one individually. Dana discovered that Kingston had its share of political and personality problems. Her opinion was that they felt like they had been "burned" by unfavorable media attention prior to her arrival.

However, in the years that followed, Dana broke a few cardinal rules of journalism when she got to know several of the council members and city employees on a personal level. She didn't feel much like raking them over the coals or "digging up dirt" on them like a hard-nosed, investigative reporter.

She began to see them for who they were, small-town politicians who cared so passionately for their town, they sometimes went overboard with their efforts. Dana didn't mind covering Kingston and her North Bartow neighbor, Adairsville. She got comfortable with the communities and the people. In fact, the slower pace of town politics, and the colorful characters she encountered made her job an easy one.

Still, she longed for bigger stories. Secure with her job and waiting on bigger scoops, Dana was informed that she had one more important news event in Kingston to cover, Confederate Memorial Day.

"What in the world could that be?" She was thinking to herself again.

Once or twice a month in Kingston was comfy and fun, but going there in broad daylight, in the middle of the week, on purpose, was starting to ask a bit too much. How would she ever get to the bigger stories if all she ever did were check police blotters, like an intern, and run over to Kingston?

The more she thought about this on her way, the madder and more uppity she got. Her foot was like lead on the pedal of her modified little gem as she stormed down Highway 411 toward the Kingston turn off. She cranked out a little more AC/DC from her stereo to calm her nerves while chugging her fourth diet cola of the day. Ironically, their hard-rockin' hit, *Highway to Hell*, was blaring from the car's speakers.[1]

"How appropriate," she laughed to herself. "That's exactly which road my career is on right now."

Okay, she was supposed to meet a couple of ladies at the museum in the park to do a feature on the upcoming Confederate Memorial Day. Dana learned the paper did one every year. What a waste of her time and journalistic abilities to drive all the way out here to re-write something that had been standard since recorded time began. If the paper did the same thing every year, why couldn't she just pull last year's story, slap a new date on it, and tag it with "staff reports," dead and alive?

Once again, the little city limits sign was on her before she knew it and she hit the brakes, as usual. She forgot to turn down her obnoxiously loud "head-banging" music while she searched for the museum. Dana remembered seeing a large plot of land in the middle of the town, if you qualify Kingston as a real town. But, she couldn't recall any museum that would certainly stand out.

Talking to herself, she said, "Okay, there's the park. There're a lot of trees, grass, a large gazebo, and a little garden shed. That must be where they keep the mowers. No museum. Must be a joke."

Then, on her second time circling the park, she slammed on her brakes. Her tires squealing just a little as her car came to a stop just beside the garden shed. Standing outside were two ladies, of what Dana considered advanced age. Of course to Dana, anyone over thirty should be eligible for Social Security.

Why were these women staring at her so hard? They were making her a little uncomfortable. Didn't they have great-grandchildren? Surely, they had seen young people in little cars before now? Then it hit her, the high-pitched, yelling sounds of her music were escaping through the sunroof and contaminating that peaceful park. Dana killed the stereo faster than someone tripping over a loose cord and yanking it from a wall.

She peeked at them through her sunglasses to see if they were still there, or if they had been little ghostly figments of her imagination. Yes sir, they were still there, still looking at her. Dana closed her eyes tightly and hung her head pretending to gather her stuff.

"I don't want to be here, I don't want to be here, I don't want to be here," she was repeating these words under her breath. "Lord, if You feel merciful and kind today, take me now, take me now, take me now."

She opened her eyes and glanced toward the spot where just seconds before the two ladies had been standing. They were gone. Hey, maybe this was just a nightmare?

Dana screamed inside her head because they were now coming toward her car. They cautiously approached it like earthlings to a spaceship from Mars. She could feel her heart beating faster. What were these ladies going to say? They didn't look too friendly. She was speeding, her music was too loud, and who knew what else was coming.

She had no choice but to get out of the car. First, she had been discovered. Second, she had killed the engine with the music, therefore as fast as her car was, it couldn't garner enough speed to race out of the park before those two got to her.

"Good day there," the thin one with the neat hair bun was waving at Dana. "Are you the girl from the newspaper?"

Busted!

"Oh, dearest Father, be with me and help me, Amen."

Then, Dana did the only thing she could do. She got out of the car and waved back. "That would be me."[2]

Notes

1. AC/DC is a hard rock, musical band that formed in Sydney, Australia, in 1973. Their single *Highway to Hell* is from their album *Highway to Hell*, 1979. http://en.wikipedia.org/wiki/AC/DC. (June 4, 2007)

2. Chapter based on author, Dana E. Davis, and her introduction to the women of the Kingston Woman's History Club. Chapters 45-49, also, are based on personal experiences of the author.

A good day . . .

"I'm Martha Mulinix, and this is Hazel Litton," the thin lady with the bun was making introductions. "And, who are you?"

"I'm Dana White from *The Daily Tribune*," Dana replied.

"Are you any relation to the White's from. . .?" Mrs. Hazel was asking the questions now, but she trailed off as Dana was overwhelmed by their interest in her.

When she regained semi-consciousness, she said, "Uh, no ma'am. My dad's family is from Tennessee. I'm not related to any Whites I know of in Georgia."

The threesome headed toward the open door of the small, white building that Dana had mistaken for the garden shed. Once inside, Mrs. Martha welcomed Dana to the museum as if she were giving a formal tour. Dana was amused.

She received the grand tour that day, which took longer than expected. Dana got lost in Mrs. Martha's recount of the history of Confederate Memorial Day. A long-time lover of history, Dana felt like she hit the proverbial jackpot of feature stories. This wasn't so bad after all. The only thing she noticed inside the museum was its smell. It smelled so old, if old can have a smell. It wasn't all that pleasant, but it also wasn't unpleasant. It was different and, in a way, mysterious and inviting.

Following the tour, Dana joined the ladies on a small bench just outside the museum. It was nice to be surrounded by lush, green grass and tall, shady pine trees. The fresh air seemed old and wise that day. It was talking to Dana like no person ever had. It was telling her to slow down a little and listen for the first time in her life.

Maybe it wasn't the Georgia breezes; perhaps it was Mrs. Martha. This small lady had the strongest voice Dana had ever heard. A retired educator could explain part of it, but it was something else. This woman commanded respect with her presence. If you ever wanted anyone's approval, it would be Mrs.

Martha's. She was a walking inspiration, and even a smart aleck, little know-it-all reporter, like Dana White, could tell this from their first meeting.

Mrs. Hazel just smiled a lot. When she told a story, or added anything to the interview that day, she made you want to sit on her lap like your favorite grandmother at bedtime. You just wanted a hug from Mrs. Hazel, and this softened the almost rude, career-woman wannabe.

What started out as a rush job, get through, yeah, yeah afternoon, turned into a life-changing experience. It was a small one, but small steps are what make up an entire life's journey.

Dana drove out of town a little slower and quieter that day. She had taken up the entire afternoon with the two ladies and didn't have time to return to the office before close of business. So, she used her emergency bag phone and called the newsroom before heading home to Lindale. Boy, was she glad that was over. But, it was far from over.

Dana's series of stories ran in the paper during the next couple of weeks leading to the big event. The only drawback to actually covering Confederate Memorial Day was having to go, on Sunday afternoon. Although the paper was "daily," it didn't print on Saturday or Sunday at that time, therefore weekends were made for fun, not work.

Armed with her notepad, camera and one guest, Dana was off to Kingston where she would blow her Sunday afternoon. Dana thought her guest was kind of forced on her that day. She did invite her under stress and duress from her mother. Dana's grandmother, Mrs. Annie Jo Woods, had lost her husband of fifty-two years just one year earlier. The entire family was spending the weekend together to lift her spirits on the one-year anniversary of his passing. And, since Dana was going to a church service, it was decided that it wouldn't be any trouble for Grandma to tag along.

Grandma had muscular dystrophy, which made it difficult for her to get up and down. The first obstacle of the day was loading grandma into the sporty Ford since it had been lowered within about half a foot off the ground. Dana dreaded their arrival where the unloading process would have to take place.

On the way to Kingston, Grandma began to chatter.

"I was born in Bartow County," she announced. This was something Dana didn't know. "My family lived in Adairsville, and my daddy ran a little trading post.

"We moved to Rome when I was very little. Daddy got sick, and my brothers moved away, so we had to be closer to more family. But, I remember going to Kingston as a child on the train. They had a lot of stores and some hotels. It was fun."

Dana was stunned. "I didn't know all that."

"Well, you do now," Grandma said.

For the rest of the trip, they chatted about Grandma's early days in Bartow County and then Floyd County before she moved to Chattooga and married Granddaddy.

Finally, the pair slowly drove into the small town.

"Wow, things have really changed," Grandma said.

"No kidding."

Upon arrival, Dana secured a parking spot, and much to her surprise, had to squeeze into one. This place was hopping compared to its usual pace. Unloading Grandma wasn't as bad as Dana had thought.

The two made their way to the church where they were greeted by a barrage of ladies handing out programs and taking names of visitors on index cards. Mrs. Martha even wrote down Grandma's name.

Once the program started, Dana realized why names were taken. Visitors were recognized. There were so many important people present. It was very impressive. Then, Dana's name was called out. She was expected to stand. How embarrassing was this? But, she and Grandma both made it through the recognition, and Grandma thoroughly enjoyed it. She was having a great time. You would have thought she knew everyone in that church.

Next, it was on to the cemetery where the real problems began. Grandma did recognize someone. He wasn't someone she knew personally. Instead, she recognized the German prince who had recently purchased Barnsley Gardens outside Adairsville.[1]

"Dana, come over here and take my picture with the prince," Grandma said while grabbing at Dana's sleeve and heading for the unsuspecting gentleman.

"No, please don't embarrass me," Dana replied. "I'm working right now, and I don't have time."

"You have a camera," Grandma wouldn't give up. "Just snap the picture. It won't take but just a second."

Before she could protest any more, Grandma had accosted the prince, who graciously posed for a snapshot. Reluctantly, Dana pretended to be a tourist taking pictures instead of a reporter. After the premier picture was taken, she continued to take the usual Confederate Memorial Day photos, including the one of the group of dignitaries at the monument, the honor guard, and the children placing flowers on the graves.

Once the day ended, and they were on their way home, Dana decided it hadn't been so bad after all. She just couldn't believe that many people had come. She still didn't have the full story.

Notes

1. In 1988, Prince Hubertus Fugger, who restored the gardens, as well as, the remains of the manor house's ruins, purchased the Barnsley Gardens estate of Godfrey Barnsley. www.barnsleyresort.com. (June 3, 2007)

Say what?

Monday morning at the paper was just as crazy as ever. Believe it or not, Dana had the top story of the weekend. Editor Lewis Justus and Publisher Charles Hurley were actually interested in the photos she'd retrieved from the Kingston ceremony.

"Here's a good one," Mr. Hurley said. "Who's the lady with the prince?"

Dana's heart sank like the Titanic. She could hear the words she would utter now forming in her mind.

"I don't know her name. She was just a lady that wanted her picture taken with the prince. In fact, I think she might have died last night."

But instead, a faint and meager, "My grandmother," erupted from her lips.

"Your grandmother," echoed in unison from the two men and about three other newsroom employees.

"Well, what's her name?" Lewis asked.

Dana longed to shout, "I don't remember," but once again, the truth pitifully came forth.

The photo Grandma had wanted to show off at the beauty parlor the next week was now the lead photo on Monday's paper. How much more humiliation could one person endure?

As usual, it wasn't quite as bad as it seemed on the surface. After Confederate Memorial Day, business in Kingston went back to its usual quiet routine. Dana continued her comfortable pace until the day she had waited for came.

Some doors opened to her. The "senior" reporter left the newspaper leaving wide open the best beats in the newsroom. These were the ones reporters reach for. Dana was up for bigger stories and more front page bylines. The only problem was that it didn't feel right. Deep down, she knew you needed to follow your heart and always do what was right.

Sentimental, but not stupid, Dana took a couple of the best beats that would ensure each story a prime spot on the front page. However, she shocked the newsroom when she refused to relinquish Kingston and Adairsville coverage to the rookie.

"Are you completely sure this is what you want to do?" Lewis asked her after the assignments had been divided.

"I'm positive," she said. "I like them. They don't bother me. We get along just fine in North Bartow."

Later on, another reporter would jokingly sneer and call her "loco."

They had gotten to her. The people of North Bartow saw a patsy and took hold. Some days, that's just how she felt. Dana would be so disgusted and depressed with the whole situation, she would seriously think about quitting, but something greater than herself wouldn't let her give up.

She was a little sad that she had to relinquish one of Kingston's feature stories just to cover one of the larger ones, but she didn't mind. The whole gist of the story was a new couple moved into Kingston, the newsworthiness; they were Yankees from New York. What a laugh!

Upon her return to the newsroom, Dana asked the new reporter how it went, and she said, "Great, they're very nice people."

When the feature ran, another reporter laughed himself silly asking, "What is a Policastro?"

It wouldn't be long until Dana would find out exactly what a Policastro was. Just after that story broke, the editor of *The North Bartow News* resigned, and Dana was reassigned and promoted. Still only twenty-three years old, and very young to hold a management position, Dana took over the operations of the small, weekly newspaper geared at the Kingston and Adairsville communities. She had followed her gut instinct and her heart, and the results had paid off.

One of her first days on the job, she drove to Kingston as the new editor. She wanted to meet and greet the people of the town in her new role. This is where she discovered the creatures known as Policastro.

There were two of them, the couple, and they had invaded the Kingston Woman's History Club Museum. Dana wanted to pick up her cell phone and give Mrs. Martha a shout to let her know the Yanks were back. They had infiltrated camp. Who knew what they were planning?

The man Policastro, known as Jim, was nailing something to the door of the museum. Dana cautiously approached. The female, known as Myrna, was hiding inside, no doubt planning an ambush.

The rustling of the leaves and the crunching of loose pine twigs gave away Dana's approach, and Jim turned around just as she reached the edge of the museum.

"Hi there," he said dropping his hammer and extending his hand. "I'm Jim Policastro. Hey Myrna, get out here, we have company."

With a smiling face and a firm handshake, Dana had encountered one of them. Myrna emerged from the museum, adjusting her glasses. She scurried past Jim to take hold of Dana's other hand. Between the tight grips they both had on the young woman, it would have been difficult to break loose.

Myrna was a fiery red head that had more energy than anyone that age Dana had ever seen. She could have given the young editor a run for her money. She and her husband obviously had more strength than their appearance gave off.

Mrs. Martha peered out from the museum. Oh, no, they had captured her. Dana wanted to shout, "Run, Mrs. Martha, run. I can hold them off for a moment."

Still in the Policastros' grip, Dana tried to introduce herself, but by this time, Mrs. Martha took charge of the situation. Explanations and formal introductions were given. Dana found herself drawn into the little museum, again, and having a wonderful time.

As it would turn out, the Policastros had visited friends nearby, bought some land, and decided to retire to the Kingston community. Myrna had also decided to retire from community service as she had spent many years in a women's club at home in New York. However, she just couldn't help herself. She met Mrs. Martha and was presented for membership. Jim couldn't help himself either. He went along for the ride with Myrna in assisting with museum projects. That's what they were doing at the museum when Dana finally discovered a Policastro.

What a first experience, the first week on the job as editor. For some reason, every new experience and every new transition in Dana's career somehow took place around the small Kingston Woman's History Club Museum.

Hello, good-bye, hello again . . .

Myrna just wouldn't give it up. She called Dana and invited her to attend a club meeting with her. Mrs. Martha and the others had invited her on occasion before now, but she had always been too busy and couldn't get away from the newsroom. Today, she had no excuse; she was the boss. Besides, Mr. Hurley had made it clear, civic duty and service is expected from editors.

What the heck? Dana gave in and joined the ladies one afternoon. Once inside one their beautiful, historic homes, she discovered the most interesting things such as antiques and beautiful sewing work. Dana couldn't tell anyone what happened at the meeting because she was too interested in the house itself. The sandwiches were great, and she made a pig of herself. The odd couple who arrived together seemed to entertain the usual crowd as much as the usual crowd entertained the odd couple, the oddballs being a displaced Yankee and a whippersnapper.

A few more meetings bounced around Kingston, and still, Dana told none of her co-workers in Cartersville about her afternoon exploits. She was learning more than any classroom could ever broach. These were ladies of class and style. They taught her about Southern tradition and what it meant to have afternoon tea. Dana learned that one's education doesn't stop with college. Instead, it is a daily process you undergo with vigor. Studying became fun. She read everything she could get her hands on, including the small, museum-published book of town memoirs, *We Remember Kingston*.

Finally, Myrna presented Dana for membership. Her indoctrination to life in Kingston was complete. Accepted by the members, she was put to work immediately. There were a few orders of business to get out of the way first. On their usual bench in the park, just outside the museum, Mrs. Martha carefully explained some of the club's activities.

"You know about the monthly meetings, of course," she was saying. Mrs. Martha paused to adjust her glasses and peer at Dana over them. "We used to give a Christmas party where we invited our husbands, but most of them are dead now. So, we just make reservations somewhere and have a nice lunch for ourselves."

Most husbands are dead! Dana was just getting started and planned to get married in November. What a bummer.

After the "business" end of Dana's new membership had been discussed, the conversation turned to one of many the young editor would have at the small museum, the history of the club.

Too young and selfish to realize what had been handed to her on a silver platter, Dana just took for granted all of the cozy afternoons spent with these ladies would last forever. When she was ready, the club would be there.

Months passed, and she continued to attend the meetings where she learned about the different duties of the club and what it meant to be a part of such a group. Then, the Christmas party arrived. The ladies made reservations at a local restaurant where the president stood to make a "special" presentation. They had gone behind Dana's back to make their Christmas party a sort of "bridal shower."

In her presentation of a beautiful crystal bowl, the president announced, "It's been so long since we had a young bride in the club. We almost forgot what to do. We're more used to burying husbands than marrying them."

A little shocked, again, Dana almost cried as she carefully unwrapped the precious gift.

The defiant and rude, young girl that had sped into their lives almost two years earlier had been transformed into a Southern lady work-in-progress. The charm of these ladies was contagious.

As Confederate Memorial Day rolled around again, Dana made sure she more than adequately had it covered in *The North Bartow News*. However, when it came time to cover the actual event, it came time to fess up to co-workers in Cartersville.

She had to "come clean" about her club affiliation and relinquish some of the coverage to another reporter. Snickers and giggles abounded, as well as, good-natured ribbing.

"So, you're one of them now," Lewis said. "That's okay, we all find our place."

Dana was proud to serve on door duty that year handing out programs to visitors and dignitaries. Her new groom, Lance, even attended the festivities where he was accosted and inducted into a fraternity all its own.

He couldn't tell exactly where the questions were coming from as a barrage of questions fell on him.

"Have you ever had back surgery? Heart surgery? Do you have a hernia? Exactly how much can you lift, boy? Come on, let's go find out."

Lance managed to mumble a few, "Uhs, and yes sirs" before they took him away to hoist tables into place and stack chairs at the museum.

The last place on earth Dana wanted to go to had turned out to be her personal retreat. Kingston possessed an unexplainable magic for her. In her mind, she decided to call Kingston the best-kept, public secret in North Georgia.

Dana continued as a club member for the next few years. The afternoon meetings in the homes of Mrs. Mattie Malone, Mrs. Martha, Mrs. Hazel Litton, and all the others gave the young woman an appreciation for antiques and the fine art of entertaining. However wonderful her time was, youth gave way to stupidity.

Dana just didn't realize what she had. She left the paper to test the waters elsewhere, but a few short years later returned to a big surprise. The women had built another museum.

She hadn't been to Kingston in almost three years, and when she drove to the little park for her first meeting with the club, she was in awe. A beautiful, new, white building proudly stood in the middle of the park. Just off to the side of the original little structure, this one had white columns and double doors. Inside, there were triple the displays of the old museum. The club was able to devote their small museum to its original intent, the Civil War years. The new museum contained everything else anyone could ever hope to know about Kingston.

And, it wasn't just the museum that had started to grow. Morrell's Corner Café was operating full swing in a renovated downtown building, serving hot meals daily. A small grocery store had returned to the downtown district, as well as a couple of more businesses.

When Dana drove into town from her usual back street route, she found the main street littered with cars. The buildings no longer looked sad and lonely. Instead, they were showing signs of rebirth and rejuvenation. She couldn't believe her eyes. But, the museum was the greatest treat of all.

She had read about Kingston's past and knew all the stories told from the women who chose to pass them on to her, but she had never given them much more thought than just stories, until now. They all had to be true. Not Sherman, Depression, wars, changing political and economic climates, and destructive forces of nature could hold down Kingston. Like the mythical phoenix rising from the ashes, the little town proved it held the same magical traits as it forever rose from the ashes.

Going back . . .

The ladies had cut the ribbon on the new Martha Mulinix Annex to the museum after Confederate Memorial Day services in 1998. In their true tradition, they held fund-raisers to pay for the new facility. They sold tapes of scenes from the town. Showing the public the world and their lives through visual images had proven to be profitable, educational, and a trademark of their style since World War I. Now, technology allowed them to disseminate it for private viewing in homes. From an impromptu art gallery in 1917, to slides and home movies in the school's cafeteria in the Sixties, to videocassettes, the ladies were all about tradition.

Technology took them a step further as they began their very own small gift shop inside the museum. They were able to print and sell postcards. A reprint of *We Remember Kingston* became another of their trademark items.

However high-tech they got, their homespun, fund-raising techniques still took the forefront. A donated, antique quilt for raffle brought in much needed funds. No one could turn down a chance for something so beautiful. Then there were the bake sales and pancake suppers at Morrell's.

While attending one of these famous pancake suppers at Morrell's, Dana recalls bringing something else to a club function that hadn't been seen in years, a baby. Lance and Dana brought their infant son, Will. He was just sitting up and experiencing new tastes. The pancake supper that evening included dinner entertainment as Will decided to try pancakes and maple syrup, and more maple syrup, and even more maple syrup. Laughter rang through the walls of the traditional Southern, corner café that evening. Two, college-educated individuals, who had proven themselves capable of management-level positions, looked like incompetent caretakers trying to control one, small child and a syrupy, sticky mess.

Dana tried to assist with the rest of the supper and clean up. It didn't work out too well after she became a walking piece of double-sided tape. That syrup was everywhere. The Davis family was causing more harm than good that night, so they were politely excused. In Woman's Club style, it was all in good fun.

Although they made their residence in Adairsville, Lance, Dana, and Will would drive to Kingston about once a week to every other week just for dinner at Morrell's. It was nice to eat inside the warm café after dark. The town was so quiet and peaceful, and the low hum and buzz of chatter inside the café would have pleased the most restless of ghosts haunting the old buildings. Kingston, once again, was in harmony with herself.

Even strolling along the street after dinner was an experience. Nowhere else on earth could you just walk out of a restaurant in a city and not fear getting mugged. Slow moving cars and other evening walkers were comfort that small-town life still exists in its most simple and pleasant form. The soft glows of light from inside the buildings took Dana back to a time she read about in the pages of the museum's records. Magic had taken hold of her. She had stepped back many years and could feel and smell Kingston like she was in her heyday.

Lance and Dana would push little Will in his stroller along the sidewalk in the cool, evening air. She could laugh a little too as they approached their new, Ford Explorer SUV. She had traded the fiery, red Ford with the loud stereo and obnoxious add-ons for a more practical family vehicle. Knowing Henry Ford had once driven out of Kingston, she laughed and thought this more "family-oriented car" is one that he could be proud of. And with this new ride, she had traded heavy metal and Southern rock for a car seat and toddler sing-alongs.

Just like a repetitive ripple in history, Dana wouldn't stay. She had unwillingly roared into the path of the Woman's Club, and now because of family and new job opportunities out of state, she reluctantly drifted out.

As in the past, she was sad and decided to say good-bye in her own way. She drove to Kingston and surveyed all that was there, and thought of all the changes she'd seen in her very short time with such an unusual and one-of-a-kind group of women. She would miss time in the museum, dinners at Morrell's, afternoon club meetings, and the antics of such a group of people.

She had to leave on a funny note. Parking for just a moment near the railroad tracks downtown, she had to laugh thinking about the day she locked her keys in the old, red Ford. She couldn't allow anyone to help. The city's maintenance men had offered assistance, but the only thing she took from them was a long piece of wire to break into her own car. Fortunately, she had left the sunroof open, so she took off her pumps, stepped onto a tire, walked across the hood like a tightrope, and crept onto the roof like a precision cat burglar.

The police arrived to check the incident since it wasn't often you see a woman sprawled on top of a car, in a dress, jamming a long piece of stiff wire through a sunroof. However, she did it, and maintained dignity. Dana knew how to maneuver in a dress like a lady, even while jimmying the lock on a car.

Of all the places and people she'd covered during her time in Bartow County, the people of North Bartow had gotten into her heart. Saying good-bye to Kingston was the hardest. She drove into nothing in 1992, and drove out of an ongoing, town revival in 1999.

No end in sight . . .

Six years and another son later, Dana was wrapping up an afternoon of cleaning and picking up her house in Middle Tennessee. The gully washing, Middle Tennessee rains were pounding the wheat fields outside her home on her family's farm. Out of breath and full of about all of the "toddler TV" she could handle, she flipped off the television and sank into a well-worn armchair.

She closed her eyes and instead of welcome silence and darkness, she began to hear voices and see a bright vision. Ladies voices were calling her name, and welcome conversations from the past were being conducted inside her head. A green, grassy park and two white buildings gleaming in the Georgia sunshine were opening their doors.

"Come back inside," they said. "Come home."

Home, where was that? Tennessee had been home since 1999, and on every corner lived a cousin. What did they mean, home? Then it hit her, she wasn't finishing what she had started. Dana had gotten sidetracked like one of the layover trains in Kingston long ago. She needed to get back "on track." But, how could she do that?

For so long, she enjoyed writing and reading, especially history. Now, she was raising kids and reading children's stories. She got up from the chair and walked to a mirror. It wasn't a pretty picture. Where did the young woman go who didn't mind climbing on top of a car to retrieve her keys? Staring back at Dana was an old woman with no makeup and a ponytail escaping the back of an old ball cap. The business clothes had long since been traded for sweats and jeans. "Oh crud," was all she could think. "Where am I?"

It didn't take long for Dana to figure out where she was, and who was calling her. She picked up the phone and called the only people she knew who could talk her back home, Mrs. Myrna Policastro and Mrs. Martha Mulinix.

She received an invitation to the 2005 Confederate Memorial Day celebration. Dana loaded up the family, and without discussion, they were driven to Georgia, still in a Ford Explorer. The only difference was that Dana had to have a red Ford, so she traded the other SUV for a brighter, shinier one. She was back!

The Saturday before Confederate Memorial Day was glorious. Dana walked into the Martha Mulinix Annex where it was "old home week." Hugs and walks down memory lane abounded. She started reading again, taking in every word from the museum's archives. She couldn't get enough.

The next months were spent making weekend trips to the museum. This time, she would arrive and stop to take in every smell, every sound, and every word that was said to her. She realized several of the ladies had died. Mrs.

Mattie was gone, Mrs. Hazel was gone, and many others were too frail to be active members. She recalled what a beautiful woman Mrs. Mattie Malone had been as she used her scrapbook for research.

She smiled looking at words from Mrs. Hazel she left behind in the museum. She thought about cleaning the cemetery with Mrs. Hazel one year when she told her the story of Marcellus Darden's tragic death.

Mrs. Flonnie Green stepped up to help with the research. She tirelessly talked to Dana in the museum and provided documents. Money and the Internet could never buy or track such first-hand information.

And, Mrs. Martha, the lady who had impacted her life so much to the point of a change in attitude toward her first job, now suffered macular degeneration. From this point forward, Dana could have no regrets. These ladies had lived life and served their community without any. No one should be allowed to tarnish their shining examples by taking them for granted.

The next two years were spent documenting their story. From generational hand-me-down stories beginning with the War Between the States to their days of activity building two museums, Dana began to capture them in the pages of a book. For Dana, this was therapeutic and recharging. The world had to know about Kingston women.

And so, she finally came full circle, as did Kingston with progress toward the future while carefully guarding their past. For more than one hundred and forty years, a continual group of women have touched lives and made tomorrow better for many.

Standing in the doorway of the Kingston Woman's History Club Museum, breezes rush by, carrying the past in and out the door of the building. Dana closed her eyes to take it all in and meditate. She opened her eyes to see and hear a wagon clicking by. She saw thousands of troops marching in the other direction on their way to a final surrender. A train blows its whistle while thundering down the tracks behind the museum. She turns in its direction, and this time it stops under the cover of darkness. Men fall from its open doors onto a depot platform. A single light guides them.

She smells smoke and hears screams of panic. Her eyes are blinded by bright orange, hot light. Then, she hears sawing and hammering with a clanging of bricks and metal tools used to lay them. A new town emerges. People and cars begin to line the streets. Funny-sounding horns greet each other. Flappers and their music fill the air. Radios blast funny shows and news from each house.

The lights go on, and later television appears. War breaks out and Kingston women come to the rescue with bandages, clothing, and whatever else is needed. The town outgrows its school and builds a new one, twice!

A park comes alive with a museum and then another. A ceremony perseveres since its conception in 1865. Dana's out of breath again. She closes and opens her eyes, takes a step backwards and enters the museum. There it is, all of it. Who couldn't love this place? She has just one warning for visitors. Be very careful because it's alive. You never know "whom" you'll meet or "when" you'll meet them. They're all around town.

Tomorrow is Better because the Kingston Woman's History Club is . . .

About the Author

Dana E. Davis is a former journalist and managing editor, who is now a work-at-home mother. Davis works as an independent graphics designer, editor, and columnist, for the monthly publication *Southern Humor*, McMinnville, Tennessee.

She grew up in North Georgia where she attended Floyd College in Rome. There, she served as editor-in-chief of the campus newspaper, *The Six Mile Post*. She also received a summer scholarship and was accepted to the Institute on Political Journalism through The Fund for American Studies at Georgetown University in Washington, D.C. in 1990 where she graduated from the program. Davis returned to Georgia to finish her bachelor's degree in publication management at the University of Georgia's Grady College of Journalism and Mass Communication in November 1991. While in college, she wrote for UGA's newspaper, *The Red and Black*, and she served on the Georgia College Press Association's board as a member and president for which she received a Georgia Press Association scholarship.

After graduating, she returned to North Georgia where she went to work as a reporter for *The Daily Tribune News* in Cartersville. In 1993, she was promoted to the managing editor of *The North Bartow News*, Adairsville (a weekly publication of Cartersville Newspapers). She left Cartersville Newspapers for a brief period, but returned in 1998.

In 1999, Mrs. Davis left Georgia to work in the public affairs office for an Air Force civilian contractor at Arnold Air Force Base, Tullahoma, Tennessee. There, she became the managing editor of *High Mach*, the base's newspaper. In 2002, she left the work force to become a work-at-home mother of two small boys. She started her freelancing services for local publications and began research for writing books. Today, she continues her own graphics and editing contracting services and writing.

She lives on her family's farm in Hillsboro, Tennessee, with her husband, Lance Davis, and two children, Will and Ben, as well as their long-time, family pet, a thirteen-year-old miniature schnauzer, O'Reilly.